Informal Learning and Literacy among Maasai Women

Informal Learning and Literacy among Maasai Women highlights the importance and role of informal education in the emancipation and development of Maasai village women in Kenya. At present, knowledge and research on the impact of informal learning and literacy on community development is limited, and there is a gap between policy level discussions and women's lived experiences. Using a postcolonial feminist framework, this book sets out to examine linkages between informal learning and literacy, human development and gender inequality.

Despite improvements in recent years, access to traditional education remains restricted for many women in rural communities across Kenya. Takayanagi's book is the first to introduce how Maasai village women utilise informal learning and literacy for collective empowerment as well as to sustain their own well-being and that of their families. It presents the perspectives of both local women and institutions and argues that women's learning is most effective when located within their own socio-cultural and political discourses, and when their voices are listened to and heard.

This ethnographic research study is a valuable resource that will contribute to the knowledge of literacy from both theoretical and practical perspectives. It is an essential read for those studying or researching information education, development studies and gender, or education, as well as for teachers, community leaders and aid workers.

Taeko Takayanagi is a JSPS Research Fellow at Waseda University in Tokyo, Japan. She received her PhD in Education from the University of Sydney and her MA in Education from the University of Manchester.

Routledge Research in International and Comparative Education

This is a series that offers a global platform to engage scholars in continuous academic debate on key challenges and the latest thinking on issues in the fast-growing field of International and Comparative Education.

Titles in the series include:

Reforming Education in Developing Countries
From Neoliberalism to Communitarianism
Izhar Oplatka

Social Justice Education in European Multi-ethnic Schools
Addressing the Goals of Intercultural Education
Cinzia Pica-Smith, Rina Manuela Contini, and Carmen N. Veloria

Education and the Public Sphere
Exploring the Structures of Mediation in Post-Colonial India
Edited by Suresh Babu G. S.

Comparative Perspectives on Refugee Youth Education
Dreams and Realities in Educational Systems Worldwide
Edited by Alexander W. Wiseman, Lisa Damaschke-Deitrick, Ericka Galegher, and Maureen F. Park

50 Years of US Study Abroad Students
Japan as the Gateway to Asia and Beyond
Sarah R. Asada

Informal Learning and Literacy among Maasai Women
Education, Emancipation and Empowerment
Taeko Takayanagi

Parental Involvement Across European Education Systems
Critical Perspectives
Edited by Angelika Paseka and Delma Byrne

For more information about this series, please visit: www.routledge.com/Routledge-Research-in-International-and-Comparative-Education/book-series/RRICE

Informal Learning and Literacy among Maasai Women

Education, Emancipation and Empowerment

Taeko Takayanagi

LONDON AND NEW YORK

First published 2020
by Routledge
2 Park Square, Milton Park, Abingdon, Oxon OX14 4RN

and by Routledge
52 Vanderbilt Avenue, New York, NY 10017

Routledge is an imprint of the Taylor & Francis Group, an informa business

© 2020 Taeko Takayanagi

The right of Taeko Takayanagi to be identified as author of this work has been asserted by her in accordance with sections 77 and 78 of the Copyright, Designs and Patents Act 1988.

All rights reserved. No part of this book may be reprinted or reproduced or utilised in any form or by any electronic, mechanical, or other means, now known or hereafter invented, including photocopying and recording, or in any information storage or retrieval system, without permission in writing from the publishers.

Trademark notice: Product or corporate names may be trademarks or registered trademarks, and are used only for identification and explanation without intent to infringe.

British Library Cataloguing-in-Publication Data
A catalogue record for this book is available from the British Library

Library of Congress Cataloging-in-Publication Data
Names: Takayanagi, Taeko, author.
Title: Informal learning and literacy among Maasai women : education, emancipation and empowerment / Taeko Takayanagi.
Other titles: Power of informal learning and literacy for women in the Maasai community, Kenya
Description: Abingdon, Oxon ; New York, NY : Routledge, 2020. | Revision of author's thesis (doctoral)–University of Sydney, 2017, titled: The power of informal learning and literacy for women in the Maasai community, Kenya. | Includes bibliographical references. |
Identifiers: LCCN 2019020449 (print) | LCCN 2019981538 (ebook) | ISBN 9781138609907 (hardback) | ISBN 9780429465970 (ebook)
Subjects: LCSH: Women, Maasai–Education. | Maasai (African people)–Education–Kenya. | Non-formal education–Kenya.
Classification: LCC DT433.545.M33 T34 2020 (print) | LCC DT433.545.M33 (ebook) | DDC 371.822089/965522606762–dc23
LC record available at https://lccn.loc.gov/2019020449
LC ebook record available at https://lccn.loc.gov/2019981538

ISBN: 978-1-138-60990-7 (hbk)
ISBN: 978-0-429-46597-0 (ebk)

Typeset in Bembo
by Wearset Ltd, Boldon, Tyne and Wear

I dedicate this study to Ryuichi, Rihito and my late daughter Hikari.

I credit many "Mamas" in Narok and those I have worked with for inspiring and encouraging me to work for international education and development.

I appreciate my Kenyan Mamas, Ms. Florence Kamau and Ms. Elizabeth Ndilai, for teaching me about Kenya as well as their great care for me during my fieldwork in the village in Narok.

Contents

List of illustrations	x
Foreword	xi
Acknowledgements	xvii
List of abbreviations	xviii
Glossary	xx

Introduction: exploring the notion of informal learning and literacy from a Maasai woman's perspective   1

1 Postcolonial feminist theory   9

Introduction 9
Postcolonial theory 11
Postcolonial feminism 18
Conclusion 21

2 Women's informal learning and empowerment in the context of development   26

Introduction 26
Informal learning and adult literacy in development 26
Women's informal learning in Africa 31
Literacy and the impact of literacy on women's well-being 33
New literacies: literacy from a socio-cultural perspective 36
Women's empowerment and agency in international development 40
Conclusion 47

3 Using an ethnographic research framework   56

Introduction 56
Feminist research 57

viii   *Contents*

Womanism – African feminism? 59
Establishing rapport and positioning myself 62
Data collection in the field 63
Data analysis 71
Ethical considerations 72
Conclusion 73

4   Socio-cultural background of the Maasai in Kenya 77

Introduction 77
Historical background of Kenya after independence from Britain 77
Government initiatives to improve education and people's well-being 78
Policy of adult and continuing education and women's development in Kenya 79
Maasai women's situation in Narok County 81
Conclusion 85

5   Narratives and process observation of village women 90

Introduction 90
Background of the research site: the village where I stayed 91
Narratives of village women 92
Analysis and discussions of the village women's narratives 101
Village women's voices on learning/literacy and well-being 113
Process observation 114
Conclusion 126

6   Interview analysis of women's group leaders and bureaucrats 133

Introduction 133
Narrative of women's group leaders 134
Analysis and discussions of the women's group leaders' narratives 139
The impact of women's group activities on well-being 146
The concept of literacy from a women's group leaders' perspective 148
Opinions about women's situation in the community and overcoming women's inequality 150
Narratives of government and NGO officers 152
Analysis and discussions of the government and NGO officers' narratives 156
The concept of literacy from a government officer's perspective: how do they see 'literacy'? 160
Conclusion 162

7 Conclusion 168

Introduction 168
Postcolonial feminist analysis: the significance of women's voices 169
Postcolonial feminist theory and informal learning and literacy in the context of international development 172
Discussion and implications of the findings 173
Women's informal learning/literacy and its impact on improving their well-being 173
Women's roles in improving well-being in their community 176
Women in Narok: changes in agency through the process of empowerment 178
Recommendations to the government, aid agencies, NGOs and future researchers 180
Directions for future research 184
Conclusion 185

Index 189

Illustrations

Figures

3.1	Wearing a Maasai beaded necklace	73
4.1	School lunch and a drinking water bottle brought from home	85
4.2	Playing with a ball in the school grounds	86
4.3	A school classroom can be used for adult education classes	87
5.1	A woman taking care of a wounded goat	119
5.2	A village dispensary in Narok	122
5.3	Adult education classes in Narok	127

Map

3.1	Map of Kenya	69

Table

3.1	Research participants	70

Foreword

Informal learning and international development

There has in recent years been a good deal of interest in informal learning – that largely unconscious, unplanned, unintentional learning everyone does during the course of everyday living which results in what have been called 'tacit funds of knowledge' and banks of skills (Moll *et al.* 1992) which we all use in negotiating our way through life. It is much larger than, and very different from, the formal and non-formal programmatic learning which is what we usually mean when we talk about 'learning'. It has been called 'the base of the iceberg' (see Rogers 2014), and it is fundamental to our sense of who we are and what we can and cannot do.

There have been and currently are a number of explorations of this informal learning in different contexts, especially in the international development field. In particular, growing interest in indigenous knowledge(s) and how it is created and passed on inter-generationally is leading to many new studies (see, for example, the special 2019 edition of *IRE*, edited by Tom *et al.*). Inge Kral's longitudinal study of an aboriginal community in Australia (Kral 2012) and Anna Robinson-Pant's comparative study of the informal learning of young farmers in Cambodia, Egypt and Ethiopia (Robinson-Pant 2016) are outstanding examples of the application of the concepts of informal learning to indigenous and developmental groups. Kyrgyz nomads and Indian pastoralists have equally been studied (Bunn 1999; Dyer and Choksi 2001). The way women in indigenous societies learn their identities, their position in their society and the roles they can and cannot play through untaught informal learning continues to attract much attention. Studies of informal learning among women in marginal and indigenous communities are in progress in Egypt with Bedouin communities and in Ethiopia and a number of other contexts (Aikman *et al.* forthcoming).

Indigenous learning

Much of this informal learning, of course, was and is experiential learning:

> Before I started school, we were herding cattle at home and it was a must that I brought home the same number of cows I went with in the morning. So I knew how to count cattle of different sizes and colours, meaning that we appreciated colour, sizes, shapes, etc. long before a teacher stood in front of us to teach numbers. This is the knowledge teachers ignored and made learning boring at times.
>
> (Banda 2016)

But some of it (especially the inter-generational elements) was 'semi-planned': as Moses instructed his Jewish community: "You shall teach these things repeatedly to your children, speaking to them when you sit at home and when you travel on the way, when you lie down and when you rise" (Deuteronomy 6:7). A recent study of the Sabar in India showed how the younger generations learnt in a structured way by observing elders or community members, following demonstrations and recreating them for themselves:

> For instance, children as young as 6–7 go on hunts with adults and are thus taught about the places to hunt; by about 10–12 they engage in making miniature versions of bow and arrows before they go on their own hunts with other Sabar adolescents. Moreover the Sabar learn within the larger landscape of jungles, and often learning is communal.… The Sabar are educated not only about basic survival skills in the forest but skills towards being a responsible member of the community.
>
> (Pallawi 2015, p. 6)

Such indigenous learning 'systems' are attracting much attention: "The international community is increasingly recognising that traditional and pragmatic ways of learning can be as efficient as Western didactic approaches" (UNESCO 2009, p. 17). But there are two dangers here. Salem points out that, although the concept of progress originally led people to denigrate and belittle native cultures, peasant communities, villages and small towns (Orr 2004, p. 193), today's interest in the 'indigenous' can lead to the 'traditional' and 'indigenous' being idealised into romantic unreality:

> In contrast to modern education, the richness of indigenous or traditional methods of education in some parts of the world as described by several scholars (cited) is reflected in its affiliation with nature and with life itself. Education in that sense is a pathway for the transformation and development of a human being, a journey to become fully human.… Traditional African education spans the whole duration of a human being's life, the whole of life is a process of learning to become fully human, to attain personhood.
>
> (Salem 2013, p. 170)

To talk in such language and, as some have, about the wholeness of indigenous learning systems may be to exaggerate.

Second, it is too easy to dichotomise the indigenous world as opposed to the modern (largely Westernised) world, and to polarise informal learning against formal and non-formal learning. In discussions of adult learning, we no longer see formal, non-formal and informal learning as separate categories; they form a continuum:

> Learning is often thought of as 'formal' or 'informal'. These are not discrete categories, and to think that they are is to misunderstand the nature of learning. It is more accurate to conceive 'formality' and 'informality' as attributes present in all circumstances of learning. The priority is then to identify these attributes, explore their relationships, and identify their effects on learners, teachers and the learning environment.
> (Colley *et al.* 2003)

> Non-formal interventions drew on both formal and informal learning processes, and it was unhelpful to characterize non-formal learning as a discrete category between the two.
> (Robinson-Pant 2016, p. 122)

Similarly the polarisation of indigenous and modern is now being revisited. It has been and in some circles still is held that

> The main causes of underdevelopment ... lie within the developing nation rather than external to it ... [that] Traditional ways of thinking and acting sustained underdevelopment ... [that] The route to modernization was to transform the people by introducing new ideas, values and beliefs through education and training programmes.
> (Blunt 1988, p. 45; citing Rogers 1976; Russell and Nicolson 1981)

But such views have been increasingly challenged: among some Western writers, the terms used are being changed: "Rather than indigenous and Western, we will use 'the universal' and 'the particular'" (Briggs 2005, p. 99; see Gustavsson 2010, 2014) or 'ethnic traditions' (Amutabi and Oketch 2009). Not everyone sees formal education like Chomsky (2006, p. 16): "far from creating independent thinkers, schools have always ... played an institutional role in a system of control and coercion". Many among the Sabar, for example, felt that 'education' (formal schooling) would "increase their *buddhi* [wisdom] and allow them not to be viewed as a *boko* (naïve, useless person as referred to by the dominant world)" (Pallawi 2015, p. 8).

Thus this is not a matter of 'either/or' – either modern or indigenous; nor is it always a question of marginalisation (although that undoubtedly exists). Many indigenous peoples occupy both worlds at the same time, traditional ideas and new knowledge being shared across different generations: "The

xiv *Foreword*

Sabar are not fearful of new knowledge but do not want to forget theirs in the making of the 'new Sabar'" (Pallawi 2015, p. 6; see also Aikman 1995). Studies in India (Chopra 2008) and in South Africa have shown how in the field of health:

> From the beginning of the colonial enterprise, biomedicine resisted amalgamation with other forms of healing and insisted on a monotherapeutic ideology and practice, whereas indigenous healing accommodated not only [modern] biomedicine, but invited pluralism within and across cultural and ethnic differences.
>
> (Decoteau 2013, p. 266)

Indigenous peoples often take hold and use in their own ways every resource which comes their way, including so-called 'modern' education and practices.

But even here the picture is complicated. It has been suggested that

> the uncritical adoption by some of the undeveloped of the modernized features of the developed occurred in tandem with the gradual abolition of their traditional ability to sustain themselves ... in a self-sufficient way of life over many years in their own places
>
> (Salem 2013, p. 143)

Some but not all: it is equally important (as Kral's study shows) that we do not see indigenous communities as homogenous – they too have their different elements, especially gender and age differences; they too have their radical and conservative elements; they too are responding in varying ways to changes in their immediate context, whether it be climate or new technologies or many other elements (for example, in some parts of the world, changing patterns of tourism are creating new challenges for indigenous groups). Through informal learning, identities are formed and reformed; roles are created and recreated in a continuous lifelong and lifewide learning process of both coping with and at the same time creating change. The different roles which formal learning (schooling), non-formal learning (for example, government and NGO training programmes provided for such communities) and self-directed learning (planned and purposeful programmes of exploration, critical reflection and trial and error resulting in the achievement of self-set goals) play in the overall learning of these women are all part of the story.

This then is the background to this in-depth study of women in Maasai societies in Kenya. One of the results of such detailed ethnographic studies of informal learning such as this is to challenge many of the concepts on which international development programmes have been built, especially the polarisation between the modern and the traditional/indigenous. It is not for me to outline here the contents of this book, only to indicate the major contribution it makes to the field, particularly of informal inter-generational learning among indigenous women. As in all good ethnographical research, in this study the voice of the women interviewed can be heard extensively, and the photographs (a useful tool of anthropological research) reveal much, observation counterbalancing interviews, checking what the women say against what they do. And – again as in all good ethnographical research – this book leads to further research questions: for example, the widespread use of mobile phones which are mentioned in this book as important can with profit be explored in greater depth, how different indigenous women learn to use mobile phones and what they do and do not do with them. There is much still to be learned from these women. But with this book, a major step forward has been taken.

Alan Rogers
University of East Anglia
March 2019

References

Aikman, Sheila (1995). Language, Literacy and Bilingual Education: An Amazon People's Strategies for Cultural Maintenance. *International Journal of Educational Development*, 15(4), 411–422.

Aikman, S., Robinson-Pant, A., and Rao, N. (eds) (forthcoming). Indigenous Women and Adult Learning, special issue of *Studies in the Education of Adults*.

Amutabi, M.N., and Oketch, M. (eds) (2009). *Studies in Lifelong Learning in Africa: From Ethnic Traditions to Technological Innovations*. New York: Edwin Mellen Press.

Banda, Dennis, University of Zambia, personal communication, 29 February 2016.

Blunt, A. (1988). Education, Learning and Development: Evolving Concepts. *Convergence*, 24(1), 37–53.

Briggs, J. (2005). The Use of Indigenous Knowledge in Development. *Progress in Development Studies*, 5(2), 99–114.

Bunn, S. (1999). The Nomad's Apprentice: Different Kinds of 'Apprenticeship' among Kyrgyz Nomads in Central Asia. In Ainley Patrick and Rainbird Helen (eds), *Apprenticeship: Towards a New Paradigm of Learning*, Kogan Page, pp. 74–85.

Chomsky, N. (2006). *Language and Mind*. Cambridge: Cambridge University Press.

Chopra, P. (2008). Parody and Power in the Gaze: Representations of the Illiterate Indian Village Woman, unpublished PhD thesis, Kings College, London.

Colley, H., Hodkinson, P., and Malcom, J. (2003). *Informality and Formality in Learning*, report for the Learning and Skills Research Centre, Leeds: University of Leeds. www.LSRC.ac.uk.

Decoteau, C.L. (2013). Hybrid Habitus: Towards a Post-Colonial Theory of Practice. In Julian Go (ed.), *Postcolonial Sociology: Political Power and Social Theory*, Vol. 24, Emerald Group Publishing, pp. 263–294.

Dyer, C., and Choksi, A. (2001). Literacy, Schooling and Development: Views of Rabari Nomads, India. In B. Street (ed.), *Literacy and Development: Ethnographic Perspectives*, London: Routledge.

Gustavsson, B. (2010). Bildung, Ubuntu and the Problem of Difference and Unity. In J. Enelo-Jansson, K. Jezierska, and B. Gustavsson (eds), *Altering Politics*, Örebro: Örebro University Press.

Gustavsson, B. (2014). Bildung and the Road from a Classical into a Global and Postcolonial Concept. *Confero*, 2(1), 109–131.

Kral, Inge (2012). *Talk, Text and Technology: Literacy and Social Practice in a Remote Indigenous Community*. Bristol: Multilingual Matters.

Moll, L., Amanti, C., Neff, D., and Gonzalez, N. (1992). Funds of Knowledge for Teaching: Using a Qualitative Approach to Connect Homes and Classrooms. *Theory into Practice*, 31(2), pp. 3–9.

Orr, David W. (2004). Orr's Laws, *Conservation Biology*. https://doi.org/10.1111/j.1523-1739.2004.01862.x, accessed 25 March 2019.

Pallawi, Sinha (2015). Emergent Education in the Homogenised World: The Significance of Integrating Indigenous Knowledge and Skills towards Future Education in India. *Learning for Sustainable Futures: Making the Connections*. https://nomadit.co.uk/conference/iuaes2014/paper/20641.

Robinson-Pant, A. (2016). *Learning, Knowledge and Skills for Agriculture to Improve Rural Livelihoods*. Paris: IFAD/UNESCO.

Rogers, A. (2014). *The Base of the Iceberg: Informal Learning and Its Impact on Formal and Non-Formal Learning*. Dortmund: Barbara Badruch.

Rogers, E.M. (1976). Communication and Development: The Passing of a Dominant Paradigm. *Communication Research*, 3, 121–148.

Russell, C.S., and Nicolson, N.K. (1981). *Public Choice and Rural Development*. Washington DC: Resources for the Future.

Salem, Abeer A.H. (2013). Negotiating Sustainability: Reclaiming Ecological Pathways to Bio-Cultural Regeneration in Egypt, unpublished PhD thesis, Prescott College.

Tom, Miye Nadya, Huaman, Elizabeth Sumida, and McCarty, Teresa L. (eds) (2019). Indigenous Knowledges as Vital Contributions to Sustainability, special issue of *International Review of Education* 65(1).

UNESCO (2009). *World Report on Investing in Cultural Diversity and Intercultural Dialogue Executive Summary*.

Acknowledgements

This book has been developed from a PhD thesis and six months' fieldwork in 2011 in Kenya. The process of writing a book has been a challenging but enjoyable time. I would never have been able to complete this study without the support and professional guidance of my supervisor, Associate Professor, Ruth Phillips, and my associate supervisor, Dr. Elizabeth Cassity, over the many months of research and writing.

This book was mainly written during my postdoc as a Japan Society for the Promotion of Science (JSPS) Fellow at Waseda University in Tokyo. And I wish to express my appreciation to JSPS for providing me with a JSPS Post-doctoral Fellowship.

My particular thanks go to Katie Peace and Sheng Bin Tan of Taylor & Francis who read full drafts of the manuscript and provided thoughtful comments and invaluable advice throughout, and motivated me from its beginnings to completion. The author also wishes to thank Pip Clubbs and the staff at Wearset for their work on the production of the book, and Steve Turrington for his copy-editing.

I would like to acknowledge the dozens of individuals all over the world, especially in Kenya, Australia and Japan, who gave their time generously while I was performing this research.

I am particularly grateful for the assistance and advice given by Prof. Fatuma Chege and Dr. Mutua Waema while I was based in Kenya for the data collection phase of the research.

I would also like to show my gratitude to Prof. Alan Rogers of the University of East Anglia for his generous contribution of a foreword.

The Joint Japan/World Bank Graduate Scholarship partially supported me to undertake the PhD studies at the University of Sydney.

I also wish to thank those who offered constant support, valued friendship and patience (Sawamura sensei, Kuroda sensei, Marvin, Archana, Remi, Marie, Shaista, Suin, Alex, Phillipa, Venice, Taka, Emiri, Sugimoto san's family, Renate, Oma, Graham, Yasuno gee, Makimura sensei, Ohishi sensei, Yamamoto sensei).

Finally I thank my family and my family in-laws for their unconditional love and support; Ryuichi, Rihito, Tokiko, Kyoko, Marin, Korin, Toshiko and Kozo.

Abbreviations

CIDA	Canadian International Development Agency
COVAW	Coalition on Violence Against Women
DAWN	Development with Women for a New Era
DFID	Department for International Development
EFA	Education for All
FAO	Food and Agriculture Organisation
FGM	*Female Genital Mutilation*
GAD	*Gender and Development*
GDP	Growth Domestic Product
GTZ	Deutsche Gesellschaft für Technische Zusammenarbeit (German Agency for Technical Cooperation)
HIV-AIDS	Human Immunodeficiency Virus Infection-Acquired Immunodeficiency Syndrome
ILO	International Labour Organization
KALA	*Kenya* Adult Learners' *Association*
KCPE	Kenya Certificate for Primary Education
KCSE	Kenya Certificate for Secondary Education
KDHS	Kenya Demographic and Health Survey
KNBS	Kenya National Bureau of Statistics
MDGs	Millennium Development Goals
MST	Movimento dos Trabalhadores Sem Terra (Landless Workers' Movement)
NGO(s)	Non Governmental Organisation(s)
OECD	Organisation for Economic Cooperation and Development
OMCT	Organisation Mondiale Contre la Torture (The World Organisation Against Torture)
Ph.D	Philosophy of Doctor
REFLECT	Regenerated Freirean Literacy Through Empowering Community Techniques
SDGs	Sustainable Development Goals
TBA	Traditional Birth Attendance
UN	United Nations
UNDP	United Nations Development Program

UNESCO	United Nations Educational, Scientific and Cultural Organisation
UNFPA	United Nations Population Fund
UNICEF	United Nations Children's Fund
UNIFEM	United Nations Entity for Gender Equality and the Empowerment of Women
UNWOMEN	United Nations Entity for Gender Equality and the Empowerment of Women
UPE	Universal Primary Education
USAID	United States Agency for International Development
WHO	World Health Organisation
WID	Women in Development

Glossary
Local language (Swahili) terms

Ugali a staple food made from maize flour with water.
Mama mother or a woman.
Manyatta a house.
Mutoto a child.
Mzzee an elder (old) man, also husband.
Shamba field, land, farm.
Shilling the currency of Kenya, abbreviated KSh.
Shuka traditional colourful piece of cloth which can be worn in a variety of ways.

Introduction

Exploring the notion of informal learning and literacy from a Maasai woman's perspective

This book is based on research conducted in Narok County, Kenya in 2011. To explore grassroots women's learning activities and their empowerment processes in relation to community development, three research approaches engaging women in a Maasai village produced a wealth of evidence about women's informal learning and literacy, and its links to gender issues and poverty in their communities. First, discourses about women's informal learning/literacy and their empowerment in the context of development will be discussed in relation to postcolonial feminist theory. Second, the research methods based on an ethnographic approach will be described, followed by the presentation of findings via a narrative and thematic analysis of interview data across two chapters. Through providing insights into a local woman's engagement with informal learning/literacy in one community, this study also aims to raise the significance of people-driven development activities.

The importance of education has been recognised by a number of international conventions, including the Universal Declaration of Human Rights in 1948 and the Dakar Framework for Action reaffirming the global 'Education for All' policy in 2000 (UNESCO 2015). Also, the United Nations declared the Millennium Development Goals (MDGs) in 2000, which included goals for improved quality of education, gender equality and women's empowerment by the target date of 2015. Women's literacy is the crucial factor in empowering women's participation in decision-making in society and in improving families' well-being. In the target year of 2015, however, challenges still remained. Some 58 million children are out of school and there are 781 million illiterate people (15 years and older) worldwide, of whom two-thirds consists of women (UNESCO 2015). Gender inequality is a strong factor in educational attainment. In a post-2015 agenda, comprising 17 goals, the Sustainable Development Goals (SDGs) have been set and agreed to by governments, international donor agencies and NGOs. SDG 4, on education, seeks to "ensure inclusive and equitable quality education and promote lifelong learning opportunities for all" (UNESCO 2015). Also, SDG 5, in relation to gender, seeks to "achieve gender equality and empower all women and girls" (UN 2015).

2 Introduction

Although men and women play different roles in society, the inequalities that exist between the genders are not entirely attributable to gender roles. Women lack equal access to resources, information and power, giving men a higher social status. Economic, social and cultural gender inequalities negatively affect the ability of women, particularly those who are in poor countries, to acquire a basic education for a better quality of life. Rather, women carry domestic unpaid and reproductive work, and tend to have a long working life from childhood to older age (Tsukada and Silvia 2009).

It is generally accepted that many women are not able to contribute fully and productively to community development because of cultural and social barriers to their participation in decision-making processes. Women's issues are multidimensional and interlinked, including socio-cultural, traditional and economic factors that affect women's status. This is especially the case in the Narok County in the Rift Valley Province, Kenya, where Maasai traditions and cultural practices are well preserved and practised. Due to the practice of female genital mutilation (FGM) and early marriage in the community, girls' participation in education is affected and restricted (Chege and Sifuna 2006; Takayanagi 2014). Moreover, girls are brought up to be subservient to men and are regarded as a gift from a father to a future husband (Chege and Sifuna 2006). Women are expected to depend first on their parents, then on their husbands and, ultimately, on their sons.

For people to have access to basic education, the Ministry of Education of Kenya established three main programmes; literacy, continuing education, community education and extension (Republic of Kenya 2010a, pp. 13–14). The literacy programme aims at providing the basic skills of reading, writing and arithmetic to illiterate adults and out-of-school youth (Republic of Kenya 2010a). Also, the government of Kenya has a new adult education curriculum aiming at certificate-oriented learning. The formal literacy centres will be most likely primary school education for adult learners to sit for the Kenyan Certificate for Primary Education. Income generating activity is focused in the literacy centre's activity. The continuing education programme targets semi-literate adult and youth to be integrated into the formal education system. They can learn school-based subjects in a non-formal setting (Republic of Kenya 2010a). The adult literacy programme also aims to advance women's empowerment through the establishment of small-scale businesses (Republic of Kenya 2010a; Bunyi 2006).

As the importance of women's roles in development projects was recognised by global communities, many aid agencies set up adult education and literacy projects for women. Women are believed to play a vital role in determining the well-being of the family and concerning education (UNESCO 2000a, 2000b; UNDP 2000). Consequently, women sought an alternative form of education through informal learning, which occurred through women's group activities. This new form of education had resulted in the emancipation of women from many forms of domination and discrimination based on gender, race and class. The women's self-directed informal learning led to women's collective empowerment. Some women became change agents in seeking solutions for improving their status and their families' well-being.

Several insights for adult literacy and development in Asia and Africa have been illuminated by the outcome of literacy examinations and improvements in the Gross Domestic Product (GDP) (UNDP 2000; UNESCO 2000a, 2000b). Critical of the application of a purely quantitative evaluation of educational projects, an ethnographic approach to explore actual literacy and numeracy practices in everyday life has been called for (Maddox et al. 2011; Street 2009; Robinson-Pant 2008; Gebre et al. 2009). In response to this call, this study adopted an ethnographic approach to build knowledge of the notion of literacy and development from the local people's perspectives. For this reason, the intention of the research was to examine people-centred development activities, whilst acknowledging tradition and culture, and hopefully moving beyond the external aid context.

There are also a number of key links between literacy and development. For instance, educated women seem to have smaller and healthier families (Bown 1990a; LeVine et al. 1991, 2012; Rao and Robinson-Pant 2006) and literate women have a positive effect on their child's schooling (Bown 1990a). Therefore functional literacy programmes targeting women have become popular with the integration of health, empowerment and income generating activities (Bown 1990a, 1990b; Carmen 1996).

Moreover, the link between literacy and the possibility of change is explicitly made in Freire's approach. Freire (1973) also saw literacy as more than reading, writing and numeracy. He argued for a literacy that was a process of "conscientization" (Freire 1973) and of "reading the world" (Freire and Macedo 1987), whereby adult learners acquire the social skills or knowledge to bring about positive changes to reduce poverty. Hence it empowers people to liberate themselves from oppressed situations. People gain self-reliance and problem solving skills to improve their well-being through literacy.

In relation to women, Freire (1985) argued that reading and writing are skills that can be used to criticise social structures that had been 'man-made', and hence women could use reading and writing skills to challenge these structures. In the context of Africa, people are rooted in their community, working to retain links with their community issues and experiences. Hence, they try to find activities and strategies by themselves to develop cooperative strategies to improve their community; for instance, women leaders make decisions that benefit 'communities rather than individuals' and 'in relation rather than dichotomously split' (Lugones 2010, p. 754). Therefore, one's priority in utilising one's skill and capacity is to improve communities rather than to profit individuals.

While the contributions of Masai women to the development of the country are significant, their work and voices remain silent in records and in scholarly works, particularly in adult education and feminist literature.

Based on this background as a context, this study explores the notion, practices and impact of informal learning and literacy and its impact on the well-being of the interviewed Maasai women in the village of Narok, Kenya, in the context of community development. It also examines how the women construct their self-directed learning and community-based development experiences, especially in regard to race, class, ethnicity and gender. This has provided an opportunity to examine how the village women have become empowered through informal learning and literacy and how they have utilised the skills gained and knowledge produced in relation to resisting traditional patriarchy to improve their well-being. Employing a theoretical framework of postcolonial feminist theory, this study made a commitment to listening to women's voices about their learning experiences in their created space.

This book is primarily built on original fieldwork conducted in Kenya, on women's experiences of informal learning/literacy integrated into community development activities in Narok County. The fieldwork for this study was conducted between April and September 2011. The reason for selecting women's groups in Narok County is because I had already established a rapport with local people during a previous research project conducted by a Japanese university between 2007 and 2009. I was therefore able to stay in the community comfortably as a researcher. As a result of this experience, I had become interested in investigating the relationship between women's informal education activities and their contribution to community development.

Kenya had gained independence from Britain in 1963 and the sociocultural situation of the Maasai had been influenced by British colonisation, as well as postcolonial systems (Coast 2002). However, the Maasai people of Narok County are dominated by their traditional lifestyle as Maasai.

This study has employed a qualitative research methodology in order to investigate women's notions and experiences of education/literacy, their needs and their strategies to enhance capacity that will prevent poverty.

This research also set out to investigate the role of formal education and the impact of informal learning (literacy) on women's power and influence in determining the well-being of their community. The key theoretical approach to the research was through a postcolonial feminist perspective. It also investigates how informal learning takes place among the women in a traditional Kenyan village, with the aim of challenging existing limitations in dominant notions of literacy. The research acknowledged the traditional, cultural and social factors that are perceived as a hindrance towards women's education and status; this was particularly achieved in the research through the method of process observation. As an invited participant researcher into activities in the community I was able to observe the interplay between traditional cultural practices and demands on the women of the village as well as how they formed strategies and resistances to those practices that were oppressive or limited their capacity to address daily challenges. The impact of women's activities and practices on bringing about a positive change in their standard of living were explored from the perspective of an autonomous development approach, in which individual women become creative and critical about their real life situation in order to find solutions for a better social and economic situation. The theoretical framework of postcolonial feminist theory, with its emphasis on the influence of colonisation on nation, race and gender, was applied to seek to have women's marginalized voices heard (Spivak 1985; Mohanty 1991).

The Kenyan government had implemented several literacy programmes since the 1960s, shifting the focus from basic literacy to functional literacy (Bunyi 2006). However, there was no clear curriculum followed in the adult education programme in Kenya (Bunyi 2006). The adult education providers who taught basic literacy and numeracy skills monitored and evaluated their own programmes. When I visited a literacy class conducted at a local church in Narok in 2008, Maasai participants were eager to gain literacy, numeracy and entrepreneurial skills. A few participants also mentioned their desire to be able to read the Bible written in Maasai and Swahili under a male literacy instructor. The government of Kenya declared a new adult education policy aiming at certificate-oriented learning, as stated by a government officer in the field data (Republic of Kenya 2010a, 2010b, 2010c). The government-run adult literacy centres were to provide adult learners with the knowledge and skills of primary school education to sit for the Kenyan Certificate for Primary Education (Republic of Kenya 2010a, 2010b, 2010c). Income generating activity was also sought to be included in the literacy centre's activity.

However, as this study demonstrates, there is capacity within a small community for some women to challenge their lack of participation in decision-making in a village community by developing their own sense of agency and contributing to development from within. Women can fully participate in small development programmes. It is also argued in this book that sustainable development needs to be owned and controlled by local people, based on their internal values. Furthermore, there should be continuous learning occurring, engaging people in learning and acting upon the knowledge gained. It is clear that at a deeper level these communities' attitudes towards literacy education are more complex. My previous research showed cases of illiterate Maasai women cooperating with each other to run community-based organisations for microcredit activities as well as for supporting girls' education. Those who are actively involved in managing women's organisations seem to gain adequate knowledge and skills, such as basic literacy, and can often run effective and efficient organisations by themselves. Although some women in Narok are not literate in a formal education setting, they have their own inherited knowledge of counting, raising children and pursuing their own learning based on their needs. Women's informal learning activities inspired the researcher to explore the value of education in their lives.

Based on previous research experiences in this context, I aimed to investigate the understandings of education and the impact of literacy on the traditional lifestyle in Narok County from a postcolonial feminist perspective,

6 *Introduction*

which attempted to find out whether power for positive changes to improve women's well-being can emerge from women's informal knowledge in their traditional community. This research also explored participants' own community-based literacy programmes and women's groups' activities in Narok County.

In order to investigate and analyse the impact of women's literacy on improvement of their well-being in Narok County, the research questions underpinning the study were:

1   What strategies and actions do women in Narok develop and employ to prevent poverty in their families and community through informal women's groups?
2   What is the nature of informal learning and literacy within the literacy and women's groups?
3   How does informal learning in the context of the women's groups open up a space from which the women can speak and be heard?
4   How do women in Narok respond to and resist oppressions that are related to patriarchal/postcolonial impositions?
5   How do their learning and community development activities manifest in their empowerment?

Overall, this study attempts to supplement the limited knowledge of the current literature by examining the gap between policy level discussions and actual women's lived experience in fighting against gender inequality and poverty within a Kenyan village context. The study of informal learning and literacy and autonomous human development through a postcolonial feminist framework in Kenya will contribute to knowledge of literacy from both theoretical and practical perspectives. How informal learning and literacy work to empower women is not well understood and can become a resource for more effective approaches to development and other poverty prevention measures. No evidence of prior documentation of the viewpoints of women in strong traditional Maasai communities in Kenya is evident in Western literature and there is limited broader scholarship on the impact of literacy on community development. There is also limited research from a postcolonial feminist perspective, where the objective is to listen to women's marginalised voices.

The results from this research provide an opportunity learning for practitioners and researchers. It may also contribute to effective international development assistance related to gender equality and poverty.

In the case of Narok County in the Rift Valley Province, Kenya, where Maasai traditions and cultural practices are well preserved and practised, women lack participation in decision-making processes. Both boys and girls are expected to help with housework such as looking after cattle and fetching fire-wood, yet girls play an additional role in taking care of younger siblings (Chege and Sifuna 2006).

In Kenya there are parallels to be drawn between national gender concerns and the objectives of community-based women's movement to improve their social situation. It is believed Kenyan women are also developing their consciousness and power by initiating needs-based development programmes (Pradervand 1989). They act through their own genuine *agency*, not just as invited participants in a government-controlled development framework (Carmen 1996).

Therefore, research on informal learning and women's empowerment in relation to international development through a postcolonial feminist approach in Kenya is innovative since it helps interpret the notion of village women's informal learning and literacy experiences in their strong traditional communities from the viewpoints of people of the Maasai in Kenya by looking at discourses, practices and impact of literacy on community development through ethnographic data. It will also determine a quantitative achievement of people for the community and the qualitative human development of individuals of/for the community through informal learning by focusing on gender issues. I believe this research will be beneficial for development agencies and community-based organisations for people while Kenya works out how the national curriculum should be reformed with consideration to their culture and traditions. I am also interested in sharing my analysis and recommendations with primary school teachers and community-based organisations so that they can manage and control their resources and development programmes.

References

Bown, L. (1990a). *Preparing the Future: Women, Literacy and Development.* Report No. 4. London: Action Aid.

Bown, L. (1990b). Women, Literacy and Development. In B. Street (ed.), *Literacy in Development. People Language Power. Education for Development.* London: Routledge.

Bunyi, W.G. (2006). *Real Options for Literacy Policy and Practice in Kenya.* Background paper prepared for the Education for All Global Monitoring Report 2006. Literacy for Life. Paris: UNESCO.

Carmen, R. (1996). *Autonomous Development: Humanizing the Landscape. An Excursion into Radical Thinking and Practice.* London: Zed Books.

Chege, F.N., and Sifuna, D.N. (2006). *Girls and Women's Education in Kenya.* Nairobi: UNESCO.

Coast, E. (2002). Maasai Socioeconomic Conditions: A Cross-Border Comparison. *Human Ecology*, 30(1), 79–105.

Freire, P. (1973). *Education for Critical Consciousness.* London: Sheed and Ward.

Freire, P. (1985). *The Politics of Education: Culture, Power and Liberation.* New York: Bergin and Garvey.

Freire, P., and Macedo, D. (1987). *Literacy: Reading the Word and the World.* London: Routledge and Kegan Paul.

Gebre, A., Openjuru, G., Rogers, A., and Street, B. (2009). *Everyday Literacies in Africa: Ethnographic Studies of Literacy and Numeracy Practices in Ethiopia.* Addis Ababa: Fountain Publishers.

LeVine, R., LeVine, S., Richman, A., Uribe, F., Correa, C., and Miller, P.J. (1991). Women's Schooling and Childcare in the Demographic Transition: A Mexican Case Study. *Population and Development Review*, 17(3), 459–496.

LeVine, R.A., LeVine, S., Schnell-Anzola, B., Rowe, M., and Dexter, E. (2012). *Literacy and Mothering: How Women's Schooling Changes the Lives of the World's Children (Child Development in Cultural Context)*. New York: Oxford University Press.

Lugones, M. (2010). Toward a Decolonial Feminism. *Hypetia*, 25(4), 742–759.

Maddox, B., Aikman, S., Rao, N., and Robinson-Pant, A. (2011). Literacy Inequalities and Social Justice. *International Journal of Educational Development*, 31(6), 577–579.

Mohanty, C.T. (1991). Under Western Eyes: Feminist Scholarship and Colonial Discourses. In C.T.R. Mohanty, Ann Russo, and L. Torres (eds), *Third World Women and the Politics of Feminism*. Bloomington: Indiana University Press.

Pradervand, P. (1989). *Listening to Africa: Developing Africa from the Grassroots*. New York: Praeger.

Rao, N., and Robinson-Pant., A. (2006). Adult Education and Indigenous People: Addressing Gender in Policy and Practice. *International Journal of Educational Development*, 26(2), 209–223.

Republic of Kenya (2010a). *The Constitution of the Republic of Kenya*. Nairobi: Government Printer.

Republic of Kenya (2010b). *2009 Kenya Population and Housing Census, Volume I A*. Nairobi: Kenya National Bureau of Statistics.

Republic of Kenya (2010c). *2009 Kenya Population and Housing Census, Volume I C*. Nairobi: Kenya National Bureau of Statistics.

Robinson-Pant, A. (2008). Why Literacy Matters: Exploring Policy Perspective on Literacies, Identities and Social Change. *Journal of Development Studies*, 44(6), 779–796.

Spivak, G.C. (1985). Can the Subaltern Speak? Speculations on Widow Sacrifice. *Wedge*, 7/8(Winter/Spring), 120–130.

Street, B. (2009). The Future of 'Social Literacies'. In M. Baynham and M. Prinsloo (eds), *The Future of Literacy Studies*, London: Palgrave Macmillan, pp. 21–37.

Takayanagi, T. (2014). The Complexity of Literacy in Kenya: Narrative Analysis of Maasai Women's Experiences. *Compare: A Journal of Comparative and International Education*, 44(5), 826–844.

Tsukada, R., and Silva, E. (2009). *Age and Gender Bias in Workloads during the Life Cycle: Evidence from Rural Ghana*. International Policy Centre for Inclusive Growth. One Pager. No. 88.

UN. (2015). *Transforming our World: The 2030 Agenda for Sustainable Development*. New York: UN.

UNDP. (2000). *Human Development Report 2000. Human Rights and Human Development*. New York: Oxford University Press.

UNESCO. (2000a). *The Dakar Framework for Action: Education for All: Meeting Our Collective Commitments*. Paris: UNESCO.

UNESCO. (2000b). *Education for All. Global Monitoring Report 2012, Youth and Skills: Putting Education to Work*. Paris: UNESCO.

UNESCO. (2015). Sustainable Development Goals for Education. http://en.unesco.org/sdgs/ed, accessed 10 December 2015.

1 Postcolonial feminist theory

Introduction

After establishing the context and motivation for this research in the previous chapter, it is important to outline and explore the theoretical framework that has informed this study.

This book focuses primarily on Maasai women's experiences in informal learning and literacy in relation to community development. As indicated in the Introduction to this book, there were several reasons why postcolonial feminist theory was selected to analyse Maasai women's life experiences. However, the two key reasons are that, one, Kenya has been strongly affected by colonisation, and later modernisation under the name of development and, two, women's voices have been largely absent from processes of planning, implementation and evaluation of development programmes (Coast 2002; Creighton and Yieke 2006; Nussbaum and Glover 1995; Razari and Miller 1995; Visvanathan *et al.* 1997; Momsen 2004).

The choice of a specifically feminist postcolonial theory relates to critical analyses that have viewed wider postcolonial theory as insufficient in explaining power relationships among social classes and gender (Allender 2002). In response to such criticisms, scholars such as Gayatri Spivak extended the theoretical bases of postcolonial theory to develop a feminist postcolonial theory. Most notably, Spivak (1985a) was very critical of the missing voices of the marginalised, especially women, in the postcolonial nation building process. Feminist postcolonial scholars have made a considerable contribution through the conceptualisation of an intersection between gender, nation, race and identity since the 1980s (Spivak 1985a; Harding 1987). Postcolonial feminist scholarship is committed to highlighting and challenging the social inequality experienced by marginalised women, especially in poor countries. Its theoretical approaches are mostly based on experiences of women in various socio-cultural, historical and political contexts. Prior to reviewing the relevant literature, it is important to note that although my topic intersects with a number of research areas, this chapter focuses mainly on literature from the field of postcolonial feminism, as it is the primary theoretical framework for this study. This chapter will first explain how postcolonial feminist theory emerged. In the following chapter I will review the literature on informal education and literacy, as that is also central to the purpose of this research.

The first section of this chapter will discuss the broader terrain of postcolonial theory as it analyses the legacies of colonialism, which includes maintaining an economic and cultural dependency between the colonised people and the former colonising country (Ashcroft *et al.* 1989, 1995, 2006). The persistent issue of gender inequality in poor countries, in terms of unequal access to education, health, public services, equal pay, legal rights and political rights, is strongly evident in most postcolonial African states. Moreover, due to the dominance of patriarchy in still strongly traditional cultures, men's power over women is often perpetuated, as women are silenced by the unacceptability of women expressing their opinions in front of men (Hodgson 2011). For at least four decades gender inequality has been the focus of women's empowerment as a key objective in the development of a postcolonial critique. The key aim of women's empowerment was to improve the status of women, towards equality of social, economic and formal citizenship. International development agencies such as the United Nations and the World Bank have focused on women's empowerment in their agendas and have attempted to integrate women into decision-making processes for development programmes (UNESCO 2000, 2014; World Bank 1997, 2012). However, it has been women's movements that have been most important in raising the key objective of the emancipation of women (Mohanty 2003; Allen 2008). Therefore feminism in postcolonial feminist theory will be the focus of this chapter.

However, it is important to note that, in response to the important work of key postcolonial thinkers such as Frantz Fanon (1967) and Edward Said (1978), the Subaltern Studies Group was established (Guha 1982). The scholarship and analysis emerging from the subaltern studies group prompted the development of a feminist critique within postcolonialism, as much of the work of the Subaltern Studies group was viewed as insufficient by feminists since it failed to explain gendered power relationships. Postcolonial feminists raised the issue of the missing voices of the marginalised throughout the world, particularly women (Spivak 1985a). Feminists also pointed out that this marginalisation meant that women were not part of nation building in postcolonial states (Spivak 1985a; Mohanty 1991). In keeping with the postmodern turn in feminism more broadly, and for the practical needs of theory, fieldwork became essential for listening to the actual voices of the oppressed (Harding and Norberg 2005). This was also important for the emergence of Southern thinkers as well as an emerging literature from poor-country feminists (Head 1977; Dangarembga 1988; Ogunyemi 1985; Parmer and Minh-ha 1990). A review of literature that deals more directly with development, foreign aid and education will be presented in Chapter 2. Lastly, postcolonial feminist theory will be illuminated to lead us to the investigation of women who are affected by social issues in poor countries, in particular.

Postcolonial theory

As postcolonial feminist theory emerged from postcolonial theory, broader postcolonial theory requires some discussion. A key point of postcolonial theory in this study is that Kenya was once one of the British colonies where the activities of Western missionaries was a form of colonisation, and Christianity imposed a different set of expectations on social as well as economic development (Achebe 1958). For example, as this study demonstrates, patriarchy has been reinforced by the Christian church, which has become an important part of the Maasai community.

Postcolonial theory emerged in the critical literature discipline in the 1960s and took some time to reach prominence, and it has become a significant approach in analysing the continuing struggle against colonisation and for social justice (Spivak 1985a).

Postcolonial theory has also been utilised as a methodological framework by key scholars interested in the politics of social identity and social and economic development (Fanon 1967; Said 1978; Bhabha 1994; Spivak 1985a). A variety of different discourses have created a large body of academic and popular literature on postcolonial theory and related topics (Ashcroft *et al.* 1989, 1995, 2006; Mongia 1996; Schwarz and Ray 2000; Young 1990). Postcolonial discourses examine and analyse various relationships between West–East, North–South, developed–underdeveloped, and coloniser–colonised (Ashcroft *et al.* 1995; Mongia 1996; Schwarz and Ray 2000). Said, Bhabha and Spivak were highly influential in conceptualising the connection between nation, culture and politics, which contributed to the creation of postcolonial theory (Young 1990).

Prior to the conceptualisation of postcolonial theory, Frantz Fanon (1967) influenced and inspired anti-colonial movements. In his book, *Black Skin, White Masks* (1967), Fanon discussed the quest for self-identity, the fight against colonisation and processes of decolonisation. As Fanon was born in Martinique, a former French colony of the Caribbean Islands, he had lived the experience of colonial racism. The official language in Martinique was French and he learnt subjects in French at school. He observed that speaking French meant that people in his country accepted French culture and the colonial master's minds as local people were forced to adopt French ways of thinking (Fanon 1967). Through the language, local people's minds were completely colonised and forced to obey their master's orders. Fanon concluded that the mastery of language affords significant power (Fanon 1967, p. 18). Frantz Fanon developed perspectives on decolonisation within postcolonial studies, seeking to demonstrate how black people were oppressed and colonised by Western cultures. It is suggested that this perspective can also be applied to examine current relationships between donor and aid recipient countries, as a number of scholars claim that, through development assistance, the relationship between the coloniser and colonised has been maintained (Ashcroft *et al.* 1995; Mongia 1996; Said 1978; Schwarz and Ray

2000). In this study this perspective can be applied more specifically as, due to the postcolonial state, educational development assistance throughout postcolonial societies has focused on formal European models of education, which act as a means of maintaining prior colonial power. This is evident in the fact that such systems fail to recognise or value traditional and informal modes of education carried out by local women aiming to resist patriarchal oppression and to preserve aspects of traditional culture (Gee 1991; Street 1995; Barton et al. 2000; Rogers 2004). For example, some women in Narok are fighting against traditional patriarchy and FGM.

Fanon also argued that local/colonised people were oppressed by outsiders/colonisers in attempts to speak of their own opinions to others. Fanon used provocative arguments to prompt people to be aware of their colonised minds. He articulated powerful ideas about liberating people within his country (Fanon 1967).

The postcolonial struggle and analysis is relevant to this study on two levels: first, because Kenya was under British colonial rule from 1895 to 1963 and, second, because it is a theoretical context from which postcolonial feminist theory emerged. While the research participants in this study did not raise the socio-cultural and political complications of colonisation, it is necessary to understand the history of Kenya, particularly in relation to education. In some literacy contexts, postcolonial theory addresses the literature produced in countries that used to be colonies of other countries, such as East Africa. Postcolonial theory raised the challenge that writers under colonial rule were educated within a system of colonisation (Sifuna 1990). This means that colonising countries like Britain educated the colonised Kenyans through the British education system. Although the importance of integration of traditional indigenous knowledge into the current formal education has been discussed for many years, Kenya has maintained a British system of education since 1963 (Sifuna 1990). This is strongly reflected in the fact that English has been used as the medium of instruction at school since 1963 (Sifuna 1990).

Postcolonial theory emerged by examining postcolonial literature and discourses in order to understand the impact of the colonisation process. It was illustrated within literature and viewed from narratives of the 'lived' experiences of colonisation and postcolonial life. Edward Said's book, *Orientalism* (1978), has been highly influential in the emergence of postcolonial theory (Mongia 1996). For Said, postcolonialism was about analysing imperialism, "the practice, the theory, and the attitudes, of a dominating metropolitan centre ruling a distant territory 'colonialism', which is almost always a consequence of imperialism, the implanting of settlements on distant territory" (1994, p. 8). Said clearly condemned the distinction between the coloniser and colonised. He described the colonised as "inhabitants of the non-Western and non-European world, which had been controlled and often settled forcibly by Europeans" (1989, p. 206). Later, Said's coloniser/colonised argument was applied to the more contemporary process of the West's impositions on the East (the Orient). In his analysis, Said pointed out that "the Orient is all absence, whereas one feels the Orientalist and what he says as presence" (1978, p. 208). Said (1978) argued that the West had constructed stereotyped views about the East. He further suggested that a long history of European colonial power and domination over colonised countries has disregarded the knowledge and life experiences of local people.

Said (1978) suggested that the positioning of the colonial subject was homogenous, for example, a homogeneous mass of Africa to be dominated by the imperial colonial powers. While there are a large number of ethnic groups, tribes and languages spoken in Africa, Said (1978) observed that Africa was seen as one large group of 'Others'. Further, Said (1978) suggested that postcolonial literature is most likely to be focused on the writings and experiences of Western men in colonial times. As Spivak (1985a) noted, female writers discussing local female opinions and life experiences were not prominent.

Western descriptions of the representation of 'the colonised' have been challenged by a number of scholars such as V.Y. Mudimbe, who authored books such as *The Invention of Africa* (1988). Also Chinua Achebe (1958), a well-known Nigerian writer, addressed misinterpretations of African culture as backward and uncivilised, by conveying the tale of the colonisation of the Igbo (one of the ethnic groups in Nigeria) from an African point of view. For example, Achebe (1977) observed that African people were portrayed as savage and ignorant in Joseph Conrad's fictional book *Heart of Darkness* (1988). Conrad represented Congolese natives as "foolish faces with unconcerned old eyes of black people" (1988, p. 8). Conrad's book reinforced racism and misconceptions about African people. This motivated Achebe to write a story about the cultural life of Igbo in Nigeria, and he published a novel called *Things Fall Apart* (1958). The novel demonstrated the impact of British imperialism and Christian missionaries through the experiences of a traditional Igbo family. As Africa was excluded from the discipline of literature, Achebe deliberately included Indigenous African writings within the field of literature. Achebe's (1977) provocative essay entitled "An Image of Africa: Racism in Conrad's Heart of Darkness" emphasised a strong criticism of how Conrad "set Africa up as a foil to Europe" (p. 251). Achebe also pointed out that "The real question is the dehumanization of Africa and Africans, which this age-long attitude has fostered and continues to foster in the world" (1977, p. 256). He asserted that the humanity of black people portrayed in the book should be addressed. He concluded that the West ought to look at people in the continent of Africa without inherited prejudices and stereotype images. Moreover, in an interview with Bill Moyers (1989), Achebe replied that "We are passing through a bad patch, and if we succeed, then even this experience of the bad patch will turn out to be an enrichment" (Moyers 1989, p. 343). Achebe confidently stated that Africa experienced the terrible colonisation by the West, yet Africa had a capacity to overcome its trauma and would make efforts to bring about social improvements. However, Olarinmoye (2013) was critical of Achebe (1977)

14 *Postcolonial feminist theory*

for representing and reinforcing traditional gender roles where women were only engaged in gendered functions such as marriage, child bearing and child rearing, hence revealing a strong patriarchal view.

Moreover, the language used in postcolonial writing (mainly the colonial master's language, for instance, English/French) was criticised by Ashcroft and others (1989). There had been a tendency towards native languages being replaced by the standard dominant language (Ashcroft 1989). Writing texts in English was already another form of exclusion of the subaltern's opinions. Spivak also noted that "the feeling of cultural identity almost always presupposes a language" (1996, p. 199). This argument led to the emergence of postcolonial writers writing in their own language, such as Ngũgĩ wa Thiong'o (1986), a Kenyan writer. Ngũgĩ wa Thiong'o notes "its [colonisation's] most important domination was the mental domination of the colonized, the control, through culture, of how people perceived themselves and their relationship to the world" (1986, p. 16). He produces novels in his mother tongue, Gikuyu, rather than in the national languages of English or Swahili. This was a way for him to fully identify himself and his roots. For him, writing in his native language rather than the colonial language of English was his political message. He encouraged other African authors to write in their native language that could be a process of "decolonizing the mind" away from the colonised mind-set to becoming a native African (Ngũgĩ wa Thiong'o 1986). He also attempted to convey the message of importance of writing about true African experiences. Ngũgĩ wa Thiong'o clearly stated that "language and literature were taking us further and further from ourselves to other selves, from our world to other worlds" (1986, p. 12). He strongly criticised the influence of a colonial language on native cultures and people. This argument remains defeated as regards the formal education system in Kenya, as the only languages used in school education are the dominant English and Swahili; this adds to diminishing the tribal or native identities. It also reflects the central relevance of postcolonial theory to this research and goes further in recognising women's specific exclusion from dominant culture.

As Parmer and Minh-ha stated, "now that more women of colour have access to education, there will be more and more rewriting work to be done on our side" (1990, p. 68). A small number of postcolonial women writers are also known in African literature, including Bessie Head (1977) (Botswana/South Africa), Tsitsi Dangarembga (1988) (Zimbabwe) and Chikwenye Okonjo Ogunyemi (1985) (Nigeria). Head (1992), in the book *The Collector of Treasures: and Other Botswana Village Tales*, described women's oppressed situation in African society. Dangarembga (1988), in the book of *Nervous Conditions*, also illustrated gender issues observed in daily lives, such as son preference in schooling and early marriage for young girls in postcolonial Zimbabwe in the 1960s. Ogunyemi's (1985) idea of 'womanism', African women's feminist ideas, will be discussed more closely later in this chapter. This approach is apt for the research focus of this study. From the 'womanism' perspective, the language of development and improvement (from the ex-colonising nations) is also a suppression of culture and denies the agency of the Maasai women who, as this research demonstrates, have their own strategies for learning and improving their economic and social status.

In addition, female postcolonial authors in Africa have produced literature that searched for an African identity. For instance, Nafissatou Diallo (1975) was the first Senegalese female author to publish a novel and an autobiography aiming to break the silence of women, the subaltern of Africa, through literature.

In an important contribution to postcolonial theory, Homi Bhabha (1994) developed the concept of hybridity based on literary and cultural theory to explain the construction of mixed culture and identity within situations of colonial opposition and inequity (Bhabha 1994, 1996). Bhabha offers his insights about the various complexities within the identification of the "Other". Bhabha constantly reminds us of the dangers of simplifying cultures or endorsing assumptions. In postcolonial discourse, the notion that any culture or identity is genuine, pure or significant can be controversial (Ashcroft et al. 1995). Bhabha himself is aware of the risks of fixity of identities within colonial thinking, stating that "all forms of culture are continually in a process of hybridity" (Rutherford 1990, p. 211). His conceptualisation of hybridity allows us to challenge our image of fixed and controlled indigenous cultures and the illusion of cultural isolation or purity. In relation to my study, the research participants found various spaces in which to develop their identities as strong women, while still committed to many traditional practices but challenging others. Interventions of colonial power have created more complex and diverse cultures in poor, postcolonial states. Cultures can be seen to interact and transform with each other in a complex way. It can be said that cultures are consequences of historical processes (Bhabha 1994). This is a key point when considering the generalised impact of feminism on women's cultural struggles for equality, as is discussed later in this book.

Another significant postcolonial writer/theorist, Stuart Hall (1992), described the West as being "a society that is developed, industrialized, urbanized, capitalist, secular, and modern" (p. 278). Consequently, Hall states that the dominant view of the West was that non-Western societies were somewhere far away from the West and could be underdeveloped and backward compared to the West (1992, p. 223). Hall's point is that like Said's description of Orientalism, dichotomies form from the Western viewpoints, which places the non-Western countries as 'other' and in need of 'development' or modernisation, to make them more like the West. This occurred during colonisation and is now perpetuated through the West being involved in development of non-Western countries. Therefore, development programmes implemented in Africa apply a Western model of improvement and they would not regard the traditional and cultural skills and organisations as important components in their implementation (Goldssmith and Mander 2001; Carmen 1996; Arowolo 2010). This study focuses on how developmental processes appear to ignore Massai women's own resistances (to patriarchy, for example) and how they develop their own literacies through informal learning in relation to the needs of their everyday lives. Therefore, postcolonial theory from a perspective of local colonised African people is useful to analyse the impact of colonisation on the colonised and to examine the socio-cultural effects in the people in Narok. Through so called development assistance, the power relationship between the coloniser and colonised can still be observed.

For marginalised and subordinated women facing multiple forms of inequalities based on gender, race and class, access to education and involvement in decision-making processes have been constrained (Moser 1993; Robeyns 2010). Such multiple inequalities intersect and have great influence on women's lives. To emphasise the status of groups of marginalised women, the term 'subaltern' was applied by Spivak (1988). Later insufficient discussion and analysis of gender perspectives in postcolonial theory were pointed out. Hence by addressing this point, postcolonial feminist theory was developed (Anderson 2002; Browne et al. 2007).

Spivak (1988) developed a new conceptualisation of the 'subaltern' in her essay, "Can the Subaltern Speak?". The term 'subaltern' was borrowed from Antonio Gramsci's application of the term, meaning a lower class of people in society who are under the hegemony of the ruling class (Ashcroft et al. 2000). Gramsci (1971) applied the term 'subaltern' in relation to social class in Italy. Subaltern is a term that commonly refers to people who are socially, politically and geographically outside of the hegemonic power structure (Gramsci 1971). He stated that "Subaltern classes are subject to the initiatives of the dominant class, even when they rebel; they are in a state of anxious defence" (Gramsci 1971, p. 21). Drawing on this meaning, subaltern people are those who are subordinated by hegemony and excluded from important positions in society. Also, subaltern groups often experience discrimination by dominant groups within their own society (Gramsci 1971; Spivak 1985). Smith (2010) suggests that Gramsci undertook an important analysis of capitalist hegemony, where Gramsci viewed slaves, peasants, religious groups, women, different races and the proletariat as the subaltern. This is why it was significant for Gramsci to understand and analyse the subaltern's emergence and processes in socio-cultural, political, historical contexts (Smith 2010). Like Gramsci's subaltern groups, colonised people have been silenced by dominant, colonising communities; they can also be viewed as subaltern. Drawing on this idea, scholarship on 'subaltern studies' emerged. For example, the Subaltern Studies Group was founded by Indian historian, Ranajit Guha (1982). However, the studies did not explain well enough subalterns' lack of autonomy and agency. Prakash further claims that "while these scholars failed to recognize fully that the subalterns' resistance did not simply oppose power but was also constituted by it, their own work showed this to be the case" (1994, p. 1480).

Spivak also argued that subaltern is not just

a classy word for oppressed, for Other, for somebody who's not getting a piece of the pie.... In postcolonial terms, everything that has limited or no access to the cultural imperialism is subaltern – a space of difference. Now who would say that's just the oppressed? The working class is oppressed. It's not subaltern....

(Kock 1992, p. 45)

Spivak raised the issue of the unequal power relations of gender and she referred to subordinated women as subaltern. Spivak especially points out the missing subordinated group in the Subaltern in this quote:

It is well known that the notion of the feminine (rather than the subaltern of imperialism) has been used in a similar way within deconstructive criticism and within certain varieties of feminist criticism. In the former case, a figure of 'woman' is at issue, one whose minimal prediction as indeterminate is already available to the phallocentric tradition. Subaltern historiography raises questions of method that would prevent it from using such a ruse. For the 'figure' of woman, the relationship between woman and silence can be plotted by women themselves; race and class differences are subsumed under that change. Subaltern historiography must confront the impossibility of such gestures.

(Spivak 1985a, p. 82)

The extent of women's empowerment to ensure that women's voices are heard in their male dominant community can be analysed by the term 'subaltern'. Spivak (1985a) noted that 'subaltern' women have been continuously excluded, and are constituted as a marginalised group in society. They stay at the lower position of the local power structure, without being uplifted to an equal status with men. Spivak (1985a) argued that subaltern women have a voice, but there is no space permitted for women to raise a voice, and their voice should be valued in society. This is a significant point in this study as it raises questions about the subordinate situation of Maasai women and how this influences women's learning and well-being. Given that postcolonial theory has evolved far beyond its original literary discourses it has been related to "questions of resistance, power, ethnicity, nationality, language, and culture and the transformation of dominant discourses by ordinary people" (Ashcroft et al. 1989). In relation to this study, women's resistance to traditional patriarchy within their Maasai community under the colonised nation of Kenya has been observed through their collective learning and action for each other and having their voice heard in their created spaces in the village. Therefore, outsiders such as development workers need to listen to and learn from the local women, which could improve the effectiveness of development programmes.

While postcolonial theory has significance in relation to integrating local people's views in educational development programmes in Africa, Spivak

(1988) pointed out that postcolonial theory does not reflect a gendered perspective. Therefore, we must incorporate feminist perspectives towards developing a postcolonial feminist approach (Anderson 2002). I discuss postcolonial feminism in the following section to provide the lens through which I embarked upon my research.

Postcolonial feminism

Postcolonial feminism is one of the critical theories that can be used to examine the intersections of race, class, and gender and other relations. With this understanding, I have paid careful attention to the complexity and experiences of village women's everyday lives, which may often be overlooked.

First, within postcolonial feminism it is often noted that a researcher's race, class, gender and culture could affect the research process, and the position of the researcher is acknowledged and incorporated into research analysis (Mohanty 1991, 1997, 2003; Kirkham and Anderson 2002). The researcher can be an influential instrument of observation in the research site and needs to be committed to analysing and interpreting the culture (Deutsch 2004). As Deutsch (2004) notes of the process of becoming a researcher, researchers should be aware that research work and writings are produced in the particular standpoints in which the researcher is positioned, hence researchers should also acknowledge the limits of objectivity. Therefore with these views in mind, I have incorporated my researcher 'positionality' as a Japanese middle-class woman and junior academic into the research process and have attempted to be responsible and accountable for how I interpret and represent the knowledge produced by the research participants in Narok.

Second, postcolonial feminist theory sets out to examine how race, gender and class relations influence social, cultural, political and economic factors, which shape the lives of subordinated women. In this study I will examine how race, tradition and gender roles influence individual experiences of learning and the daily life of Maasai women. Through village women's narratives I will be able to examine and gain a deeper understanding of the barriers and facilitators that have influenced the village women in seeking a solution to improve their well-being and in particular their strategies for avoiding poverty for themselves and their children.

The aim of feminist research is not only to generate a more accurate account of women's everyday experiences, but also seek to change the oppressive conditions in which they live (Narayan 1997; Mohanty 1991, 1997, 2003; Kirkham and Anderson 2002; Fine 2010; Evans 2002; Phillips 2009). Feminist research is politically driven in that it challenges the dominant forces influencing women's lives (Mohanty 2003). The aim of this study is not only to explore women's informal learning and community development activities, but also to seek to improve the conditions in which they live, so that women practice and gain access to learning and literacy. This postcolonial feminist perspective "recognises the need for knowledge construction from the perspective of the marginalised female subject whose voice has been muted in the knowledge production process" (Kirkham and Anderson 2002, p. 10). Feminist research methods also aim at giving close attention to "what was spoken, what was implied and what was not spoken about" (Denzin and Lincoln 1994).

In addition, Spivak (1985b) also developed the idea of 'strategic essentialism'. This was necessary in the context of an intrinsically post-structuralist theory of postcolonial feminism, as strategic essentialism can be engaged by a collective group of the subaltern (or women) to work toward structural change, while at the same time criticising the category for being assumed to be a homogeneous group of people (Spivak 1985b). The term 'essentialism' refers here to the risk of 'restoring' subaltern voices, creating stereotyped impressions of their diverse cultures (Spivak 1985b). She said, "one must nevertheless insist that the colonized subaltern subject is irretrievably heterogeneous" (Spivak 1985b, p. 79). This relates to wider debates in feminism, in the postmodern critiques of radical and other structural feminisms that tended to generalise all women's experiences of being women (Fine 2010; Evans 2002; Spender 1985; Mohanty 2003; Phillips 2009).

However, Spivak (1999) also suggests that essentialism could be used strategically by groups to make it easier for the subaltern to be heard and understood by the majority. For instance, if women's groups have their own goals and activities to change their unfair situation in communities, the most common needs are addressed in working for improvements. The subaltern group of people are structurally marginalised and individual voices would not be effective enough to bring about social change. Yet, collective voices as a group could influence and lead social change. Spivak analysed the European metaphysics of Kant and Hegel in her book called *A Critique of Postcolonial Reason* (1999), and observed that they seem to exclude the subaltern from social discussions, and also prevent non-Western scholars from occupying positions as fully human subjects. Based on her analysis of the major philosophers, Spivak (1999) suggested non-Western people as well as the subaltern had been historically excluded from philosophical discourses (Spivak 1999).

Within Spivak's discussion of strategic essentialism, it is implied that the marginalised people themselves create a group for formulating their own identity and to further advance their own well-being. This relates to the key question of this study: that is whether a family and community are benefited in a sustainable way based on grassroots informal women's groups. The Maasai women use strategic collective action based on collective voices; they, as a group, take initiatives in order to bring about social change.

After studying postcolonial theory and the concept of subaltern, Spivak (1988) criticised subaltern studies and postcolonial scholarship when she observed a young Bengali woman's suicide in South Asia. Some widows will commit suicide to honour their husbands culturally. Spivak (1988) used this example and claimed that this type of suicide was a woman's wrong effort at self-representation, and some women are not able to express themselves in the South Asian patriarchal society:

> Nor does the solution lie in the positivist inclusion of a monolithic collectivity of 'women' in the list of the oppressed whose unfractured subjectivity allows them to speak for themselves against an equally monolithic 'same system'.
>
> (Spivak 1988, p. 278)

As Spivak observed, some postcolonial debates as well as Subaltern studies had left 'women' out of their discourse. Spivak also observed that women had been constructed "both as object of colonialist historiography and as subject of insurgency, the ideological construction of gender keeps the male dominant" (Spivak 1988, p. 287). Therefore, "If, in the context of colonial production, the subaltern has no history and cannot speak, the subaltern as female is even more deeply in shadow" (Spivak 1988, p. 287).

A postcolonial feminist view is that women's issues have been historically discussed from a view of generalising and universalising, which could lead to a possible misunderstanding of women's actual situations, especially, women of colour (Mohanty 1991). Postcolonial theory has prompted scholars to reconsider key aspects of tradition and culture in the everyday lives of women in postcolonial states, such as Kenya (Spivak 1985a; Mohanty 1997). Mohanty (1991, 1997) questions Spivak's suggestion of the generalisation of 'women' and asserts that we should recognise differences in women's subordinate experiences in a diversity of historical, cultural and social contexts. Mohanty's position reminds us to consider the continuing struggles of indigenous people for their identity formation in the globalized world, by looking at the impact of the perspectives of colonial thought and patriarchal power (Pierson et al. 1998; Young 2001). The important point to draw from this discussion is that women in postcolonial countries may experience specific gender issues that differ from women in the West.

Moreover, Narayan (1997) explored and examined how the cultures and feminist agendas of poor countries have been misinterpreted, and she also contributed to the cultural politics of discussions of 'Westernisation' in poor-countries contexts. Narayan strongly claims that "Westerners are sadly ignorant about Third-World (sic) cultural contexts and hence suffer from parochial limitations of vision" (1997, p. 125). She found that Westerners' commitment to learning about other cultures is limited and they tend to be attached to stereotyped images of poor countries, which can limit one's exploring knowledge about the 'real' poor countries and often would result in misinterpretation about cultures of poor countries (Narayan 1997). Postcolonial feminists claimed that mainstream Western feminists used to ignore the voices of women of colour, non-Western women for many years, thus creating resentment from feminists in poor nations (Spivak 1985a; Mohanty 1991). However, due to the influence of postmodern theory and the demand for recognition of diversity and difference, feminist approaches have changed in that women's issues are now analysed by gender, social classes and ethnic identities (Narayan 1997).

Despite the critical view of them from authors such as Mohanty, many Western feminists do write in support of the postcolonial feminist project. For example, Haraway (1991) critiques gendered discourses observing that they are "deeply indebted to racism and colonialism" and she encourages women to act upon bringing about equal status in the world. Her words are meant for people who "need and hope to live in a world less riddled by the dominations of race, colonialism, class, gender and sexuality" (Haraway 1991, p. 1). Also Hoogvelt, another European postcolonial feminist scholar in the development literature, takes a global perspective and suggests that a large number of views of the oppressed can be reported through cultural theory, considering multiple identities and traditions (1997, p. 157). She states that postcolonial discourses cause us to reconstruct the identities of marginalised people (Hoogvelt 1997). I engaged in this type of critical reflection in order to conduct my research with village women in Kenya. Through narratives constructed by the research participants, I was able to analyse their positions and identity.

However, in many poor countries, scholars' theories of postcolonialism can provide an outlet for citizens to discuss various experiences endured during colonialism (Said 1989). Such experiences include: migration, slavery, suppression, resistance, representation, difference, race, gender, place and responses to the influential discourses of imperial Europe (Said 1989). Postcolonial feminists see the parallels between recently decolonized nations and the state of women within patriarchy – both take the perspective of a socially marginalized subgroup in their relationship to the dominant culture (Spivak 1988; Mohanty 1991, 1997; Narayan 1997).

Conclusion

In this chapter, an examination and discussion of postcolonialism and postcolonial feminism provide the theoretical foundations for this study. A discussion of postcolonial theory was central in considering not only the impact of colonisation on postcolonial states and to create a framework for listening to the voices of marginalised people, but to also consider the processes of ongoing colonial impositions through 'development, especially in regard to education'. The discussion about African writers like Achebe (1958) and Ngũgĩ wa Thiong'o (1986), who contributed to critical analyses of English literature discriminating against African cultures and people, reflect a similar trajectory as for the politicisation of Western literary theories. This politicisation led to political commentary by key thinkers in postcolonial literary analysis (for example Spivak, Said, Hall and Bhaba).

As a research methodology, a postcolonial feminist perspective assisted in placing Maasai women's marginalised experiences at the focal point of analysis with its strong emphasis on listening to the voices of the subaltern (Spivak

1985a). It also established the effects of historical forces, together with the present social and political processes in Kenya as a postcolonial state, that influence the Maasai women's educational experiences and activities. Therefore postcolonial feminist theory is applied here on two distinct levels: first, as a way of doing feminist research and, second, as a way of viewing the wider forces at play in the village women's lives.

Even though the Maasai have strong cultural and traditional practices, because of other cultures' influence, their society is changing or, as Bhaba (1994) would describe it, 'hybridising'. This is specifically evident in relation to development programmes imposed by outsiders that have also stimulated cultural changes for the Maasai.

References

Achebe, C. (1958). *Things Fall Apart*. Oxford: Heinemann Educational Publishers.
Achebe, C. (1977). An Image of Africa: Racism in Conrad's 'Heart of Darkness'. *Massachusetts Review*, 18. Rpt. in *Heart of Darkness, An Authoritative Text, Background and Sources Criticism* (1961), 3rd edn, Ed. Robert Kimbrough, London: W.W. Norton and Co. (1988), pp. 251–261.
Allen, A. (2008). Power and the Politics of Difference: Oppression, Empowerment and Transnational Justice. *Hypatia*, 23(3), 156–172.
Allender, T. (2002). Robert Montgomery and the Daughter Slayers: A Punjabi Educational Imperative, 1855–65. *South Asia: Journal of South Asian Studies*, 25(1), 97–119.
Anderson, J. (2002). Toward a Post-Colonial Feminist Methodology in Nursing Research: Exploring the Convergence of Post-Colonial and Black Feminist Scholarship. *Nurse Researcher*, 9(3), 7–27.
Arowolo, D. (2010). The Effects of Western Civilization and Culture on Africa. *Afro Asian Journal of Social Sciences*, 1(1), 1–13.
Ashcroft, B., Griffiths, G., and Tiffin, H. (1989). *The Empire Writes Back: Theory and Practice in Post-colonial Literatures*. London: Routledge.
Ashcroft, B., Griffiths, G., and Tiffin, H. (1995). *The Post-Colonial Studies Reader*. London: Routledge.
Ashcroft, B., Griffiths, G., and Tiffin, H. (2000). *Post-Colonial Studies: The Key Concepts*. London: Routledge.
Ashcroft, B., Griffiths, G., and Tiffin, H. (eds). (2006). *The Post-Colonial Studies Reader* (2nd edn). London: Routledge.
Barton, D., Hamilton, M., and Ivanic, R. (eds). (2000). *Situated Literacies: Reading and Writing in Context*. London: Routledge.
Bhabha, H.K. (1994). *The Location of Culture*. London: Routledge.
Bhabha, H.K. (1996). Cultures In-Between. In S. Hall and P. Du Gay (eds), *Questions of Cultural Identity*, London: Sage Publications, pp. 53–60.
Browne, A.J., Smye, V., and Varcoe, C. (2007). Postcolonial Feminist Theoretical Perspectives and Women's Health. In M. Morrow, O. Hankivsky, and C. Varcoe (eds), *Women's Health in Canada: Critical Perspectives on Theory and Policy*, Toronto, ON: University of Toronto Press, pp. 124–142.
Carmen, R. (1996). *Autonomous Development: Humanizing the Landscape. An Excursion into Radical Thinking and Practice*. London: Zed Books.

Coast, E. (2002). Maasai Socioeconomic Conditions: A Cross-Border Comparison. *Human Ecology*, 30(1), 79–105.

Conrad, J. (1988). *Heart of Darkness: An Authoritative Text, Backgrounds and Sources, Criticism* (3rd edn). New York: W.W. Norton & Company.

Creighton, C., and Yieke, F. (2006). *Gender Inequalities in Kenya*. Paris: UNESCO.

Dangarembga, T. (1988). *Nervous Conditions*. Seattle: Seal Press.

Denzin, N.K., and Lincoln, Y.S. (1994). *Handbook of Qualitative Research*. London: Sage.

Deutsch, N.L. (2004). Positionality and the Pen: Reflections on the Process of Becoming a Feminist Researcher and Writer. *Qualitative Inquiry*, 10(6), 885–902.

Diallo, N.N. (1975). *De Tilène au Plateau, a Dakar childhood*. Dakar: Les Nouvelles Editions Africaines.

Evans, M.S. (2002). Re-Viewing the Second Wave. *Feminist Studies*, 28(2), 258–267.

Fanon, F. (1967). *Black Skin, White Masks*. Translated by Charles Lam Markmann. New York: Grove Press.

Fine, C. (2010). *Delusions of Gender: How our Minds, Society, and Neurosexism Create Difference*. Norton: W.W. Norton & Company.

Gee, J.P. (1991). What is Literacy? In Candace Mitchell and Kathleen Weiler (eds), *Rewriting Literacy: Culture and the Discourse of the Other*, New York: Bergin and Garvey, pp. 3–11.

Goldsmith, E., and Mander, J. (eds). (2001). *The Case against the Global Economy and for a Turn Towards Localization*. London: Earthscan.

Gramsci, A. (1971). *Selections from the Prison Notebooks*, edited and translated by Quintin Hoare and Geoffrey Nowell Smith. London: Lawrence & Wishart.

Guha, R. (1982). *Subaltern Studies No. 1: Writings on South Asian History and Society*. Delhi: Oxford University Press.

Hall, S. (1992). The West and the Rest: Discourse and Power. In S. Hall and B. Gieben (eds), *Formations of Modernity*, Cambridge: Polity Press, pp. 275–331.

Haraway, D. (1991). *Simians, Cyborgs, and Women: The Reinvention of Nature*. New York: Routledge.

Harding, S. (1987). *Feminism and Methodology*. Bloomington: Indiana University Press.

Harding, S., and Norberg, K. (2005). New Feminist Approaches to Social Science Methodologies: An Introduction. *Signs: Journal of Women in Culture and Society*, 30(4), 2009–2015.

Head, B. (1992). *The Collector of Treasures: And Other Botswana Village Tales*, African Writers Series. London: Heinemann.

Hodgson, L.D. (2011). *Gender and Culture at the Limit of Rights*, Studies in Human Rights Series. Philadelphia: University of Pennsylvania Press.

Hoogvelt, A. (1997). *Globalization and the Postcolonial World: The New Political Economy of Development*. Baltimore: Johns Hopkins University Press.

Kirkham, S., and Anderson, J. (2002). Postcolonial Nursing Scholarship: From Epistemology to Method. *Advances in Nursing Science*, 25(1), 1–17.

Kock, D.L. (1992). An Interview with Gayatri Chakravorty Spivak. *A Review of International English Literature*, 23(3), 77–92.

Mohanty, C.T. (1991). Under Western Eyes: Feminist Scholarship and Colonial Discourses. In C.T.R. Mohanty, Ann Russo, and L. Torres (eds), *Third World Women and the Politics of Feminism*, Bloomington: Indiana University Press.

Mohanty, C.T. (1997). Under Western Eyes. In A. McClintock, A. Mufti, and E. Shohat (eds), *Dangerous Liaisons, Gender, Nation and Postcolonial Perspectives*, Minneapolis and London: University of Minnesota Press, pp. 255–277.

Mohanty, C.T. (2003). *Feminism without Borders: Decolonizing Theory. Practicing Solidarity*. Durham and London: Duke University Press.

Momsen, J. (2004). *Gender and Development*. London: Routledge.

Mongia, P. (1996). *Contemporary Postcolonial Theory*. London: Arnold.

Moser, C. (1993). *Gender Planning and Development: Theory, Practice and Training*. London: Routledge.

Moyers, B. (1989). Chinua Achebe: Nigerian Novelist. In S.B. Flowers, *A World of Ideas*, New York: Doubleday, p. 343.

Mudimbe, V.Y. (1988). *The Invention of Africa: Gnosis, Philosophy, and the Order of Knowledge*. Bloomington: Indiana University Press.

Narayan, U. (1997). *Dislocating Cultures: Identities, Traditions, and Third-World Feminism*. New York: Routledge.

Ngũgĩ wa Thiong'o. (1986). *Decolonising the Mind*. Portsmouth: Heinemann Educational Books.

Nussbaum, C.M., and Glover, J. (1995). *Women, Culture, and Development: A Study of Human Capabilities*. Oxford: Clarendon Press.

Ogunyemi, C.O. (1985). Womanism: The Dynamics of the Contemporary Black Female Novel in English. *Signs*, 11(1), 63–80.

Olarinmoye, A.W. (2013). The Images of Women in Yoruba Folktales. *International Journal of Humanities and Social Science*, 3(4), 138–149.

Parmer, P., and Minh-ha, T.T. (1990). Woman, Native, Other. *Feminist Review*, 36(3), 65–74.

Phillips, R. (2009). Food Security and Women's Health: A Feminist Perspective for International Social Work. *International Social Work*, 52(4), 485–498.

Pierson, R.R., Chaudhuri, N., and McAuley, B. (1998). *Nation, Empire, Colony: Historicizing Gender and Race*. Bloomington: Indiana University Press.

Prakash, G. (1994). Subaltern Studies as Postcolonial Criticism. *The American Historical Review*, 99(5), 1475–1490.

Razari, S., and Miller, C. (1995). *From WID to GAD: Conceptual Shifts in the Women and Development Discourse*. Geneva: United Nations Research Institute for Social Development.

Robeyns, I. (2010). Gender and the Metric of Justice. In H. Brighouse and I. Robeyns (eds), *Measuring Justice: Primary Goods and Capabilities*, Cambridge: Cambridge University Press, pp. 215–236.

Rogers, A. (2004). Looking Again at Non-Formal and Informal Education: Towards a New Paradigm. In *Encyclopedia of Informal Education*. www.infed.org/biblio/non_formal_paradigm.htm.

Rutherford, J. (ed.). (1990). *Identity: Community, Culture, Difference*. London: Lawrence & Wishart.

Said, E. (1978). *Orientalism*. London: Routledge & Kegan Paul.

Said, E. (1989). Representing the Colonized: Anthropology's Interlocutors. *Critical Inquiry*, 15(2), 205–225.

Said, E. (1994). *Culture and Imperialism*. London: Vintage Books.

Schwarz, H., and Ray, S. (2000). *A Companion to Postcolonial Studies*. Malden: Blackwell Publishers.

Sifuna, D.N. (1990). *Development of Education in Africa: The Kenyan Experience.* Nairobi: Initiatives Ltd.
Smith, K. (2010). Gramsci at the Margins: Subjectivity and Subalternity in a Theory of Hegemony. *International Gramsci Journal*, 1(2), 39–50.
Spender, D. (1985). *For the Record: The Making and Meaning of Feminist Knowledge.* London: Women's Press.
Spivak, G.C. (1985). Can the Subaltern Speak?: Speculations on Widow Sacrifice. *Wedge*, 7/8(Winter/Spring), 120–130.
Spivak, G.C. (1985b). Subaltern Studies: Deconstructing Histroriography. *Subaltern Studies*, 4, 330–363.
Spivak, G.C. (1988). Can the Subaltern Speak? In C. Nelson and L. Grossberg (eds), *Marxism and the Interpretation of Culture*, Basingstoke: Macmillan Education, pp. 271–313.
Spivak, G.C. (1996). Postcolonialism, Marginality, Postcoloniality and Value. In P. Mongia, (ed.), *Contemporary Postcolonial Theory: A Reader*, London: Arnold, pp. 198–222.
Spivak, G.C. (1999). *A Critique of Postcolonial Reason: Toward a History of the Vanishing Present.* Cambridge, MA: Harvard University Press.
Street, B.V. (1995). *Social Literacies: Critical Approaches to Literacy in Development, Ethnography and Education.* London: Longman.
UNESCO. (2000). *Education for All. Global Monitoring Report 2012, Youth and Skills: Putting Education to Work.* Paris: UNESCO.
UNESCO. (2014). *Education for All. Global Monitoring Report 2013, Teaching and Learning: Achieving Quality for All.* Paris: UNESCO.
Visvanathan, N., Duggan, L., Nisonoff, L., and Wiegersma, N. (1997). *The Women, Gender and Development Reader.* London: Zed Books.
World Bank. (1997). *Women's Education in Developing Countries: Barriers, Benefits, and Policies.* Baltimore, MD: Johns Hopkins University Press.
World Bank. (2012). *World Development Report 2012: Gender Equality and Development.* Washington, DC: World Bank.
Young, R.J.C. (1990). *White Mythologies: Writing History and the West.* London: Routledge.
Young, R.J.C. (2001). *Postcolonialism: An Historical Introduction.* Oxford: Wiley-Blackwell.

2 Women's informal learning and empowerment in the context of development

Introduction

In Chapter 1, the theoretical framework for this book was established via a review of literature relevant to the development of postcolonial feminism. The main messages arising from a postcolonial feminist perspective are, first, that there is no universal experience of women's oppression; and, second, that in postcolonial states women are generally still of a subaltern status and that it is a task of postcolonial feminism and feminist researchers to create spaces for subaltern women to speak from and be heard. An important role of postcolonial feminist research is the focus on social justice. This perspective places women's experiences at the centre of analysis by examining daily experiences of marginalisation and power (Anderson 2002).

As the focus of this study is women's self-directed learning and literacy, this chapter analyses meanings of formal, non-formal and informal education and literacy. It presents a review of the meanings of literacy and its significance in socio-economic contexts. The importance of recognition of women's empowerment, agency and autonomy in the context of development is also put forward and examined in the chapter. Finally, as this study seeks to investigate Maasai women's experiences of informal learning, literacy and development in their traditional patriarchal context, intersections of poverty, racial and ethnic marginalisation and economic marginalisation and gender will also be discussed.

Informal learning and adult literacy in development

My intention in this book is to explore why women's informal learning and literacy are vital for a country's development. While non-formal/informal education and literacy targeting adults had been neglected by governments and international donor agencies in the 1990s, in the post-Dakar decades, ministries of education in poor countries and aid agencies have shown an interest in provision of quality non-formal/informal education to disadvantaged and vulnerable groups of people (Rogers 2004; Hoppers 2006). Such education approaches have become important to meet various educational needs, therefore financial and technical support from international aid agencies were provided to education and development organisations in poor countries such as Kenya (Lauglo 2001; Hoppers 2005).

As stated above, there are three major education approaches: formal, non-formal and informal. Formal education is structured education programmes that take place at schools. Non-formal education is organised educational programmes outside of formal education systems such as language or skills classes. Informal education is lifelong learning educational activities occurring in everyday life at home and in work places. On the one hand, formal education is defined as "the highly institutionalized, chronologically graded and hierarchically structured 'education system', spanning lower primary school and the upper reaches of the university" (Coombs and Ahmed 1974, p. 8). Critically, formal educational programmes are systematised and organised. Formal education programmes are primarily classroom-based and delivered for the most part by teachers trained by an accredited teacher training institution. The colonisation process used formal schooling and literacy instruction to promote a type of education that followed the colonisers' education, privileging European culture, languages and religion (Freire 1970). The Kenyan writer, Ngũgĩ wa Thiong'o (1986) also observed that colonial schooling and language education can be seen as a vehicle of colonisation. This was through his own schooling experience where he was forced to learn English, the colonial language, but not Gikuyu, his mother tongue.

On the other hand, non-formal education "is any organized, systematic, educational activity carried on outside the framework of the formal system to provide selected types of learning to particular subgroups in the population, adults as well as children" (Coombs and Ahmed 1974, p. 8). Non-formal education can be viewed as literacy education with skills development or flexible learning opportunities provided by governments and non-governmental organisations. There is a third education system called informal education. Coombs and Ahmed define it as follows:

> Informal education as used here is the lifelong process by which every person acquires and accumulates knowledge, skills, attitudes and insights from daily experiences and exposure to the environment – at home, at work, at play; from the example and attitudes of family and friends; from travel, reading newspapers and books; or by listening to the radio or viewing films or television. Generally, informal education is unorganized and often unsystematic; yet it accounts for the great bulk of any person's total lifetime learning – including that of even a highly 'schooled' person.
>
> (1974, p. 8)

It is unorganised and unstructured learning, hence it is part of a lifelong learning process.

UNESCO defines informal learning as follows:

Informal learning is learning that occurs in daily life, in the family, in the workplace, in communities and through interests and activities of individuals. Through the recognition, validation and accreditation process, competences gained in informal learning can be made visible, and can contribute to qualifications and other recognitions.

(2012, p. 8)

Informal learning plays a vital role in the development of professional skills of individuals and people can benefit from it to improve one's well-being. Edwards and Usher (2001) explored the application of informal learning in one's life, arguing that community-based informal learning has become a reasonable resource for those who have engaged in the development of skills and multiliteracies. Informal learning takes place based on one's personal needs, and the autonomy of a learner is seen as an advantage in informal learning (Papen 2012). Hence a learner controls one's own learning process and it can be a meaningful experience in which a learner becomes more familiar and capable within one's own cultural setting (Yanchar *et al.* 2013).

Furthermore, informal education has links to notions of traditional education in Africa. Traditional education is passed from one generation to another via verbal communication and cultural rituals. Even though Western education was imposed on Africa by colonisation, including studies of European languages, history and literature, the culture and tradition of a community has been transferred in the form of traditional education. Also, people in Africa acquire knowledge about agriculture, food preparation, health care, conservation and herbal medicine through traditional informal learning (Omolewa 2007). To preserve traditional knowledge, Omolewa (2007) highlighted the significance of the integration of traditional knowledge into the current school curriculum, adopting elements of story-telling and dancing. A local language as a medium of instruction in educational institutions is also recommended so that learners acquire the contents of knowledge and skills effectively (Mulumba and Masaazim 2012).

Rogers (2004) suggests that formal and non-formal education are included in wider areas of informal learning. While formal education is organised in primary, secondary and higher educational institutions with a formal curriculum, informal learning is taking place throughout one's life. Therefore informal learning is unstructured, incidental learning and the most significant learning activities happen in the everyday of people's lives (Rogers 2003). Jeffs and Smith (1997, 2005, 2011) support this view and summarise informal education by suggesting that it "works through, and is driven by, conversation" and "is spontaneous and involves exploring and enlarging experience, and can take place in any setting". Smith (1999, 2008) also regards informal learning as self-directed learning and suggests that "people might seek to 'teach themselves' through conversation, through constructing some sort of learning plan".

Discussing informal group learning, Hemmings asserted that "remarkable things can happen when we come together in small groups" (2011, p. 280). It is also suggested that through informal learning, people try to work for the well-being of their colleagues and lead change that affects people's lives (Jeffs and Smith 2005, pp. 95–96). Adults learn through involvement in community development and also learn for local community development (Fragoso *et al.* 2011).

Also supporting informal learning, Rogers argues that we need lifelong learning to lead to social change and overcome disadvantages:

> The reason why some people are poor and remain outside the dominant groups is not their lack of education but the fact that they are being 'excluded' by the elites, by the oppression of the systems (including formal education) through which the dominant groups exert power. What is needed is to change the systems as well as provide learning opportunities for the excluded.
>
> (2006, p. 130)

Jackson *et al.* (2011) suggests that current debates on life-long learning "do not explicitly address gender as an issue" (p. 247). Further, it is observed that women's groups are effective in building individual confidence, empowerment and leading solidarity among women in development programmes (Jackson *et al.* 2011).

This is an important aspect of adult learning, as noted by Coombs (1968) that adults learn based on their needs to solve daily issues. Informal learning along with adult literacy acquisition is observed in Maasai women's everyday lives. This is described extensively in the Maasai women's interviews discussed later in this book. The radical nature of informal education also helps people become empowered to challenge social issues and liberate people from oppressed situations (Richardson and Wolfe 2001). Richardson and Wolfe suggest that:

> informal and formal education are not opposites. Just as education in the classroom has informal elements, so informal education may use formal methods and styles. However, informal education has the capacity to act as a counterbalance to schooling, especially when formal education is centralised and controlled.
>
> (2001, p. 2)

Adults learn based on their needs, using previous knowledge, and apply acquired skills and knowledge in order to solve problems immediately. Merriam *et al.* (2007) highlight that learning activities are highly related to culture, therefore, the responsibility of all community members "to teach and to learn" (p. 237) and further observed that "informal learning, which adults engage in on a daily basis, hardly counts as "real learning" in a formal school setting. The Maasai women in Narok County identified urgent issues in their village and organised a small women's group to overcome the issues. There was not an obvious instructor who directed the group members in what to do, rather they all believed in mutual cooperation and acted upon solutions together. Through analysing social issues, taking initiatives for solving the issues and reflecting the outcomes, the women in Narok have experienced a form of empowering. The interviewed women's voices highlighted a sense that their self-determined learning consequently brings about positive change to overcome underlying social problems. The Narok women became active agents of social change through informal learning. "Individual and collective agency are necessary to make gender inequitable society more equitable" (Maslak 2008 p. 119). Maslak notes that "agency reflects the engagement of participants – individually and collectively – in this entire process from critical analysis and knowledge construction to changing attitudes and meanings, to planning and carrying out strategic activities" (2008, p. 119). Resistance to oppressed situations through agency is indicated in the village women's grassroots movements introduced in Chapter 5. Women's informal groups introduced in this study can be seen to serve as an emancipatory function (Maslak 2008).

Based on research conducted in Africa and the Middle East, King (1982) shows that in the absence of formal education, people acquire skills through families and peers based on everyday life experiences. People with limited literacy and numeracy skills may find it difficult to participate in a formal educational course to gain particular skills, yet for them a less formal and informal type of learning system to acquire skills might be more comfortable and effective (Beddie and Halliday-Wynes 2010). A good example of the effectiveness of informal learning is demonstrated in Robertson's (1984) findings on the benefits of non-formal education of schooled girls in Ghana, who were selling goods at the market, suggested that formal schooling was not useful for the girls to gain trading knowledge, rather these girls acquired trading skills through informal education.

However, Hodkinson (2010) raises a concern about the formalisation of informal education, where some educators and policy-makers try to specify, measure and control the process of learning. Hodkinson argued that "what matters more are important questions about the value and purposes of what is being learned, and to whom" (2010, p. 46). Literacy rates are

> a replacement for personal trust.... The desire to express literacy through numbers is currently driven by policies and an imaginary which is based in the vision of a global order in which nations compete for position within a capitalist marketplace.
>
> (Hamilton 2012b, pp. 25, 27)

In other words, Hodkinson (2010) is suggesting that due to the drive for countries to use literacy as a measure of development in a market place, the intrinsic interpersonal values of informal education, such as trust, can get lost.

While there are primarily three types of education systems, informal learning plays a significant role in the acquisition of skills and knowledge of individuals particularly where people have restricted access to formal learning. As will be noted in later chapters some women in this study use informal learning effectively to improve their standard of living.

Women's informal learning in Africa

The focus of this book is on the experience of informal learning and literacy in Kenya. As such, it is important to develop an understanding of the specificities of the practices of informal learning in the context of Africa.

In Africa, in spite of active participation in the agricultural area, women are restricted from property ownership, land tenure systems, access to finance, education and social welfare services, due to socio-cultural factors (Kiptot and Franzel 2011; Oduro et al. 2011; Hodgson 2011). Several studies provide empirical data for us to consider. Inequalities between men and women in assets, wages, education and employment still exist in Kenya (Chiuri 1996). The assets or resources can be the means of production such as land and labour or capital/finances in the form of cash and/or credit. It is claimed that the traditional patriarchal systems in Africa were reconstructed under colonialism (1895–1963) in ways that benefited men, disadvantaged women, and strengthened male control over female labour and productivity (Chiuri 1996; Kiptot and Franzel 2011; Oduro et al. 2011; Hodgson 2011). Local chiefs became colonial functionaries who regained the power to allocate land (Chiuri 1996). In examining the formal education system, it is evident that it has been sustained by foreign aid, and African governments have perpetuated Western-style education systems within their own countries. Thus, the primary beneficiaries of formal education in Africa tended to be high-class or privileged individuals, not the wider population (Psacharopoulos 1994).

Despite the hardship most women in Africa face, there are a number of autonomous grassroots groups established by women that are committed to mobilising resources to sustain women's groups and activism. Local community and faith-based organisations provide opportunities for informal learning (Trutko et al. 2014). Such organisations also provide an opportunity for the organisations' participants to engage in informal network building. This has been true for some church and grassroots women's groups in Narok, as described by women's voices in this study. It can be said that the informal learning process is community-based rather than individual (Popov 2009). After becoming empowered through informal learning, women excise their agency in response to oppressive daily situations (Papen 2002).

Adebimpe and Temitope (2014) in Nigeria emphasise that if local small-scale business women have access to networks and associations providing informal capacity development opportunities, their small businesses will improve. Hence, outside agencies need to support the learning needs of local women entrepreneurs (Davis 2012).

Daniels (2003) investigated women's capacity for leadership and community development in an impoverished area of South Africa and found that a collaborative learning environment was effective for the participants. This means that collaborative learning can be seen to enhance women's ability and cooperation. Furthermore there is a case study showing that women in South Africa undertook self-directed learning processes for knowledge sharing of midwifery information and built a networking system to solve problems (Pimmer et al. 2014).

As informal learning can be seen as traditional African education, Omolewa (2007) reminds us that story-telling, and proverbs, which are the elements of indigenous learning strategies, can be included into what the current modern educational system offers.

A positive argument that informal learning and literacy contribute to community and individual development emerges in the long-term ethnographic work of Uta Papen (2002). Papen (2003) commends the significance of informal learning and literacy based on a study conducted in Namibia that showed that informal learning and literacy were found to be a social practice instead of just a means of writing and reading. Papen (2003) also found that informal learning and literacy are connected to human rights and social justice and the embodiment of power. Further, by examining local tour guides for safari tours for Western tourists, it was evident that local tour guides gained knowledge from their daily interactions with tourists, which Papen described as informal on-the-job training. Although Papen did not regard orality or traditional learning in Africa as the most important component in knowledge creation, she observed that "both talk and text were significant in shaping the dynamics making in this event and it is impossible to assign fixed authority to either of them" (2003, p. 144).

This is also demonstrated well from the village women's voices in this study. The local women brought a value to the field of women's entrepreneurship, which promotes social justice, accountability, creating opportunities, providing access to local resources, and building the management capacities of women. Women's rights, empowerment, health and reproductive rights, water, education and agriculture have been prioritised by many women's groups in the research site, Kenya, which is described in Chapters 5 and 6.

Given that this study is focused primarily on how informal learning asserts women's capacity to foster community development in Kenya, women's empowerment is valued as a capacity that enables social change and women's level of agency within communities. Women's social networks and their role as the managers of social relations put them in a central position within their communities to act as agents of change and community development (Carmen 1996).

Literacy and the impact of literacy on women's well-being

In addition to the effectiveness of informal learning discussed in the above section, central to this study is a view of literacy that is widely seen as an important component in human development, especially people's empowerment and agency. A large number of international organisations and donor agencies over the last 60 years have invested in numerous literacy projects in poor countries under varied frameworks with a variety of aims (UNESCO 2000, 2005; UNDP 2003). There are important global policy frameworks in the field of education and literacy, for example, Education for All (EFA) and the Millennium Development Goals (MDGs) (UNESCO 2000; UNDP 2003). Although the Dakar Framework for Action on Education for All focused on the education field from early childhood to adult literacy, the United Nations' MDGs limited its education focus to universal primary education emphasising gender equality (UNESCO 2000). Since the MDGs were finalised in 2015, a new set of global policies were developed. The 17 United Nations Sustainable Development Goals (SDGs), which were based on the evaluation of the Millennium Development Goals, have been adopted by governments, international donor agencies and NGOs and have an established target year to achieve the new goals, set for 2030 (UN 2015). The sustainability Goal 4 of Education states: "ensure inclusive and equitable quality education and promote lifelong learning opportunities for all" (UN 2015). Expansive aspects of education also are included in the goals of health, growth and employment, sustainable consumption and production, and climate change (UNESCO 2015). The SDGs recognise more diverse approaches to ensure the promotion of the quality of education. Further, Goal 5 aims to "promote gender equality and empower women" (UN 2015). The revised goal in the SDGs recognises that gender discrimination has excluded women from formal education but also implies that informal learning is also recognised as an important means of gaining knowledge and literacy in diverse forms.

Given the research focus on women's literacy in this study, it is important to explain the meanings of literacy. The meaning of literacy can be revealed in socio-cultural, historical and political perspectives and its meaning differs between communities, cultures and societies (Street 2001). In simple terms, literacy is mostly understood as the acquisition of reading and writing skills (UNESCO 2015). In this sense, literacy is a fundamental learning need that comprises knowledge, information skills such as computer skills, values and attitudes necessary for individual, family and community awareness and development (Smith 1994, 2008). However, gender inequality in educational attainment varies substantially across ethnic and geographical lines. In most communities in Africa, culture dictates who has access and control of assets and resources, including formal education, and these rights are largely limited to men (Nyaga 2008). Therefore, informal learning and literacy are central to women's emancipation in Africa.

Additionally, literacy and its impact on development have been investigated in diverse socio-cultural contexts and from varied perspectives, from the personal to community levels (Bartlett 2008; Dyer 2008; Papen 2002; Street 2001; Maddox 2007; Robinson-Pant 2008). Scholars have examined definitions of literacy and how it is practised in various work-related, educational and religious institutions (Maddox 2005, 2007), as well as in homes and everyday life (Barton *et al.* 2000; Bartlett 2008). Uta Papen, who has conducted ethnographic research into literacy in Namibia for many years, noted that "Literacy is both an agent and a channel of globalization and change" (2009, p. 6). In Papen's understanding, literacy reflects elements of social and cultural practices applied in particular socio-cultural contexts. People develop certain skills to cope with social demands within their context. Therefore Papen (2009) asserts that it is important to observe and listen to local people's views on the role of literacy in one's life. Furthermore, women's empowerment and agency perspectives of literacy are a dominant discourse in the literature of women's development. It is argued that by participating in literacy classes, women develop high self-confidence and empowerment, and can become a change agent in addressing and analysing the issues, and seeking possible solutions to social problems (Robinson-Pant 2008; Stromquist 1995, 2013). This study is concerned with the notion, role and impact of literacy on Maasai women's everyday lives and sets out to demonstrate how Maasai women in Kenya have developed self-empowerment via informal learning and literacy. When women become empowered, they question their subordinate situation in a patriarchal society, and are prompted to act and reflect on actions (Freire 1970). This leads to collective action against social injustice.

While international organisations such as UNESCO have been a key influence in the development of the notion of literacy in *formal* literacy programmes, it is crucial to acknowledge women's informal learning processes. Literacy has multiple meanings and plays a variety of roles in human development. Multiple and ethnographic literacies are discussed in the application of literacy and numeracy skills (Street 2001; Maddox 2007; Gebre *et al.* 2009; Papen 2005, 2012). However, these tend to concentrate on the wider benefits of literacy and the impact of core areas of learning such as writing, reading and mathematics in people's everyday live. The Maasai women have formed their own life experiences and knowledge developed through informal learning processes that assist them in coping with their everyday life in Kenya.

Thus, often basic skills of those defined as literate are not adequate for employment within the formal sector. Clodomir Santos de Morais (Carmen and Sobrado 2000, p. 17) criticises functional literacy, arguing that poor people need another type of literacy, "entrepreneurial literacy, which will allow them to develop self-managing organisations based on the division of labour" (Carmen and Sobrado 2000, p. 17). Carmen and Sobrado (2000) noted that the root cause of poverty is primarily linked to unemployment in poor countries. It is also evident that economic opportunities are often limited to educated people in Africa (Vavrus 2003; Ighobor 2013). Hence, gaining literacy skills should be a process that people go through as a 'capacitation (learning)' process through organised groups, thus possibly creating jobs themselves. Other scholars have also questioned a single literacy, arguing that one needs to look at multiple literacies (Street 2001; Papen 2002, 2005). Within a socio-cultural view of literacy, literacies are seen as social and cultural practices in which reading and writing are used in different socio-cultural settings (Street 2001; Papen 2002, 2005). In the development context, Gebre *et al.* (2009) have illustrated how contexts such as markets, families, small-scale businesses and farming determine what counts as 'everyday literacies', by observing how people in Africa practice literacy and numeracy in their everyday lives. Gebre *et al.* (2009) emphasise that so-called illiterate adults do engage in literacy and numeracy activities. People use signs, symbols and pictures to record something or indicate some messages (Gebre *et al.* 2009). Based on their existing knowledge and life experiences, they form their own literacy and numeracy skills. Gebre *et al.* (2009) argue that the application of literacy and numeracy in people's everyday lives is more vital than the process of learning literacy (Gebre *et al.* 2009).

Clearly, it is significant to recognise different perspectives on the meaning of literacy, and Freire (1973) claimed that literacy means more than the core skills of reading, writing and mathematics and suggests that adult learners acquire social skills or knowledge to bring about positive changes to reduce poverty. For Freire literacy is more about the process of 'conscientisation' (building critical awareness) (Freire 1973) and 'reading the world' (understanding community issues) (Freire and Macedo 1987), hence it influences people in liberating themselves from oppressed situations. In order for the subaltern to have a voice they would need to engage in 'conscientisation'. Postcolonial advocates promote the potentialities of agency, and strategies must be found to create an active, dynamic feminism that can make a difference in areas such as the relationship between informal learning, literacy and development (Goetz 1997). It has been recognised that people gain self-reliance and problem solving skills to improve their well-being through literacy.

Consequently, in the autonomous model of communication, learners are active and identify what they would like to know about (Carmen 1996). Freire's (1970) theory of linking education to social change is central to this study. The literacy approach contributes to "the process of learning to perceive social, political and economic contradictions and taking actions against the oppressive elements of reality" (Archer and Cottingham 1996, p. 5). Freire noted that literacy starts from the objective of transforming citizens' political and social situations, as well as acknowledging that learning letters gives people the ability to read and write in the world (Freire and Macedo 1987).

While learners are taught to obey a master's will and conform to society (the aim of conventional previous literacy approaches), for Freire (1970), literacy programmes ought to encourage learners to be critical thinkers. He called this a process of critical thinking, 'conscientisation', and argued that the social system oppresses people's opinion of the political and social situation and their potential capacity as human beings. Freire (1985) also strongly insisted that literacy should help people build confidence to solve problems by making their own decisions rather than depending on others and, in addition to this, he reminded us that people are able to identify and examine root causes. Hence, non-literate people are seen not as objects in a passive learning style, but as subjects with the ability to exercise agency. Literacy is more than the academic skills of reading, writing and mathematics.

In recognising literacy as a social skill to transform reality it gives power to people to act for social justice. There are multiple literacies practiced in different socio-cultural settings and its effectiveness to improve people's wellbeing needs to be recognised. Hence the next section discusses further aspects of literacy. First New Literacies from a socio-cultural perspective are discussed. This also highlights the importance of an ethnographic approach to understanding how literacy is practiced in one's everyday life in a particular socio-cultural context. Second, how women become empowered to make decisions autonomously through literacy learning is examined.

New literacies: literacy from a socio-cultural perspective

In addition to Freire's conscientisation aimed literacy approach, Street (1984) developed the concept of New Literacies, which focuses on everyday meaning literacies in the context of a particular socio-cultural setting. The inclusion of an ethnographic perspective to analyse the application of literacy and numeracy skills has become significant. Street (1984) suggests that social conditions and cultural interpretations of literacy should be valued.

Scribner has also focused on literacy as a cultural system and examines its influence on modes of thought; he observed that literacy is a "social achievement, an outcome of cultural transmission acquired in the course of participation in socially organized activities" (1984, p. 72). When the socio-cultural nature of literacy is accepted, literacies are found in any language of diverse communities (Rogers 1994; Street 1984, 1993; Willinsky 1990). As Street (1984, 1993, 2001) argues, Western linguists ignore "wider parameters" of kinship, traditional systems and political structures.

The New Literacy approach looks beyond a formal literacy learning setting to informal learning as learning takes place in everyday life. In promoting an ethnography of literacy, Hymes suggests that "facets of the cultural values and beliefs, social institutions and forms, roles and personalities, history and ecology of a community may have to be examined in their bearing on communicative events and patterns" (1994, p. 12).

As Street notes,

> The rich cultural variation in these practices and conceptions leads us to rethink what we mean by them and to be wary of assuming a single

literacy where we may simply be imposing assumptions derived from our own cultural practice onto other people's literacies

(2001, p. 430)

Street further explains:

> What has come to be termed the "New Literacy Studies" (NLS) (Gee 1991; Street 1995) represents a new tradition in considering the nature of literacy, focusing not so much on acquisition of skills, as in dominant approaches, but rather on what it means to think of literacy as a social practice. This entails the recognition of multiple literacies, varying according to time and space, but also contested in relations of power … and asking "whose literacies" are dominant and whose are marginalized or resistant.
>
> (2003, p. 77)

Therefore, criticising the traditionally great division between oral and literate communities, Street (1984) suggested that it needs to be recognised that all people regardless of their ideas of literacy engage in all sorts of oral and literacy practices (Robinson-Pant 2008). Literacy, here, is regarded as a social practice. In supporting the concept of New Literacy, Irvine (1996) proposes that a postcolonial curriculum be developed based on a particular sociopolitical context, reflecting any marginalised group of people within a dominant community. As New Literacy Studies is based on the deep understanding of literacy practices applied in local contexts, there is a difficulty in engaging such research with policy (Pahl and Rowsell 2006, p. 5). Therefore this study focuses on documenting the processes of individual agency and empowerment rather than evaluating change (Basu *et al.* 2008).

Although the meaning of literacy has been associated with books and writing and reading taught formally at school, New Literacy regards literacy as social practice undertaken in everyday lives at home and work. For instance, Barton and Hamilton (1998) reported, through an ethnographic study approach, that people in Lancaster, UK, read books for their children, took notes down during meetings, wrote diaries and poems at home. Further, Barton and Hamilton (1998) showed how people's interests led literacy practices and how and what people used literacy for. In addition, they criticised the adult literacy survey conducted by the OECD, saying that culture was regarded as an obstacle and the text criteria did not represent everyday life items. Hamilton and Pitt (2011) argued that formal learning is more valued over informal learning, and standardised and measurable evaluation is preferred. The starting point of policy is not everyday practice of literacy but existing institutional structures and goals (Hamilton 2012a, p. 179).

Formal education and learning have reinforced dominant literacy types, giving advantage to those who practiced dominant literacies in their own homes. The role of education has been reinforced by the choice of dominant literacies, both of which maintained the status quo regarding access to knowledge and power in a society (Auerbach 1992; Street 1984, 2001).

In most societies, even those adults who are unable to read and write are still able to cope with literacy interactions, using many different strategies. As Rogers observed, "All adults – literate and non-literate – are engaged in literacy practices, dealing with literacy events" (1994, p. 47). In this context, Robinson-Pant points out that ethnographic researchers may "promote the 'non literacy' aspects of adult education" (2008, p. 794).

In summary, this section has explored the way that literacy activities are organised and can be owned by local people based on their needs. Through their learning processes, they develop not only literacy skills but also abilities such as confidence, self-reliance and critical awareness. Literacy should focus on a more human development side that results in learners being more independent.

Literacy programmes for women: the impact of literacy on women's empowerment and agency

For girls, poverty exacerbates levels of discrimination, exclusion and neglect they may already face as a result of their gender. This is true when a girl tries to obtain an education, which is vital to breaking the cycle of poverty. Once girls are educated, educated women have greater agency, which benefits their children's nutrition, sanitation and schooling (Bown 1990b; LeVine *et al.* 2012; UNESCO 2014). However, exercising agency is complex in different socio-cultural contexts.

Despite obstacles to women's literacy, if appropriate educational activities are organised with women, there are positive effects from literacy projects on social, economic and personal change (Bown 1990a; LeVine *et al.* 1991; Rao and Robinson-Pant 2006). From a women's and a development perspective, literacy has been associated with lower child mortality rates and improvement in child nutrition (Bown 1990a; LeVine *et al.* 1991; Rao and Robinson-Pant 2006). Educated women have smaller and healthier families (Bown 1990a; LeVine *et al.* 1991) and therefore functional literacy programmes targeting women have become popular with the integration of health, empowerment and income generating activities (Bown 1990a; Carmen 1996). Stromquist (1997) found through a study of literacy programme participants in Brazil that the participants developed awareness of their environments and confidence in social activities. Egbo (2000) reported that literate women in Nigeria had greater participation in the meetings of family and community and raised their voices in the decision-making process. It is suggested that women participating in a literacy programme tend to become empowered by experiencing greater self-esteem and self-confidence.

First, research has also suggested that literate women have a positive effect on their child's schooling (Bown 1990a). A strong correlation has also been made between the level of women's educational attainment and employment as well as other forms of income generation (World Bank 1997). The importance of the link between women's health and literacy, from a functional view of literacy, in which the woman's reproductive role as a good mother is highly emphasised, Rao and Robinson-Pant (2006) claimed a woman's individual views on literacy remained unheard. Further, scholars have questioned the notion of a single literacy, arguing that one needs to think in terms of multiple literacies (Street 2001; Papen 2002, 2005). Robinson-Pant (2009) warned of risks in applying the one kind of adult literacy imposed by UNESCO.

However, Puchner (2003) argues that even if some women are empowered to give an opinion in the meetings of family and community, socio-cultural issues still restrict and limit a space for women to speak out. In some communities, the dominant group still controls access to and the use of literacy skills by women (Puchner 2003).

Second, a significant finding is that literacy also enhances comprehension abilities in modalities other than reading when literate mothers listen, for example, to radio health messages (Levine et al. 2012). Levine et al. (2012) observed that literacy skills for women play an important part in reducing risks to their children's health and improving children's development. Vavrus supports the view of wider benefits for women from literacy and suggests that an educated woman can take "an active role in controlling her fertility, practicing safe sex and protecting the environment" (2003, p. 41). She noted, however, that women's choices about child bearing, reproductive health and environmental conservation are shaped by socio-cultural and economic circumstances (2003, p. 41). This re-emphasises the need for development and literacy programmes to include strategies for women's emancipation.

Street (2001) makes an important observation about the meaning of literacy when he observed that "knowledge: the ways in which people address reading and writing are themselves rooted in conceptions of knowledge, identity, being" (Street 2001, p. 7). Plus, meanings and practices of literacy are "always rooted in a particular world-view and a desire for that view of literacy to dominate and to marginalise others" (Street 2001, p. 8). Papen (2005) asserts that in designing a literacy project in poor countries, we need to know the implications of literacy skills in learners' everyday life and their notion of literacy.

Furthermore, participants in literacy programmes can be more motivated to gain literacy skills if the objective of literacy is linked to livelihood, internal solidarity and cultural values (Trudell and Klaas 2010). The research findings discussed above are well observed in Narok County; the research participants have shown their way of learning and literacy in their local context.

Oral culture has been in present in Africa for centuries, as it is for the Maasai in Kenya, utilising the spoken word to record, communicate and exchange knowledge (Carmen 1996). Given that orality is one of the communications methods the Maasai village women have been engaged with, the concept of orality should be described. While writing is to visualise verbal expressions, and is part of communication (Goody 1968), Ong (1982) further points out since words come from the lips of human-beings, writing simply transcribes verbal words. Literacy has become a technology to transfer verbal words to print. In oral cultures people verbally transfer knowledge of traditional and cultural practices from generation to generation. Invented manuscript cultures have been neglecting the effectiveness and importance of orality. Much of Africa is made up of oral culture societies. Many Africans hold understandings of sayings, proverbs and stories, rather than comprehending written letters. In such cultures, oral stories comply with human needs to keep customs, experiences and observations in a community (Carmen 1996).

Foley (1997) warns of the dangers of simply dividing oral and literate practices, and Finnegan asserts that "'orality' and 'literacy' are not two separate and independent things", orality and literacy are both communication tools to exchange information and knowledge (1988, p. 175).

We can conclude from this discussion that there needs to be a balance between orality and literacy that should apply under appropriate conditions. The key point here is to establish a further dimension within the mechanisms of informal learning and literacy and its role in development in communities in poor countries. Some of these arguments will be carried forward in the next section which examines the debates on women's empowerment and agency in the context of development.

Women's empowerment and agency in international development

This section describes the key themes in the literature that focuses on women's development such as empowerment, autonomy and agency. Empowerment, autonomy and agency are indispensable to women's development processes, which were also central themes emerging from the narratives of village women in Narok.

Empowerment

Although in feminist literature empowerment is a debated concept (Phillips 2015), due to diverse applications in development discourses, it has played a strong role in claiming autonomy for women.

'Empowerment' has been a primary concern in women-focused development that has been encouraged by international organisations to achieve women's development. In defining the concept of empowerment, Friedmann observed that

> the objective of an alternative development is to humanize a system that has shut them out, and to accomplish this through forms of everyday resistance and political struggle that insist on the rights of the excluded

population as human beings, as citizens, and as peoples intent on realizing their loving and creative powers within.

(1992, p. 13)

Further, Chambers, expanding Friedman's view on empowerment, suggested that "Empowerment means that people, especially poorer people, are enabled to take more control over their lives, and secure a better livelihood with ownership and control of productive assets as one key element" (2003, p. 11). Moreover, Kabeer claims that "empowerment refers to the expansion in people's ability to make strategic life choices in a context where this ability was previously denied to them" (1999, p. 437). As will be noted in later chapters in this book, empowerment has been gained by Maasai women through their efforts to establish power over their domestic economies that had hitherto been dominated by patriarchal tradition over female autonomy at all levels. To achieve this the Maasai women become empowered through informal learning and literacy to improve their everyday lives by resisting the domination of patriarchal power.

Relating Kabeer's (1999) point to the purpose of this study, the ability of women to act within their communities as agents of change for community development is related to that which they have been empowered to do. Oxaal and Baden (1997, p. 14), hence, suggest that empowerment is related to strengthening grassroots organisations and the involvement of marginalised social groups. Although facing wide criticism when applied on a large scale (Phillips 2015), some researchers argue that microcredit plays a role of empowering women by gaining income in poor countries (Oxaal and Baden 1997; Malhotra *et al.* 2002). This is because women have lower access to finance than men in many African countries and tend to rely more on informal sources of capital and personal money management than men (Aterido *et al.* 2011). Regarding women's development, it is possible for organisations to use microfinance as a tool to connect women to larger collectives and processes that are empowering (Sengupta 2013). In a microfinance programme, women are motivated to engage in a collective action for the satisfaction of basic needs. Compared to men, women tend to prefer higher social spending on children's schooling, family's well-being and poverty alleviation (World Bank 2004; Voola 2013). The research participants in this study were also involved in a village-based microfinance model or small business programmes. This discussion is supported by Huiskamp and Hartmann-Mahmud's (2007) study, in which social spending helps to secure gender-specific types of insurance and maintain solidarity within a society. In this study, the village women created an opportunity to increase their income by building links among women and cooperating with each other.

Moreover, studies illustrate women as carers and nurturers with a tendency to spend a substantial portion of their income on the health and education of their children (Mayoux 1999; Pitt and Khandker 1998; Voola 2013). Hence, targeting women is seen as a powerful way of assisting children. However, it is criticised as the "patriarchal hold on family's productive assets needs to be challenged" (Garikipati 2008, p. 2638) and the need for women to develop a capacity to control over their financial activities (Goetz and Gupta 1996; Voola 2013). As will be noted in Chapters 5 and 6 of this book, this point is well illustrated in some of the research participants' interviews as the Maasai women sought out autonomy through their own lending system.

Some researchers argue that microcredit programmes were reported as successful for some women, and access to credit has contributed to gaining economic empowerment of women, but not the sole determinant of women's empowerment, autonomy and agency (Feiner and Barker 2007; Phillips 2015). Microcredit encouraged women to work harder in craft making or chicken rearing which has not actually resulted in breaking out of poverty (Feiner and Barker 2007; Phillips 2015). This is because microcredit programmes have been implemented under neoliberal development programmes and also aimed at increasing individual empowerment to control household assets and resources, rather than collective action to challenge power structures. Furthermore, Feiner and Barker observed the problem of an individual empowerment approach and argued that "microcredit programmes do nothing to change the structural conditions that create poverty", and instead reinforce the "individual myths of wealth and poverty" (2007, p. 237). This individualistic nature of the concept of empowerment is clearly stated in the Human Development Report 2014:

> While empowerment is quintessentially individual, a useful analogy can also be drawn for societies. If social cohesion is not strong and there is ethnic and other fragmentation, a society's capacity for collective action is much reduced in responding to adverse events.
>
> (UNDP 2014, p. 24)

This emphasises the individualistic idea of empowerment and does not recognise collective action, which often takes place in traditional communal communities, like the Maasai in Kenya (Phillips 2015). This study is directly linked to concerns about the way empowerment is observed in informal women's group activities in Narok.

Furthermore, empowerment requires power to change a difficult situation. Feminist scholarship suggests that marginalised women need power to challenge patriarchal structures and social injustice (Moglen 1983). Allen, a feminist and philosopher, suggests a notion of power that is at the basis of the definition of empowerment and explains it in three distinct ways; power over, power to and power with. This is beneficial as it demonstrates the importance of agency in relation to those seeking to 'empower' someone (1998, pp. 33–35). Her explanation of the forms is:

> Power-over: the ability of an actor or set of actors to constrain the choices available to another actor or set of actors in a nontrivial way;

Power-to: the ability of an individual actor to attain an end or series of ends;
Power-with: the ability of a collectivity to act together for the attainment of a common or shared end or series of ends.

(1998, p. 125)

First, the example of power-over can be likened to that of a coach's exercise of his or her power over his or her players for the coach's benefit (Allen 1998). One controls power over the other. Second, power-to is meant in the sense that one has power to solve a problem in spite of one's subordinate status. Third, collective empowerment is the goal of power-with, in which people organise a programme with a common purpose to achieve their goals (Allen 1998).

These conceptualisations suggest that with power one can negotiate about gender, race and ethnicity (Knudsen 2006, p. 67), and such notions of power become fundamental to an understanding of the intersectional position embedded in the lives and practices of the agency of women in Narok. In the case of the Maasai women, they are engaged in a 'power with' process – they use collective empowerment effectively rather than rely on individual empowerment, which is often part of the colonising education process or the intent of neoliberal informed development programmes.

Based on the discussion of collective action, this study examines how several grassroots level non-governmental initiatives are empowering women to make individual and collective choices as active agents to produce desired outcomes for themselves and their communities. Sen and Grown clearly state: "recognition not just of poor women's work but of its *centrality* to such development processes is essential" (1987, p. 83). It is clear that women have been seen more as objects than as subjects in many communities (Sen and Östlin 2011). Poor women should be recognised as having a capacity to plan, implement and evaluate, having control over the whole development process. This makes collective action by women within communities developing their empowerment.

In addition, in calling for a grassroots women's movement in Kenya, Maathai raised a concern that

> historically our people have been persuaded to believe that because they are poor, they lack not only capital, but also knowledge and skills to address their challenges. Instead they are conditioned to believe that solutions to their problems must come from "outside".

(2004)

She added that "culture may be the missing link in the development of Africa. Africans, especially, should re-discover positive aspects of their culture. In accepting them, they would give themselves a sense of belonging, identity and self-confidence" (2004). Culture is central to African feminist and social development. In Maathai's view, useful aspects of culture should be the basis for the planning and implementation of development programmes in Africa, and people's collective action would induce a positive change. Also in order to address the complex issues of deforestation and global climate change, Maathai established the Green Belt Movement. One result is that projects such as 'tree nurseries' have been established and managed by rural women in Kenya. In recognition of Maathai's work, more than 15 countries in Africa have participated in the Pan-African Green Belt Network (Maathai 2004).

Socio-cultural norms and customary practices can limit women's ability and participation in household decision-making processes and economic opportunities (World Bank 2012). However, women's empowerment, autonomy and agency being cultivated by learning and grassroots development projects can affect women's livelihood. Regarding the relationship between empowerment and agency, Alsop *et al.* (2006) describes empowerment as an explanation of agency. Kabeer (1999) emphasises that the process of empowerment are completed with an exercise of agency while acknowledging the importance of access to resources, including employment, and its impact on final well-being. According to Kabeer (2000), a key aspect of women's empowerment is whether one has power and ability to make choices. Malhotra (2003, p. 3) elaborates on Kabeer's point that agency is the ability to act on what one values as an important aspect of empowerment. Hence, "agency is defined as the ability to make decisions about one's own life and act on them to achieve a desired outcome, free of violence, retribution, or fear. The ability to make those choices is often called empowerment" (World Bank 2012, p. 13). According to Carmen, the concept of agency implies "people acting autonomously as subjects, as distinct from people being acted upon as objects and possibly being used as participants in interventionist initiatives, projects and programmes which are not theirs" (1996, p. 3). The motivation for human agency comes from within not from the outside, as individuals take initiative in organising development activities. Agency for some women is about being "conscious actors, not passive subjects in the various situations in which they find themselves" (Ralston 2006, p. 184). Therefore, empowered women take initiative to solve social issues, in which Sen suggests, "what a person is free to do and achieve in pursuit of whatever goals or values he or she regards as important" (1985, p. 206).

Lastly, autonomy in turn becomes an outcome of empowerment, which is a common notion in development. Women can act independently and women's autonomy illustrates outcomes of moving away from patriarchy. It shows an understanding of the ways in which individual women make a decision, act and organise independently.

While women's cultivated agency is a significant focus of the outcome of an empowerment process, Allen (1998) is critical of women's empowerment discourses that tend to focus on women's motherhood, and a flow of development programmes 'for' women is that they were established on the basis of assumptions that women's major roles are housekeeping and childcare.

This suggests an oppressive, fixed idea of womanhood in development. Therefore, Young (1997) points out that women's empowerment may be considered in two ways: in an individual sense, a woman achieves more control over her own life, including family decisions or expenditures; and, in a collective sense, where women as a group work together to overcome social structures that restrict them in society, such as in community mobilisation for advocacy campaigns, or in the case of this study informal learning to strengthen capacity to manage to stay out of poverty. Allen (2008) suggests, therefore, that collective empowerment of women to negotiate in a patriarchal community is a critical approach. Collective empowerment is not about developing a new initiative to lead to a bigger solution, but connecting efforts and strengthening membership within a working group to lead to small but continuous positive change, much like the informal groups amongst the Maasai women who participated in this study. This point is significant in exploring how Maasai women utilise their collective voices in a created space to take collective actions. Individual empowerment is effective for women to make certain decisions, yet collective empowerment is also necessary when women need to take a positive social action through a group and attempt to bring about positive change in a community.

As women of the Maasai have experienced the influence of the intersectionality of ethnicity, class and gender in their everyday lives and these aspects are intricately interlinked, the following section explores the concept of intersectionality and how it relates to Maasai women's life experiences.

Intersectionality of ethnicity, class, gender and poverty

This complex and transnational examination of the Maasai women's struggles in their lives highlights the historical and cultural variability of gender relations as they intersect with race, class and nation. The intersections of these relationships can be used as an additional tool for data analysis within the primary theoretical framework of postcolonial feminist theory.

Mohanty (2003) criticised the homogeneous categorisation of women of colour and how "Third-World Women" (*sic*) have been presented in literature. Kimberle Crenshaw (1989) put forward the idea of intersectionality through the examination of discrimination of black women in the USA. Crenshaw (1989), after researching employment discrimination faced by black women in the United States, asserted that the overlapping of race and gender issues for women of colour had been largely neglected by the feminist movement. Her assertion of the significance of multi-dimensional oppression was adopted by the black feminist movement in the late 1980s (Cooper 2015). Crenshaw further claimed that existing discriminations in a society were seen as multiple forms of discriminations towards gender, race, religion, nation and class, hence we need to consider each discrimination not individually but interdependently. Therefore, Crenshaw made clear that intersectionality showed "the need to account for multiple grounds of identity when considering how the social world is constructed" (1991, p. 1245). "Simultaneous and linked" social identities of race, gender and class were addressed through the analytical form of intersectionality (Browne and Misra 2003, p. 488). The intersectionality approach contributes to feminist research and to understanding injustice at structural levels through analysing individuals' struggles and experiences. One needs to understand those experiences as interconnected and reliant on one another. Wilkins (2004) stated: "Both structurally and individually, gender, race, and class necessarily inflect each other so that a person is never simply a woman or a man, but rather a black, middle class woman, or a white working class man" (p. 5). Therefore, we must negotiate diverse identities depending on the context and situation.

The everyday lives of the interviewed Maasai women for this study have been shaped by simultaneous effects of race, gender, class and culture and have challenged the male-dominant community by collective empowerment highlighted in Chapters 5 and 6. The Maasai women's subordinated situations need to be understood in their socio-cultural context. Thus, any attempt to analyse the intersection of race, class, gender and nation require the uncovering of the traditional and cultural erasures of the Maasai in Kenya. The research participants' own voices are well represented, as they are subordinated Maasai females in a traditional patriarchal community. While scholars established and discussed intersectionality as applied to analyse women's subordinated situations in their socio-cultural context, development agencies must also recognise the need for an intersectionality analysis for multiple identities of programme beneficiaries: "An intersectionality approach [...] addresses the manner in which racism, patriarchy, class oppression and other discriminately systems create inequalities that structure the relative positions of women, races, ethnicities, class and the like" (United Nations 2001). For instance, in the research site of the village in Kenya where the Maasai are dominant, an international NGO, World Vision, had implemented a child-sponsorship project, under which the organisation assisted in girls' education and in eradicating FGM practices through advocacy campaign. This NGO project appears to be an example of how development agencies integrate an intersectional perspective into their work, in which marginalised poor Maasai girls were given a formal education opportunity to be self-empowered and independent and also went through a training to refuse the cultural practice of FGM.

Despite Crenshaw's (1989, 1991) assertion of the usefulness of intersectionality within feminist research, Davis (2008), Nash (2008) and Schurr and Segebart (2012) recognise that the concept of intersectionality is still ambivalent when applied as a theoretical framework. While Crenshaw (1989, 1991, 2012) argued that by focusing on one's identity, intersectionality helps to unpack women's lived experiences of subordination and oppression, Peter Kwan criticises that "intersectionality tells us little about fiscal, emotional, psychological, and other conditions nor the subjectivity of those caught in the trajectories of intersecting categories" (2000, p. 687). Kwan's opinion implies that intersectionality helps us understand one's personal structural identities but is not sufficient to know the target person as an individual (Cooper 2015), thus an intersectional approach as a methodology is not well established. Furthermore, Nash summarises four major problems of intersectionality: "the lack of a defined intersectional methodology; the use of black women as quintessential intersectional subjects; the vague definition of intersectionality; and the empirical validity of intersectionality" (2008, p. 1). Although black women's standpoint is useful to analyse multilayered discrimination, intersectionality per se is rather vague to analyse women's subordination experiences from the view of diverse dimensions of social identities. Nash further asserts that intersectionality scholarship serves to "subvert race/gender binaries in service of theorizing identity in a more complex fashion" (2008, p. 2).

Although there are some criticisms of intersectionality, it can be a productive tool for analysing development and feminist research, as Butler and Scott (1992, p. xiii) state that "feminist theory needs to generate analysis, critiques, and political interventions, and open up a political imaginary for feminism".

Maasai women's experiences of informal learning and development highlight the historical and cultural variability of gender relations as they intersect with class, ethnicity and nation. Moreover, through intersectional perspectives on Maasai women's subordinated situation, the women's experiences on education and human rights are influenced by socio-cultural aspects of society, national and community politics, gender and constructed gender power relationships. To overcome the systematised gender discrimination, silenced women cultivate agency and become empowered to create a space to raise their voices in Narok, Kenya, as this book highlights in Chapters 5 and 6. The key skills for building their own agency are the development and usage of informal learning and literacy.

While recognising the multiple identities of targeted subordinated people and groups, the integration of an intersectional analysis into research and development practices can be challenging. The answers generated by this study supplement the existing literature and contribute to a more complete understanding of the complexity of Maasai women's learning and community development experiences.

Conclusion

This chapter has provided a critical analysis of the role of women's informal learning and literacy in the context of development. This chapter has also summarised the conceptual lenses of informal learning and literacy theory within an African context. Highlighting traditional education methodologies that have taken place in Africa, the significance of orality was discussed. This argument led to a suggestion that informal learning and literacy are not a category of fixed concept but rather can be conceived and practiced depending on social, cultural, historical and political contexts. This position also highlights the need both in practice and policy, to concede that not all women are alike. Following on from the everyday experiences of learning and community, the development activities of village women are inextricably interwoven and an individual woman's experience should be respected. Women's collective empowerment was also examined, how women were united to challenge traditional patriarchy through grassroots women's movements. As outlined in Chapter 2, women's development and informal learning and literacy policy and practice has failed to investigate and address this complex multilayered phenomenon of learning in the context of African women. Therefore, there is a need to re-envision the notion of village women's informal learning and literacy through women's grassroots activities from the perspective of intersectionality of race, class and gender.

This chapter again reminds us to listen to local women's experiences on their learning and literacy application for their life to improve their wellbeing.

The subsequent chapter will look at how the theoretical framework of postcolonial feminist theory and women's informal learning and literacy facilitates or contributes to the design of the research methodology for the purposes of this study.

References

Adebimpe, A.A. and Temitope, H.A. (2014). Women in Small Scale Business in Nigeria: Challenges in Accessing Credit Facilities. *A Journal of Culture and African Women Studies*.

Allen, A. (2008). Power and the Politics of Difference: Oppression, Empowerment and Transnational Justice. *Hypatia*, 23(3), 156–172.

Allen, A. (1998). Rethinking Power. *Hypatia*, 13(1), 21–40.

Alsop, R., Bertelsen, M., and Holland, J. (2006). *Empowerment in Practice from Analysis to Implementation*. Washington, DC: World Bank.

Anderson, J. (2002). Toward a Post-Colonial Feminist Methodology in Nursing Research: Exploring the Convergence of Post-Colonial and Black Feminist Scholarship. *Nurse Researcher*, 9(3), 7–27.

Archer, D., and Cottingham, S. (1996). *Action Research Report on REFLECT: The Experiences of Three REFLECT Pilot Projects in Uganda, Bangladesh, El Salvador*. London: Overseas Development Administration.

Aterido, R., Beck, T., and Iacovone, L. (2011). *Gender and Finance in Sub-Saharan Africa: Are Women Disadvantaged?* Policy Research Working Paper Series 5571, Washington, DC: World Bank.

Auerbach, E.R. (1992). *Making Meaning, Making Change: Participatory Curriculum Development for ESL Literacy*. Washington, DC: National Clearinghouse on Literacy Education, Centre for Applied Linguistics.

Bartlett, L. (2008). Literacy's verb: Exploring What Literacy is and What Literacy Does. *International Journal of Educational Development*, 28(6), 737–753.

Barton, D., and Hamilton, M. (1998). *Local Literacies: Reading and Writing in One Community*. London: Routledge.

Barton, D., Hamilton, M., and Ivanic, R. (eds). (2000). *Situated Literacies: Reading and Writing in Context*. London: Routledge.

Basu, K., Maddox, B., and Robinson-Pant, A. (2008). Literacies, Identities and Social

Change: Interdisciplinary Approaches to Literacy and Development. *Journal of Development Studies*, 44(6), 769–778.
Beddie, F., and Halliday-Wynes, S. (2010). Informal and Non-Formal Learning in Vocational Education and Training. In *International Encyclopedia of Education* (3rd Edition), pp. 240–246.
Bown, L. (1990a). *Preparing the Future: Women, Literacy and Development*. Report No. 4. London: Action Aid.
Bown, L. (1990b). Women, Literacy and Development. In B. Street (ed.), *Literacy in Development. People Language Power. Education for Development*. London: Routledge.
Browne, I., and Misra, J. (2003). The Intersection of Gender and Race in Labor Markets. *Annual Review of Sociology*, 29(1), 487–513.
Butler, J., and Scott, J.W. (eds). (1992). *Feminists Theorize the Political*. New York: Routledge.
Carmen, R. (1996). *Autonomous Development: Humanizing the Landscape. An Excursion into Radical Thinking and Practice*. London: Zed Books.
Carmen, R., and Sobrado, M. (2000). *A Future for the Excluded: Job Creation and Income Generation by the Poor: Clodomir Santos de Morais and the Organization Workshop*. London: Zed Books.
Chambers, R. (2003). *Challenging the Professions: Frontiers for Rural Development*. Rugby: Practical Action.
Chiuri, W. (1996). The Effect of Change in Land Tenure and Resources Management on Gender Relations and the Subsequent Changes in Highland Ecosystems: A Case Study of Iruri Kiamariga Community in Nyeri District Kenya, unpublished doctoral dissertation, University of Waterloo, Canada.
Coombs, P. (1968). *The World Educational Crisis: A Systems Analysis*. Oxford: Oxford University Press.
Coombs, P., and Ahmed, M. (1974). *Attacking Rural Poverty*. Baltimore: Johns Hopkins University Press.
Cooper, B. (2015). *Intersectionality*, Oxford Handbooks Online. Oxford: Oxford University Press.
Crenshaw, K. (1989). Demarginalizing the Intersection of Race and Sex: A Black Feminist Critique of Antidiscrimination Doctrine, Feminist Theory and Antiracist Politics. *University of Chicago Legal Forum* 1989: 139–167.
Crenshaw, K. (1991). Mapping the Margins: Intersectionality, Identity Politics, and Violence against Women of Color. *Stanford Law Review*, 43(6), 1241–1299.
Crenshaw, K. (2012). From Private Violence to Mass Incarceration: Thinking Intersectionality about Women, Race, and Social Control. *UCLA Law Review*, 59, 1419–1472.
Daniels, D. (2003). Learning about Community Leadership: Fusing Methodology and Pedagogy to Learn about the Lives of Settlement Women. *Adult Education Quarterly*, 53(3), 189–206.
Davis, K. (2008). Intersectionality as Buzzword: A Sociology of Science Perspective on What Makes a Feminist Theory Successful. *Feminist Theory*, 9(1), 67–85.
Davis, Paul J. (2012). The Global Training Deficit: The Scarcity of Formal and Informal Professional Development Opportunities for Women Entrepreneurs. *Industrial and Commercial Training*, 44(1), 19–25.
Dyer, C. (2008). Literacies and Discourses of Development among the Rabaris of Kutch, India. *Journal of Development Studies*, 44(6), 863–879.

Edwards, R., and Usher, R. (2001). Lifelong Learning: A Postmodern Condition of Education? *Adult Education Quarterly*, 51(4), 273–287.

Egbo, B. (2000). *Gender, Literacy and Life Chances in Sub-Saharan Africa*. Clevedon: Multilingual Matters.

Feiner, S.F., and Barker, D.K. (2007). Microcredit and Women's Poverty, In B. Rakocy, A. Reuss, C. Sturr, and the Dollars and Sense Collective (eds), *Real World Globalization* (9th ed.), Boston: Dollars and Sense, pp. 236–240.

Finnegan, R. (1988). *Literacy and Orality: Studies in the Technology of Communication*. Oxford, UK: Blackwell Publishing.

Foley, A.W. (1997). *Anthropological Linguistics: An Introduction*. Oxford: Basil Blackwell.

Fragoso, A., Kurantowicz, E., and Lucio-Villegas, E. (eds) (2011). *Between Global and Local: Adult Learning and Development*. Frankfurt am Main: Peter Lang.

Freire, P. (1970). *Pedagogy of the Oppressed*. New York: Continuum.

Freire, P. (1973). *Education for Critical Consciousness*. London: Sheed and Ward.

Freire, P. (1985). *The Politics of Education: Culture, Power and Liberation*. New York: Bergin and Garvey.

Freire, P., and Macedo, D. (1987). *Literacy: Reading the Word and the World*. London: Routledge and Kegan Paul.

Friedmann, J. (1992). *Empowerment: The Politics of an Alternative Development*. New York: John Wiley & Sons.

Garikipati, S. (2008). The Impact of Lending to Women on Household Vulnerability and Women's Empowerment: Evidence from India. *World Development*, 36(12), 2620–2642.

Gebre, A., Openjuru, G., Rogers, A., and Street, B. (2009). *Everyday Literacies in Africa: Ethnographic Studies of Literacy and Numeracy Practices in Ethiopia*. Addis Ababa: Fountain Publishers.

Gee, J.P. (1991). What is Literacy? In Candace Mitchell and Kathleen Weiler (eds), *Rewriting Literacy: Culture and the Discourse of the Other*, New York: Bergin and Garvey, pp. 3–11.

Goetz, A.M. (1997). *Getting Institutions Right for Women in Development*. London: Zed Books.

Goetz, A.M., and Gupta, S.R. (1996). Who Takes the Credit? Gender, Power, and Control over Loan Use in Rural Credit Programmes in Bangladesh. *World Development*, 24(1), 45–63.

Goody, J. (1968). *Literacy in Traditional Societies*. Cambridge, UK: Cambridge University Press.

Hamilton, M. (2012a). The Effects of the Literacy Policy Environment on Local Sites of Learning. *Language and Education*, 26(2), 169–182.

Hamilton, M. (2012b). *Literacy and the Politics of Representation*. London: Taylor and Francis.

Hamilton, M., and Pitt, K. (2011). Challenging Representations: Constructing the Adult Literacy Learner over 30 Years of Policy and Practice in the United Kingdom. *Reading Research Quarterly*, 46(4), 350–373.

Hemmings, H. (2011). *Together: How Small Groups Achieve Big Things*. London: John Murray.

Hodgson, L.D. (2011). *Gender and Culture at the Limit of Rights*, Studies in Human Rights Series. Philadelphia: University of Pennsylvania Press.

Hodkinson, P. (2010). Informal learning: A contested concept. In P.P.B. McGaw (ed.), *International Encyclopedia of Education* (3rd edn), Oxford: Elsevier, pp. 42–46.

Hoppers, W. (2005). Community Schools as an Educational Alternative in Africa: A Critique. *International Review of Education*, 51(2), 115–137.

Hoppers, W. (2006). *Non-Formal Education and Basic Education Reform: A Conceptual Review.* Paris: UNESCO, IIEP.

Huiskamp, G., and Hartmann-Mahmud, L. (2007). As Development Seeks to Empower: Women from Mexico and Niger Challenge Theoretical Categories. *Journal of Poverty*, 10(4), 1–26.

Hymes, D. (1994). Toward Ethnographies of Communication. In J. Maybin (ed.), *Language and Literacy in Social Practice: A Reader*, Avon, UK: Multilingual Matters, pp. 11–22.

Ighobor, K. (2013). *Africa Renewal May: Africa's Youth: A 'Ticking Time Bomb' or an Opportunity?* New York: UN.

Irvine, P. (1996). *Forty Miles and Four Hundred Years: Toward a Post-Colonial Curriculum for Native American Students*, unpublished manuscript, University of Rochester, Rochester. New York.

Jackson, N.J., Betts, C., and Willis, J. (2011). Surrey Lifewide Learning Award: A Learning Partnership to Support Lifewide Learning. In N.J. Jackson (ed.), *Learning for a Complex World: A Lifewide Concept of Learning, Education and Personal Development.* Authorhouse.

Jeffs, T., and Smith, M.K. (2005). *Informal Education. Conversation, Democracy and Learning.* Ticknall: Education Now.

Jeffs, T., and Smith, M.K. (1997, 2005, 2011). What is Informal Education? In *Encyclopedia of Informal Education.* http://infed.org/mobi/what-is-informal-education, accessed 12 May 2016.

Kabeer, N. (1999). Resources, Agency, Achievements: Reflections on the Measurement of Women's Empowerment. *Development and Change*, 30(3), 435–464.

Kabeer, N. (2000). Social Exclusion, Poverty and Discrimination: Towards an Analytical Framework. *IDS Bulletin*, 31(4), 83–97.

King, K. (1982). Formal, Nonformal and Informal Learning: Some North South Contrasts. *International Review of Education*, 28(2), 177–187.

Kiptot, E., and Franzel, S. (2011). *Gender and Agroforestry in Africa: Are Women Participating?* ICRAF Occasional Paper No. 13. Nairobi: World Agroforestry Centre.

Knudsen, S.V. (2006). Intersectionality: A Theoretical Inspiration in the Analysis of Minority Cultures and Identities in Textbooks. In E. Bruillard, B. Aamotsbakken, S.V. Knudsen, and M. Horsley (eds), *Caught in the Web or Lost in the Textbook?* Caen: IUFM de Caen, pp. 61–76.

Kwan, P. (2000). Complicity and Complexity: Cosynthesis and Praxis. *DePaul Law Review*, 49, 687.

Lauglo, J. (2001). *Engaging with Adults: The Case for Increased Support to Adult Basic Education in Sub-Saharan Africa.* Washington DC: World Bank. Africa Region Human Development Working Paper Series.

LeVine, R.A., LeVine, S., Richman, A., Uribe, F., Correa, C., and Miller, P.J. (1991). Women's Schooling and Childcare in the Demographic Transition: A Mexican Case Study. *Population and Development Review*, 17(3), 459–496.

LeVine, R.A., LeVine, S., Schnell-Anzola, B., Rowe, M., and Dexter, E. (2012). *Literacy and Mothering: How Women's Schooling Changes the Lives of the World's Children (Child Development in Cultural Context).* New York: Oxford University Press.

Maathai, W. (2004). Nobel Lecture, Oslo, 10 December 2004. www.nobelprize.org/nobel_prizes/peace/laureates/2004/maathai-lecture-text.html.

Maddox, B. (2005). Assessing the Impact of Women's Literacies in Bangladesh: An Ethnographic Inquiry. *International Journal of Educational Development*, 25(2), 123–132.

Maddox, B. (2007). Secular and Koranic Literacies in South Asia: From Colonisation to Contemporary Practice. *International Journal of Educational Development*, 27(6), 661–668.

Malhotra, A. (2003). Conceptualizing and Measuring Women's Empowerment as a Variable in International Development, Measuring Empowerment: Cross-disciplinary Perspectives, Washington, DC, 4–5 February.

Malhotra, A., Sidney, R.S., and Carol, B. (2002). *Measuring Women's Empowerment as a Variable in International Development*. International Centre for Research on Women and the Gender and Development Group of the World Bank. Washington, D.C.: World Bank.

Maslak, M.A. (ed.). (2008). *The Structure and Agency of Women's Education*. Albany: State University of New York Press.

Mayoux, L. (1999). Questioning Virtuous Spirals: Micro-Finance and Women's Empowerment in Africa. *Journal of International Development*, 11(7), 957–984.

Merriam, S.B., Caffarella, R.S., and Baumgartner, L.M. (2007). *Learning in Adulthood: A Comprehensive Guide* (3rd edn). San Francisco, CA: Jossey-Bass.

Moglen, H. (1983). Power and Empowerment. *Women's Studies International Forum*, 6(2), 131–134.

Mohanty, C.T. (2003). *Feminism without Borders: Decolonizing Theory. Practicing Solidarity*. Durham and London: Duke University Press.

Mulumba, B.M., and Masaazim, M.F. (2012). Challenges to African Development: The Medium of Instruction in Uganda's Education System. *Pedagogy, Culture and Society*, 20(3), 435–450.

Nash, J. (2008). Re-Thinking Intersectionality. *Feminist Review*, 89, 1–15.

Ngiug wa Thiong'o. (1986). *Decolonising the Mind*. Portsmouth: Heinemann Educational Books.

Nyaga, S.N. (2008). Correlation between indigenous Communities' Concept of Development and Their Response to Contemporary Paradigms of Sustainable Development. *Chemchemi International Journal of the Kenyatta University School of Humanities and Social Sciences*, 5, 105–123.

Oduro, A.D., Baah-Boateng, W., and Boakye-Yiadom, L. (2011). *Measuring the Gender Asset Gap in Ghana*. Accra, Ghana: University of Ghana and Woeli Publishing Services.

Omolewa, M. (2007). Traditional African Modes of Education: Their Relevance in the Modern World. *International Review of Education*, 53(5/6), 593–612.

Ong, W.J. (1982). *Orality and Literacy: The Technologizing of the Word*. London: Routledge.

Oxaal, Z., and Baden, S. (1997). *Gender and Empowerment: Definitions, Approaches and Implications for Policy*, Bridge Report No. 40. Sussex: Institute of Development Studies.

Pahl, K., and Rowsell, J. (eds) (2006). *Travel Notes from the New Literacy Studies: Instances of Practice*. Clevedon: Multilingual Matters.

Papen, U. (2002). *TVs, Textbooks and Tour Guides: Uses and Meanings of Literacy in Namibia*, unpublished PhD thesis, King's College, London.

Papen, U. (2005). Literacy and Development: What Works for Whom? or, How Relevant is the Social Practices View of Literacy for Literacy Education in Developing Countries? *International Journal of Educational Development*, 25(1), 5–17.

Papen, U. (2009). Literacy, Learning and Health: A Social Practices View of Health Literacy. *Literacy and Numeracy Studies*, 16(2), 19–34.

Papen, U. (2012). *Literacy and Globalization: Reading and Writing in Times of Social and Cultural Change*. London: Routledge.

Phillips, R. (2015). How 'Empowerment' May Miss Its Mark: Gender Equality Policies and how They Are Understood in Women's NGOs. *Voluntas: International Journal of Voluntary and Nonprofit Organizations*, 26(4), 1122–1142.

Pimmer, C., Brysiewicz, P., Linxen, S., Walters, F., Chipps, J., and Gröhbiel, U. (2014). Informal Mobile Learning in Nurse Education and Practice in Remote Areas. A Case Study from Rural South Africa. *Nurse Education Today*, 34(11), 1398–1404.

Pitt, M.M., and Khandker, S.R. (1998). The Impact of Group Based Credit Programs on Poor Households in Bangladesh: Does the gender of participants matter? *Journal of Political Economy*, 106(5), 958–996.

Popov, O. (2009). *Gender Aspects of Informal Learning in a Local Mozambican Community*, Working Papers in Teacher Education. Umeå School of Education, Umeå University, SE-90187 Umeå, Sweden.

Psacharopoulos, G. (1994). Returns to Investment in Education: A Global Update. *World Development*, 22(9), 1325–1343.

Puchner, L. (2003). Women and Literacy in Rural Mali: A Study of the Socio-Economic Impact of Participating in Literacy Programmes in Four Villages. *International Journal of Educational Development*, 23(4), 439–458.

Ralston, H. (2006). Citizenship, Identity, Agency and Resistance among Canadian and Australian Women of South Asia. In Evangelia Tastsoglou and Dobrowolsky (eds), *Women, Migration and Citizenship; Making Local, National and Transnational Connections*, Aldershot, UK: Ashgate Press, pp. 183–200.

Rao, N., and Robinson-Pant, A. (2006). Adult Education and Indigenous People: Addressing Gender in Policy and Practice. *International Journal of Educational Development*, 26(2), 209–223.

Richardson, L.D., and Wolfe, M. (eds). (2001). *Principles and Practice of Informal Education: Learning through Life*. London: Routledge-Falmer.

Robertson, C. (1984). Formal or Non-Formal Education? Entrepreneurial Women in Ghana. *Comparative Education Review*, 28(4), 639–658.

Robinson-Pant, A. (2008). Why Literacy Matters: Exploring Policy Perspectives on Literacies, Identities and Social Change. *Journal of Development Studies*, 44(6), 779–796.

Robinson-Pant, A. (2009). Changing Discourses: Literacy and Development in Nepal. *International Journal of Educational Development*, 30(2), 136–144.

Rogers, A. (1994). *Using Literacy: A New Approach to Post-Literacy Materials*. Education Research. Serial No. 10. London: Overseas Development Administration.

Rogers, A. (2003). *What is the Difference? A New Critique of Adult Learning and Teaching*. Leicester: NIACE.

Rogers, A. (2004). Looking Again at Non-Formal and Informal Education: Towards a New Paradigm. In *Encyclopedia of Informal Education*. www.infed.org/biblio/non_formal_paradigm.htm.

Rogers, A. (2006). Escaping the Slums or Changing the Slums? Lifelong Learning and Social Transformation. *International Journal of Lifelong Education*, 25(2), 125–137.

Schurr, C., and Segebart, D. (2012). Engaging with Feminist Postcolonial Concerns through Participatory Action Research and Intersectionality. *Geographica Helvetica*, 67(3), 147–154.

54 Women's informal learning and empowerment

Sen, A. (1985). Well-Being, Agency and Freedom: The Dewey Lectures 1984. *Journal of Philosophy*, 82, 169–221.

Sen, G., and Grown, C. (1987). *Development, Crises and Alternative Visions: Third World Women's Perspectives*. New York: Monthly Review Press.

Sen, G., and Östlin, P. (2011). Gender Inequality in Health. In WHO, *Improving Equity in Health by Addressing Social Determinants*, Geneva: WHO, pp. 59–87.

Sengupta, N. (2013). Poor Women's Empowerment: The Discursive Space of Microfinance. *Indian Journal of Gender Studies*, 20(2), 279–304.

Smith, M.K. (1994). *Local Education: Community, Conversation, Action*. Buckingham: Open University Press.

Smith, M.K. (1999, 2008). Informal Learning. In *Encyclopedia of Informal Education*. http://infed.org/mobi/informal-learning-theory-practice-and-experience, accessed 15 March 2016.

Street, B.V. (1984). *Literacy in Theory and Practice*. New York: Cambridge University Press.

Street, B.V. (1993). The New Literacy Studies, guest editorial. *Journal of Research in Reading*, 16(2), 81–97.

Street, B.V. (1995). *Social Literacies: Critical Approaches to Literacy in Development, Ethnography and Education*. London: Longman.

Street, B.V. (2001). *Literacy and Development: Ethnographic Perspectives*. London: Routledge.

Street, B.V. (2003). What's "New" in New Literacy Studies? Critical Approaches to Literacy in Theory and Practice. *Comparative Education*, 5(2), 77–91.

Stromquist, N.P. (1995). Romancing the State: Gender and Power in Education. *Comparative Education Review*, 39(4), 423–454.

Stromquist, N.P. (1997). *Increasing Girls' and Women's Participation in Basic Education*. Paris: Unesco, International Institute for Educational Planning.

Stromquist, N.P. (2013). Education Policies for Gender Equity: Probing into State Responses. *Education Policy Analysis Archives*, 21(65), 1–31.

Trudell, B., and Klaas, A. (2010). Distinction, Integration and Identity: Motivations for Local Language Literacy in Senegalese Communities. *International Journal of Educational Development*, 30(2), 121–129.

Trutko, J., O'Brien, C., Wandner, S., and Barnow, B. (2014). *Formative Evaluation of Job Clubs Operated by Faith and Community-Based Organizations: Findings from Site Visits and Options for Future Evaluation* (Final report submitted to the Chief Evaluation Office, U.S. Department of Labor). Washington, DC: Capital Research Corporation, Inc. and George Washington University.

UIL (UNESCO Institute for Lifelong Learning). (2012). *CONFINTEA VI/United Nations Literacy Decade Country Reports*. Hamburg: UIL.

UN. (2001). *Gender and Racial Discrimination*, Report of the Expert Group Meeting, 21–24 November 2000, Zagreb, Croatia. www.un.org/womenwatch/daw/csw/genrac/report.htm.

UN. (2015). *Transforming our World: The 2030 Agenda for Sustainable Development*. New York: UN.

UNDP. (2003). *Human Development Report 2003. Millennium Development Goals: A Compact among Nations to End Human Poverty*.

UNDP. (2014). *Human Development Report 2014. Sustaining Human Progress: Reducing Vulnerabilities and Building Resilience*. New York: Oxford University Press.

UNESCO. (2000). *The Dakar Framework for Action. Education for All: Meeting Our Collective Commitments*. Paris: UNESCO.
UNESCO. (2005). *Literacy for Life. EFA Global Monitoring Report 2006*. Paris: UNESCO.
UNESCO. (2012). *Shaping the Education of Tomorrow: 2012 Report on the UN Decade of Education for Sustainable Development*, abridged. Paris: UNESCO.
UNESCO. (2014). *Education for All Global Monitoring Report 2013. Teaching and Learning: Achieving Quality for All*. Paris: UNESCO.
UNESCO. (2015). *Sustainable Development Goals for Education*. http://en.unesco.org/sdgs/ed, accessed 10 December 2015.
Vavrus, F. (2003). *Desire and Decline: Schooling amid Crisis in Tanzania*. New York: Peter Lang Publishing.
Voola, P.A. (2013). *Beyond the Economics of Gender Inequalities in Microfinance: Comparing Problem Representations in India and Australia*, unpublished PhD thesis, University of Sydney.
Wilkins, A.C. (2004). Puerto Rican Wannabes: Sexual Spectacle and the Marking of Race, Class, and Gender Boundaries. *Gender and Society*, 18, 103–121.
Willinsky, J. (1990). *The New Literacy: Redefining Reading and Writing in the Schools*. New York: Routledge.
World Bank. (1997). *Women's Education in Developing Countries: Barriers, Benefits, and Policies*. Baltimore, MD: Johns Hopkins University Press.
World Bank. (2004). *Gender and Development in the Middle East and North Africa: Women in the Public Sphere*. MENA Development Report. Washington, DC: World Bank, Middle East and North Africa Region.
World Bank. (2012). *World Development Report 2012: Gender Equality and Development*. Washington, DC: World Bank.
Yanchar, S.C., Spackman, J.S., and Faulconer, J.E. (2013). Learning as Embodied Familiarization. *Journal of Theoretical and Philosophical Psychology*, 33(4), 216–232.
Young, I.M. (1997). Unruly Categories: A Critique of Nancy Fraser's Dual Systems Theory. *New Left Review*, 222, 147–160.

3 Using an ethnographic research framework

Introduction

An ethnographic approach was determined to be the most useful in exploring and documenting Maasai women's experiences of literacy. Togetherness and solidarity to bring about a positive change through informal women's groups were key themes of exploration. Interviews and process observation revealed the cooperative and collective sharing of resources, knowledge and expertise among village women in Kenya. This said, qualitative studies of Maasai women's life and learning experiences have been limited.

The chapter discusses the research framework and the methodological decisions taken based on the socio-cultural context of Maasai women in Kenya. The purpose of the study was to explore, from a postcolonial feminist perspective, the role of informal learning and literacy as a key means for village women to move out of and resist poverty, and to examine the primary linkages between informal learning/literacy, human development and gender inequality in Narok County, Kenya, through local women's and institutional perspectives.

Given the nature of the research, an ethnographic framework was employed for this study as it ensures women's voices are heard and aligns with postcolonial feminist theory. This study attempted to understand Kenyan women's struggles in their everyday lives, and their experiences of informal learning and literacy integrated into their community development activities in Narok County. This research explored the notion of literacy for the women in the District, their needs, their experiences to improve their living conditions and the activities of women's groups.

As discussed in the literature review chapters, the exploratory analysis of the informal conversations with women based on these broad questions helped to identify specific phenomena among women in Narok County. Cases of women's experiences were examined by using an ethnographic approach in the field.

Moreover, feminist researchers suggest that women's insights have been little recorded as social science knowledge, hence women's individual experiences need to be approached and listened to (Narayan 1991; Mohanty 2003).

While the participants of this study are mostly women in Kenya, Ogunyemi's (1985) idea of 'womanism', a perspective of women in the context of Africa, will be discussed under feminist research. Then, the researcher's positioning during the fieldwork in the village will be explained. The field research in this study was based on an ethnographic approach using the methods of process observation and semi-structured interviews. Process observation is to observe people's behavioural patterns or processes of a group (Conole 1978). Semi-structured interviews can be conducted based on an untied structure using open-ended questions to find out about particular topics (Lindlof and Taylor 2002). As this study proceeded by applying observation and interview techniques through ethnography, each method will be explained in the next section in detail. Finally, ethical considerations regarding the research participants are also addressed.

Feminist research

The postcolonial feminist perspective of inquiry helped me explore the intersecting forces that influence women's everyday life and understanding of their learning issues. In addition, I was able to illuminate how power relations, race, class and gender influence women's learning and community development experiences by:

1   Asking semi-structured interview questions constructed to explore whether research participants view themselves as having learning opportunities and access to learning. By asking certain questions such as: Did you go to school? If not, why? This supported my understanding of the historical and cultural factors that shape the women's social position and thus their learning experience.
2   Gathering information about the activities that affect women and their families' well-being. I was able to explore with the research participants as to whether through these learning and community development activities women developed empowerment and agency.
3   Asking questions to explore whether gender issues affected their life experiences helped me to understand the significance of gender roles in their village context.

In order to clarify the importance of a feminist approach this section discusses how feminism has been debated and applied to research contexts in poor countries. Theoretically it is an important discussion because it is the lens through which this study is seen and it reflects the researcher's position or standpoint. The focus of the discussion below is the theoretical connection between feminism and doing research and, in particular, doing postcolonial feminist research.

Focusing on the notion of essentialising tendencies in feminism, Mohanty (2003) critiqued the political project of Western feminism in its discursive construction of the category of the 'Third World woman' (*sic*) as a hegemonic entity. Mohanty (2003) stated that Western feminisms have tended to gloss over the differences amongst Southern women, when experiences of oppression are very diverse, and contingent on geography, history and culture. Mohanty (2003) argues that multicultural feminism is required. As Narayan and Harding also state.

> [P]ostcolonial feminist concerns transform mainstream notions of experience, human rights, the origins of philosophic issues, philosophic uses of metaphors of the family, white antiracism, human progress, scientific progress, modernity, the unity of scientific method, the desirability of universal knowledge claims....
>
> (1998, p. 1)

In other words, researchers must aim to examine situations of women from different perspectives. Connell (2007) has recognised the heterogeneity and multiplicity of masculinities, and reminds us to recognise the significance of the context without falling into a world of homogenous and independent cultures and places. Alexander and Mohanty argue that:

> [T]he experience of repression can be, but is not necessarily, a catalyst for organising. It is, in fact, the *interpretation* of that experience within a collective context that marks the moment of transformation from perceived contradictions and material disenfranchisement to participation in women's movements.
>
> (1997, p. xl)

Mohanty also noted that feminist researchers should consider that there can be no apolitical scholarship. Further, she criticised "a notion of gender or sexual difference or even patriarchy which can be applied universally and cross-culturally" (1991, p. 51). Feminist researchers should be aware of the influence of politics and power in their practices and recognise obvious power relations between males and females at different levels of society.

Narayan (1997) explained how a cultural change occurs in traditional communities from women's perspectives by looking at the conversion to Christianity and the practice of female genital mutilation in poor country contexts. Narayan further argued that "there is no need to portray female genital mutilation" as an "African cultural practice" or dowry murders and dowry related harassment as a "problem of Indian women" as that can eclipse the fact that not all "African women" or "Indian women" confront these problems, or confront them in identical ways, or in ways that "efface local contestations of these problems" (Narayan 1997, p. 104). She thus reinforces the need for multiplicity in understanding the way women experience oppression in diverse contexts and in diverse ways.

There is a constant need to remind researchers to question and critically reflect on ideas we formulate from our research study. I have examined my own subjectivity within my research to reflect on the ways that strategic essentialism could be used for my research.

Womanism – African feminism?

Western feminists often make assumptions about the homogenisation of gender and much postcolonial and feminist scholarship seems to include limited discussion on recognising the historical context of African cultures, traditions and languages (Ogunyemi 1985; Oyewumi 2005; Tamale 2006). Oyeronke Oyewumi suggests: "If gender is socially constructed, then gender cannot behave in the same way across time and space" (2005, p. 11). Oyewumi critiques Western feminists' views on African women as a "homogeneous, bio-anatomically determined group, which is always constituted as powerless and victimized", regardless of what culture the body grew up in (2005, p. 11). Redefining feminism to ensure its relevance to the African context is crucial for African feminism. African feminism is important in this research as it provides a position from which to understand feminist identity within Africa and provides insight into how women in Africa negotiate other aspects of individual and cultural identity.

In Filomina Chioma Steady's notable work, she views African feminism as:

> emphasizing female autonomy and cooperation; nature over culture; and the centrality of children, multiple mothering, and kinship.... It also questions features of traditional African cultures without denigrating them, understanding that these traditional features might be viewed differently by the various classes of women.... [I]f African feminism is to succeed as a human reformation project, it cannot accept separatism from the opposite sex. Eschewing male exclusion, then, becomes one defining feature of African feminism that differentiates it from feminism as it is conceptualized in the West.... African feminism is not antagonistic to men but challenges them to be aware of those aspects of women's subjugation that differ from the generalized oppression of all African people.
>
> (1981, p. 28)

As well as not being about women only, African feminism also asserts that African women should use their own voices, instead of having Western scholars to speak for them. African feminism aims to seek identity and agency together with African men, liberating all African people from various forms of colonisation. Instead of avoiding male counterparts, the involvement of men in gender equality movements is emphasised (Nnaemeka 2005). A further principal is that by playing dynamic women's roles, women become active agents rather than victims of situations.

Nevertheless, in an argument for recognising a specifically *African* womanhood, Kanogo (2005) suggested that despite women's lower position in

Kenyan society, women were not totally passive at home or in the community. Kanogo (2005) observed that women were flexible enough to adapt to colonial or postcolonial circumstances; for instance, depending on the situation, they went to look for employment in the cities or maintained household chores in accordance with their husbands' or parents' demands (Kanogo 2005). While most women remained struggling beneath patriarchal power and subordination to men, some obtained an education or brought about a new gendered practice in their traditional community (Kanogo 2005). This illustrates that there are potential paths among women to think about new ways of experiencing gender and womanhood as well as social change. As will be described in later chapters, this view of 'African womanhood' is supported by many of the strategies employed by the research participants who seek to resist patriarchy and seek economic independence in order to support their children. It is clear that African feminist scholarship and postcolonial scholarship are complementary as a theoretical approach to the analysis of education and development.

Moreover, the Nigerian writer and scholar, Ogunyemi (1985, p. 65) developed the alternative concept, 'womanism', to meet the specific requirement of feminist perspectives in Africa. Supporting Mohanty's (2003) challenge to wider feminisms, to consider essential points of culture and ethnicity, it can be said that Ogunyemi's concept of 'womanism' is a localised feminist theory that seeks to represent the African social and cultural environment. Ogunyemi's definition of the concept is that:

> Womanism is black centred; it is accommodationist. It believes in the freedom and independence of women like feminism; unlike radical feminism, it wants meaningful union between black women and black men and black children and will see to it that men begin to change from their sexist stand.
>
> (1985, p. 65)

In her view, instead of rallying to obtain women's equal rights to African men, African women seek transformations that will see their work collaboratively with men towards creating spaces of female power in socio-cultural areas (Ogunyemi 1985). More precisely, Ogunyemi stated that:

> With the world power structure as it is, what would the relevance be of a black female character's struggle to be equal to such a black man as, for example, ... on the African side, as Ngugi wa Thiong'o's treacherous male ... or Chinua Achebe's insecure Okonkwo[1]?
>
> (1985, p. 68)

In other words, Ogunyemi (1985) claims that African women do not seek equal status with African men as suggested by Western feminism. Rather, African womanists should seek to create a harmonious society with considerations for race and ethnicity. Here, women try to accommodate the self-pride of men and accept men as their partners. Therefore, Ogunyemi's (1985) central concern in African feminism is more about compromise and collaboration. It is also emphasised that women consider a communitarian perspective over an individual one (Oyewumi 2003). Moreover, gender in the African context is about gendering, a process of gender reconstruction in everyday interactions (Oyewumi 2010). This point is also emphasised by Tamale (2006, p. 41) who states that "the connectivity across African women's differences and specificities" is vital to achieve a more equitable and democratic society. Oyewumi's (2010) concerns remind us that culturally defined strategies exist in collective struggles seeking social transformation for bringing about a better society. Oyewumi's (2010) point of view on African feminism is an apt frame for analysis of the village women's voices reported in Chapter 5 of this book. It demonstrates women's integrity and how women may seek autonomy within their community. It also suggests that women should not stop living life due to oppression, and it shows that women in Africa seek dignity and freedom under justice and equality as human beings (Mangena 2003). Women and men work together in partnership rather than one in which women seek power through the exclusion of men.

African feminists from a postcolonial feminist perspective have special relevance in this research because their views acknowledge the lived experiences of subordinated women in a patriarchal society, hence women can generate knowledge about equality and social justice (Tamale 2006). African feminism represents a clear statement and vision for women in Africa. Wane also highlights that "indigenous knowledge in Africa is a living experience informed by ancestral voices of cultural norms, values and beliefs of people, and the knowledge is collectively and communally shared" (2008, pp. 190–191). This affirms the view that communal culture is central in knowledge ownership. Such an agenda fits with recommendations that emerged from the research reported in this book as it demonstrates the inclusion of local women's own strategies to combat poverty through literacy and informal learning based on their experiences and traditional knowledges. The overlay of African feminism or 'womanism' provides a suitable dimension for the multiple subtle forms of resistance to oppression that the Masai village women demonstrated throughout the study.

In the history of women's social and collective action in Africa, one cannot forget the Nobel Peace laureate, Professor Wangari Maathai, of Kenya. With her environment issues-based non-governmental organisation (NGO) named the Green Belt Movement, she promoted human rights, gender equality, peace and democracy in Kenya. In her Nobel Peace lecture given in 2004, as a woman activist, she stated that:

> I am especially mindful of women and the girl child. I hope it will encourage them to raise their voices and take more space for leadership. I

know the honour also gives a deep sense of pride to our men, both old and young.

In her view, although women are primary care-givers in Africa, women's opinions have been less regarded in male-dominated decision-making in Kenya. She suggests that women's feasible outcomes from action will influence men. Maathai (2004) also emphasised the significance of promoting democracy in Kenya to have an equitable society between men and women. This opinion was supported by Tamale (2006), who has called for a strong commitment to political engagement of the women's movement. Tamale (2006, p. 40) affirmed that women's subordination is a political issue to be addressed and she encouraged women's groups working for gender equity to adopt a political agenda (Tamale 2006). This perspective of African feminism demands an engagement beyond the traditional domain for women in Maasai villages and must be seen as a long-term strategy that builds on the local communal strengths that are the focus of this research on informal learning and ideas of literacy. However, all of the African feminists open up a space for traditional culture to work with feminist goals.

Establishing rapport and positioning myself

Establishing a good rapport with all stakeholders is crucial to conduct successful fieldwork (Charmaz 2006). A researcher needs to respect research participants and make an effort to understand the foundations on which their views are based (Charmaz 2006). Respecting and understanding research participants' views is also urged by Ospina et al. (2008), who argues that the researcher/researched hierarchy has been an issue in research practices; some researchers attempt to relinquish their control over the lived experience and knowledge of the researched in order to establish a connection between researcher and researched. It is also helpful to have a relaxed unstressful interview process, where interviewees are comfortable speaking about their experiences with confidence. As part of this research and as a researcher I was very aware that I might bring certain biases, values and beliefs into this research process. However, based on the researcher's previous fieldwork experience in Narok County, the researcher had developed a clear understanding of the community and was well-known in the community. Former experience helped the researcher establish a rapport with research participants with minimal difficulty. During my previous research visits, I was positioned as an underprivileged foreign woman (or rather girl) by local people in the district. They regarded me as a hopeless and unfortunate woman since I was physically much smaller than them, did not have my own family and did not own any cattle or goats. Interestingly, this helped me, as an outsider-researcher, to be part of the community and to settle down in the village.

Reflexivity is an acknowledged and introspective process where researchers constantly challenge themselves to see how their own perspectives are affecting the research method, analysis or interpretations (Brown 1994). Therefore, my interactions in the research process and theoretical insights required regular self-reflection. I valued the women's voices and narratives because my own experiences, my cultural background, my beliefs, values and social position do have an influence on the entire research process.

Given the significance of African feminism considered for this study and the researcher's positioning, the following section will describe this research framework of ethnography and its approaches of interviews and process observation.

Data collection in the field

Data collection was conducted in Kenya during one six-month trip between April and September 2011, 37 interviews were conducted with members of women's groups, literacy centres, women's group leaders in their community and with government organisations. I had a local interpreter for interviews with village women. I had known her personally since I first conducted fieldwork in 2006 and she assisted me in connecting with her community people and her colleagues. I had asked her for assistance as an interpreter for my fieldwork since 2006, hence she understood my fieldwork and the purpose of my study conducted in Narok. During the long-term fieldwork for my PhD studies, I explained about the purpose of my study and the contents of interview questions. Through this briefing session, we made sure that the contents of the interview questions were clearly understood and the researcher would adjust the time of interview to the interpreter's and interviewee's schedule. An interpreter may shape the interview in ways the researcher did not intend, and also the interpreter may distort interview responses rather than facilitate understanding (Mosley 2013), however, the research needs to consider a variety of issues rather than assuming that organising interviews with an interpreter would produce low-quality data (Mosley 2013). A language is not just a tool for translating messages, but carries particular socio-cultural meanings (Bhabha 1994; Bassnet 1994; Temple 1997). The local interpreter played a role in enabling the researcher to ascribe meanings to the women's voices and also to teach local habits and culture (Temple 1997). The local interpreter and I had a discussion on my research and the interviewed data occasionally in the field, thus making sure that all the interview questions were covered. Also the interpreter helped me understand their tradition and culture by elaborating the interviewed women's replies/stories to me, if there were particular comments which related to their community's tradition. Spivak (1999) argues that there is no central and consistent generalized "native voice" and demonstrates that rather there is a multiplicity of voices within every culture.

Spivak (1999) suggests that when representing the other, intellectual activists might use a method of "speaking to" a particular community through imagined dialogue as a way to stay ethically reflexive. Moreover, it is possible to bring in sexist and postcolonial assumptions and misconceptions that must be unlearned through dialogue (Spivak 1999). Therefore, the researcher practiced constant internal reflexivity, which occurred both in the writing process and through interactions in the village, and was required to continually combat deeply embedded thought patterns.

As the primary goal of ethnography is to seek to comprehend the sociocultural contexts of a particular society (Atkinson et al. 2001), ethnography was appropriate for my study. By participating in women's group activity, observing and interviewing local people, I attempted to understand the lives of local people in Kenya.

Ethnographic research has broad implications for many fields, including education. Basu et al. (2008) and Robinson-Pant (2008) have both described the importance of ethnographic research to capture the actual opinions of indigenous organisations in poor countries. In her argument, Robinson-Pant (2008) states that results of ethnographic research can influence the literacy discourse and practices of development organisations involved in implementing literacy programmes. Professional development evaluators and staff developers can also use this approach to understand needs in a specific community, experiences, viewpoints and goals of people. Such information can enable them to design useful and worthwhile programmes for policy practitioners, community workers and educationalists to ultimately improve people's living conditions.

An ethnographer should be flexible and reflexive (Bryman 2001). The role of an ethnographer is to learn from local people, adopting their lifestyle and not controlling their decisions on everyday practices or customs. Also, an ethnographer needs to reveal what s/he has observed and her/his experiences staying in a particular community from time to time.

In the case of Narok County in Kenya, ethnographic/anthropological research on education and development has been very limited. Sawamura (2008) has highlighted that many research studies have relied heavily on quantitative data, and also the majority of academics as well as development practitioners seem to be interested in attainment of the levels of productivity and efficiency of literacy programmes.

To understand Maasai women's thinking and behaviours in literacies, this ethnography-based research primarily relies on both techniques of observation (a researcher takes part in everyday life in a particular community) and interviews (Agar 1996). Fontana and Frey state that observation and interviews seem to "go hand in hand" (2003, p. 74), because of the nature of ethnography. These techniques were mainly used to collect data, which is described in the process of data collection.

Therefore, this study's approach was based on Spradley's (1979) standpoint that the researcher stayed in a village, learning about Maasai culture and experiencing their everyday lives in order to understand Maasai women's perceptions.

Process observation

The fieldwork was carried out in a six-month period in Kenya. Not only qualitative interviews but also process observation were used as a data collection method in this ethnographic study. Process observation can be defined as "a technique of observing the behavioral patterns or human processes of a group" (Conole 1978, p. 11). In relation to their informal inference by nature, Brady and Collier (2004) state that casual process observation is "[a]n insight or piece of data that provides information about context, process or mechanism, and that contributes distinctive leverage in causal inference" (pp. 227–228). According to Narayanasamy and Ramesh (1997), through the process observation method, a researcher gathers data by documenting and reflecting on events and incidents in the community. This means that the researcher acts as an observer who watches and documents what is occurring during a particular process. The researcher documents the processes within the village that contributed to informal learning and literacy. To do this, the researcher acts passively, noting in a diary of research experiences, which produces a rich description of the studied group's mechanism and its descriptive context in a natural setting (Brady and Collier 2004). Research participants speak their own language and use everyday concepts to explain their own perspective (Geertz 1973; Burgess 1984). A researcher seeks to find meanings in their situations as well.

Although the purpose of participant observation is to collect field data by watching local people's behaviour and habits within their natural setting (Thyer 2009), my participation as a researcher was based on invitations to observe such processes of learning. As McCall and Simmons discuss, the participant observer's role "is not a single method but rather a characteristic style of research which makes use of a number of methods and techniques – observation, informant interviewing, document analysis, respondent interviewing and participation with self-analysis" (1969, p. 1). My approach was to only document events and activities in which I was invited to participate in the village. Therefore, the processes of observing during data collection included being present at discussions, conversations, telephone calls, teaching and learning activities in the community, then writing, reading and recording what was observed.

Lastly, Williams (1988, p. 136) warns us of the possible paternalism involved in the participant observation method, and the arrogance of the researcher invading another group's world to get information in order to relay it to the outside world; this had influenced my decision to only observe processes to which I was invited. In the initial stage of the research project, research participants were told that the researcher would get involved in various community activities on the basis of permission or invitation from local people. Therefore, participation in daily life varied depending on their available time and place. Upon invitation from participants, I also participated in tea breaks, going shopping, visiting their friends' houses and so on. I got involved in daily situations, observed people, looked at things and listened to local people. I also made an effort to document incidents and episodes in my field notes.

Interviews

Many ethnographers use interviews to supplement the material gained by participating in the usual round of social encounters and experiences. As Madison (2005) states, interviewing is "a dynamic process fundamental to ethnography" (p. 35). This study initially used semi-structured interviews with research participants to understand their notion of literacy and views about improving their life conditions, together with informal conversations throughout the research project. Semi-structured interviews took place on the basis of an untied structure using open-ended questions to explore certain topics (Lindlof and Taylor 2002). The individual interview provided a unique opportunity to reflect each participant's own life.

In this study, the interview themes were initially based on broad topics and interview questions were focused to grasp further specific insights within the themes. The broad questions for interviewing members of women's groups were:

- Can you tell me about yourself and your experience in learning and the women's group?
- How has your involvement in your women's group changed your lifestyle, family or community?
- What do you think about the benefits of learning and/or literacy skills?
- What is your idea of an ideal community?

As Patton (1987) observed, good questions in interviews must be open-ended, neutral, sensitive and clear, with plain language used in questions about the participants' background, experience of participating in women's group activities, the perceptions of literacy education and development of their own community. For the purpose of record, appointments with primary and secondary participants were made formally. The interview transcriptions were used for an in-depth analysis. Detailed notes were taken to record an interviewee's explanation and to reflect the researcher's opinion.

My proficiency in the local languages of Maa and Swahili is at the level of greetings and self-introduction. I was able to read basic Swahili, yet my reading comprehension was rather limited and needed assistance from a local literate person. With my limited level of Maa and Swahili, I first greeted a research participant in Maa and introduced myself in Swahili, and I communicated with an interviewee asking about their name, age and occupation to open the interview. The interpreter was one of the well respected and known females in the village and wherever we had an interview with a village woman, the research participants were welcoming and accommodating to us.

All the women's group leaders and government-related people spoke fluent English. Most of the interviews were conducted at the research participants' offices, a local literacy centre, women's groups meeting venues and local cafes.

Individual interviews were scheduled for between 30 and 60 minutes, with flexibility. I held each interview at a location most convenient and comfortable for my participants.

It was difficult at times to reach the participants, as they had busy home and work schedules and lives, but I was able to find space and time from each participant for her individual interviews. It was also the reason I met them at locations they preferred in order to make it easier for them to participate in the interviews. I then attempted to conduct a second round of individual interviews in order to ask more questions about issues and points brought up in the first individual interview. However, it was impossible to schedule the second interviews due to the research participants' engagement in their jobs, household chores and so on.

All data was recorded through written notes only as the researcher has developed skills in this method of recording data due to her extensive prior experience in this context. The researcher attempted to write down all the interviewee's comments in a notebook. The researcher asked a question one by one and writes the research participant's reply down in the notebook through the interpreter accordingly. Once the particular question was answered and recorded in the notebook, then the researcher and the interpreter moved to the next question. However, when the participants consented to being photographed, a digital camera was used during women's group activities to detail some of the observations of processes in the village. The photographs of programme activities in the district added another dimension when analysing data regarding gender relations in the practices of community development.

Selection of field sites and research participants

Women's' grass root organisations in Narok County in the Rift Valley Province in Kenya, East Africa, were studied in-depth to understand socio-cultural conditions and women's experiences of their literacy and community development activities. The reason for the selection of the women's groups in Narok County as the research site in Kenya is because the researcher was able to stay in their community without any problems, having conducted fieldwork several times previously in their community between 2007 and 2009,[2] whilst employed as a researcher for Hiroshima University. The researcher's former experience meant she was already familiar to the community. Women's group leaders had also expressed their interest in the research topic. The energy, enthusiasm and willingness of the women's leaders and participants of women's groups for the topic of the research were key factors in the site selection for the study. A second aim of identifying the location was that it is a community where culture and tradition are well preserved, and it is an indigenous population with low literacy rates among women in Kenya.

The research questions that framed the study evolved from involvement in the research project during 2006 and 2009. As a result of this experience, I became interested in investigating the relationship between women's informal learning and literacy activities and their contribution to community development and poverty prevention.

As described in what follows, Narok County is located in south-west Kenya, along the Great Rift Valley, where the Maasai are dominant (see map of Kenya in Figure 3.1). The Maasai speak Maa (the Maasai language), which historically had no written script. However, the Latin alphabet has been used to record Maa, especially in transcribing the Bible. Most people can communicate in Swahili and/or English.

Recruitment process of research participants

Criteria for selection of the range of primary participants were the following:

1   Kenyan women, aged 18 years or older (regardless of education levels), who are members of women's groups and/or have attended adult literacy centres;
2   Women's group leaders in the community, or church-, school-, community-based organisations;
3   Government officers involved in literacy and/or gender and development programmes.

Research participants are summarised in Table 3.1.

The village women participants in Narok County were recruited by a general invitation to members of the village women's group through the agency of the local school-teacher who is part of the community. Individual women expressed their interest in participating in the research to the local teacher, and she passed this on to the researcher. This was conducted orally rather than through written communication due to two factors: first, the women are mostly illiterate in the traditional sense and, second, they do not speak a language that is written. Therefore, local teachers introduced the researcher to a village-based literacy centre, enabling the researcher to conduct interviews with voluntary participants who attended the literacy centre. In addition to the above target participants, ethnographic data was collected from several other local people, development work-related organisations and government officials to supplement the data obtained from the primary participants. To gather the second cohort of government officers, aid workers and school teachers, snowball sampling was applied (Wright and Stein 2005; Noy 2008). This was because email was unreliable and not assured for each group.

Using an ethnological research framework 69

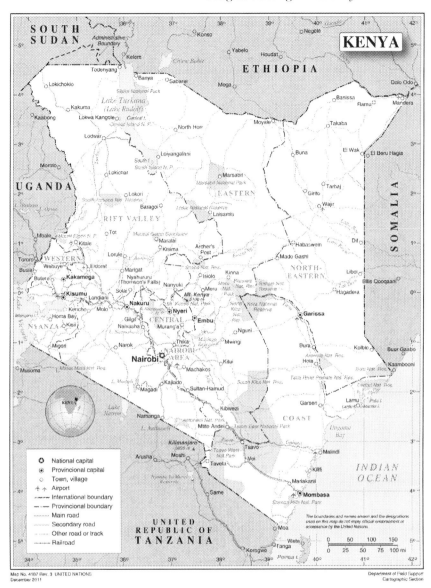

Map 3.1 Map of Kenya.

Snowball sampling is used to reach research participants through introductions given by trusted insiders (Wright and Stein 2005). Noy (2008) defines snowball sampling in this more concrete way: "A sampling procedure may be defined as snowball sampling when the researcher accesses informants through contact information that is provided by other informants" (Noy 2008, p. 330). To put it in a different way, a researcher uses a chain of

Table 3.1 Research participants

Research method	Open-ended questions	Narrative interviews	Narrative interviews	Process observation
Participants	Literacy, education, gender and development officers, Church leaders	Leaders of women's groups	Participants of literacy/women's groups	The whole community
Number of participants	10	12	15	About 100
Recruitment method	Snowballing	Through literacy/women's groups	Through literacy/women's groups	Community leaders, literacy/women's groups

recommendations to access more potential participants. Once participants were reached, the researcher explained the purpose of the study and ensured that the research participants understood that their participation was entirely voluntary. Participants also had the opportunity to contact the researcher with any questions about the research study.

Data analysis

In analysing the data, I established a process of qualitative cross-referencing, and evaluated the accuracy of the data according to the convergence of different data sources (Fetterman 2009). In addition to interviews, informal conversations, field notes, documents such as organisation minutes, policy documents were included in the analysis process (Fetterman 2009).

The information collected from the interviews was analysed thematically and as narrative case studies. First of all, narrative analysis was applied to evaluate interviews about the sequences of everyday life of participants via key themes. The process covered analysis of the stories that people use to understand their lives and the world around them (Bryman 2001). Narrative analysis best matched the needs of my research question, exploring women's experiences of informal learning and literacy and development activities in a traditional community. Narrative analysis is often employed to refer to both an approach – one that emphasises the examination of the storied nature of human recounting of lives and events – and to the sources themselves, that is the stories that people tell in recounting their life experiences (Czarniawska 2004). Narrative analysis also works well in the broader theoretical framework of postcolonial feminism – the importance of own 'voice' – as it focuses upon language as being not merely a technical device for establishing meaning, but deeply and subjectively constitutive of reality (Riessman 1993), thus, opening a space for local women to speak from. Narrative analysis aims to see how research subjects impose order upon and make sense of their flow of life experiences (Riessman 1993).

Research participants had more than one year's experience of informal learning and literacy and community development activities through their women's group. Second, to supplement the thematic analysis of data, case studies were drawn from some of the interviews. The case studies are summaries of the written notes recorded by the researcher. These case studies highlight the circumstances and views of the participants. The participants' choices and decision-making processes on informal learning and literacy, and community activities, were illuminated as well. The data of process observation was recorded in a research trip diary. Whenever the researcher had a question of whatever kind on the observed information, he/she attempted to clarify it with local people. Information obtained from the process observation data was combined. Ethical considerations are discussed in the next section.

Ethical considerations

As most of the research participants of this study exist in a vulnerable situation, it was necessary to consider the ethical aspects of this study.

In this research, all data will be kept in a secure and locked location for seven years. All identifying information has been kept for future use. I have coded to link informants' details with the data collected and kept identifying information separate from the raw data, to ensure anonymity.

While privacy refers to a person's interest in controlling other people's access to information about research participants, confidentiality means agreements with persons about what may be done with their data (Sieber 1992), which constitutes informed consent. These considerations were included in the application for ethics approval from the University of Sydney Human Ethics Committee. Also, I obtained a research permit under the number NCST/RRI/12/1/SS-011/538 from the government of Kenya.

The University's Human Ethics Committee approved protocols to conduct interviews in Kenya for the research. In the actual research, ethical systems were put in place as follows. All research participants had a briefing session about the research project and their written consent was received prior to interviewing in English, as English is the official language in Kenya. For illiterate participants, a local interpreter read a project information sheet and the project was explained, including the purpose of the research study, so that all research information was clearly understood. The local interpreter also read a consent form, and the participant's agreement on the form was recorded by a thumbprint in ink on a special box on the consent form. It should be noted that Maa is not a written language, hence it was unnecessary to translate the documents. It was also explained that their participation in research was voluntary, and that they had a right to withdraw at any time during the conduct of the research. As noted earlier, my research approach was adjusted to the research participants' situation at their convenience, hence interpretation into Maa needed to be spontaneous in the field. The interview transcripts and field notes have been kept on a password protected computer. Confidential information on participants has not been collected or recorded. As Norton (2000) suggested, assistance in assignments, translation or transportation was offered in return for the research participants' valuable time. This exchange contributed to establish the rapport between participants and the researcher.

In the case of my fieldwork in Narok County, I observed the reactions of some village women to the procedure of an agreement on a consent form. For instance, when my interpreter and I explained the summary of research and a written consent form to a research participant in the village, some women looked surprised and told the interpreter that they were keen to answer questions without any formal paperwork because the interpreter and researcher had become friends of theirs. Some women even expressed interest in being photographed with their actual names. For a few village women, it

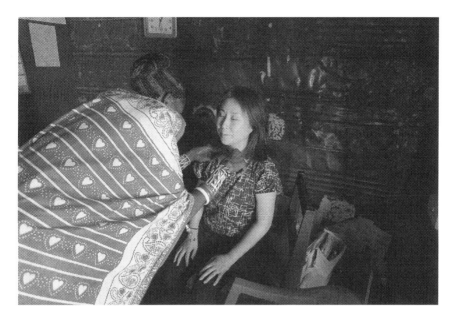

Figure 3.1 Wearing a Maasai beaded necklace.

was an honourable thing to have a photo taken and be part of a publication. My fieldwork meant that an anthropological or ethnographic approach to research in this village depended highly on mutual trust and/or a cultivated friendship between an outside researcher and village people. The whole process of data collection with Western-oriented ethics provided me with an opportunity to reconsider the ethical procedure developed in Australia. This echoes what Robinson-Pant (2005, p. 116) suggests, that "Taking a cross-cultural perspective on ethics can lead to greater understanding about the values that underpin our research approach so that we can learn to articulate how those values inform our ethical stance". Therefore the content and process of informed consent should be developed based on a "collective decision" between the researcher and research participants (Chilisa 2009, p. 423). It would be more effective to work with local academics to develop a culturally appropriate ethical procedure in future. Moreover, academics who are interested in conducting fieldwork in Africa should be critical about Western-oriented research procedures.

Conclusion

This chapter has detailed the methodology utilised in this research. I conducted semi-structured interviews with 15 village women, 12 women's group leaders and ten government-related people over a six-month period in 2011. The interviews were analysed as narratives of the lived experiences of the research participants. An additional methodology was process observation, detailing my research in the village.

The next chapter, Chapter 4, will describe socio-cultural and economic factors and traditional practices affecting Maasai women's subordinate situation in Kenya.

Notes

1 Okonkwo is the tragic hero in Achebe's book, "Things Fall Apart" (1958).
2 The project was called "Comparative Study on Education and Society in Africa: New Development Emerging from Fieldwork (2005–2008: Project Leader, Prof. Nobuhide SAWAMURA)" and funded by the Japan Society for the Promotion of Science.

References

Agar, M. (1996). *The Professional Stranger: An Informal Introduction to Ethnography* (2nd edn). New York: Academic Press.

Alexander, M.J., and Mohanty, T.C. (eds) (1997). *Feminist Genealogies, Colonial Legacies, Democratic Futures*. New York: Routledge.

Atkinson, P., Coffey, A., Delamont, S., Lofland, J., and Lofland, L.H. (2001). *Handbook of Ethnography* (2nd edn). London: Sage.

Bassnet, S. (1994). *Translation Studies*. London: Routledge.

Basu, K., Maddox, B., and Robinson-Pant, A. (2008). Literacies, Identities and Social Change: Interdisciplinary Approaches to Literacy and Development. *Journal of Development Studies*, 44(6), 769–778.

Bhabha, H.K. (1994). *The Location of Culture*. London: Routledge.

Brady, H.E., and Collier, D.C. (2004). *Rethinking Social Inquiry: Diverse Tools, Shared Standards*. Lanham, Md.: Rowman and Littlefield.

Brown, S. (1994). Research in Education: What Influence on Policy and Practice? *Knowledge and Policy*, 7(4), 94–107.

Bryman, A. (2001). *Social Research Methods*. Oxford: Oxford University Press.

Burgess, R.G. (1984). *In the Field: An Introduction to Field Research*. London: George Allen & Unwin.

Charmaz, K. (2006). *Constructing Grounded Theory: A Practical Guide through Qualitative Analysis*. London: Sage.

Chilisa, B. (2009). Indigenous African-Centred Ethics: Contesting and Complementing Dominant Models. In M.D. Mertens and P. Ginsberg (eds), *Handbook of Social Research Ethics*, Thousand Oaks, CA: Sage, pp. 407–425.

Connell, R. (2007). *Southern Theory: The Global Dynamics of Knowledge in Social Science*. Australia: Allen & Unwin.

Conole, L. (1978). Process Observation. *Asia Pacific Journal of Human Resources*, 16(2), 11–17.

Czarniawska, B. (2004). *Narratives in Social Science Research*. Thousand Oaks, CA: Sage.

Fetterman, M.D. (2009). *Ethnography: Step-by-Step (Applied Social Research Methods)*. Thousand Oaks, CA: Sage.

Fontana, A., and Frey, J.H. (2003). The Interview: From Structured Questions to Negotiated Text. In K.N. Denzin and S.Y. Lincoln (eds), *Collecting and Interpreting Qualitative Materials* (2nd edn), California: Thousand Oaks, pp. 61–105.

Geertz, C. (1973). *The Interpretation of Cultures*. London: Hutchinson.
Kanogo, T. (2005). *African Womanhood in Colonial Kenya 1900–50*. Oxford: James Currey; Nairobi: EAEP; Athens: Ohio University Press.
Lindlof, T.R., and Taylor, B.C. (2002). *Qualitative Communication Research Methods* (2nd edn). Thousand Oaks, CA Sage.
Maathai, W. (2004). *Nobel Lecture*, Oslo, 10 December 2004. www.nobelprize.org/nobel_prizes/peace/laureates/2004/maathai-lecture-text.html.
Madison, D.S. (2005). *Critical Ethnography: Method, Ethics and Performance*. Thousand Oaks, CA: Sage.
Mangena, O. (2003). Feminism (Singular), African Feminisms (Plural) and the African Diaspora. *Agenda*, 58, 98–100.
McCall, G.J., and Simmons, J.L. (1969). *Issues in Participant Observation*. Reading, Massachusetts: Addison Wesley.
Mohanty, C.T. (1991). Under Western Eyes: Feminist Scholarship and Colonial Discourses. In C.T.R. Mohanty, Ann Russo, and L. Torres (eds), *Third World Women and the Politics of Feminism*. Bloomington: Indiana University Press.
Mohanty, C.T. (2003). *Feminism without Borders: Decolonizing Theory. Practicing Solidarity*. Durham and London: Duke University Press.
Mosley, L. (ed.). (2013). *Interview Research in Political Science*. Ithaca: Cornell University Press.
Narayan, U. (1991). Finding Our Own Voices: The Need for Non-Western Contributions to Global Feminism. *Women and Language*, 10, 8–10.
Narayan, U. (1997). *Dislocating Cultures: Identities, Traditions, and Third-World Feminism*. New York: Routledge.
Narayan, U., and Harding, S. (1998). Introduction. Border Crossing: Multicultural and Postcolonial Feminist Challenges to Philosophy (Part1). *Hypatia*, 13(2), 1–6.
Narayanasamy, N., and Ramesh, R. (1997). Process Observation in PRA: Guidelines and Reflections. *PLA Notes* (1996), 26, 56–58, London; International Institute For Environment and Development.
Ngũgĩ wa Thiong'o. (1986). *Decolonising the Mind*. Nairobi: Heinemann.
Nnaemeka, O. (2005). *Female Circumcision and the Politics of Knowledge: African Women in Imperialist Discourses*. Connecticut: Greenwood Publishing Group.
Norton, B. (2000). *Identity and Language Learning: Gender, Ethnicity and Educational Change*. Harlow, England: Longman.
Noy, C. (2008). Sampling Knowledge: The Hermeneutics of Snowball Sampling in Qualitative Research. *International Journal of Social Research Methodology*, 11(4), 327–344.
Ogunyemi, C.O. (1985). Womanism: The Dynamics of the Contemporary Black Female Novel in English. *Signs*, 11(1), 63–80.
Ospina, S., Hadidy, E.W., and Hofmann-Pinilla, A. (2008). Cooperative Inquiry for Learning and Connectedness. *Action Learning: Research and Practice*, 5(2), 131–147.
Oyewumi, O. (2003). Ties that (Un)Bind: Feminism, Sisterhood and Other Foreign Relations. *A Journal of Culture and African Women Studies*, 1(1), 1–18.
Oyewumi, O. (2005). *African Gender Studies: A Reader*. New York: Palgrave Macmillan.
Oyewumi, O. (2010). *Gender Epistemologies in Africa: Gendering Traditions, Spaces, Social Institutions, and Identities*. New York: Palgrave Macmillan.
Parpart, J., Rai, S., and Staudt, K. (2002). *Rethinking Em(power)ment: Gender and Development: Gender and Development in a Global/Local World*. London: Routledge.

Patton, M.Q. (1987). *How to Use Qualitative Methods in Evaluation*. Newbury Park, CA: Sage.
Riessman, C.K. (1993). *Narrative Analysis*. Newbury Park, CA: Sage.
Robinson-Pant, A. (2005). *Cross Cultural Perspectives on Educational Research*. Berkshire: Open University Press.
Robinson-Pant, A. (2008). Why Literacy Matters: Exploring Policy Perspectives on Literacies, Identities and Social Change. *Journal of Development Studies*, 44(6), 779–796.
Sawamura, N. (2008). Qualitative Approach in the Study of Educational Development: Grasping the Realities through Fieldwork. In N. Sawamura (ed.), *Advancing the Study of International Cooperation for Educational Development: Practice and Challenges towards Achieving Education for All*, Tokyo: Akashi Shoten, pp. 27–47.
Sieber, J.E. (1992). *Planning Ethically Responsible Research: A Guide for Students and Students and Internal Review Boards*. Thousand Oaks, CA: Sage.
Spivak, G.C. (1999). *A Critique of Postcolonial Reason: Toward a History of the Vanishing Present*. Cambridge, MA: Harvard University Press.
Spradley, J.P. (1979). *The Ethnographic Interview*. New York: Holt, Rinehart and Winston.
Steady, F.C. (1981). *The Black Woman Cross-Culturally*. Cambridge, Massachusetts: Schenkman Publishing Co.
Tamale, S. (2006). African Feminism: How Should *We* Change? *Development*, 49, 38–41.
Temple, B. (1997). Watch Your Tongue: Issues in Translation and Cross-Cultural Research. *Sociology*, 31(3), 607–618.
Thyer, B. (2009). *The Handbook of Social Work Research Methods*. California: Sage.
UN (United Nations). (2001). *Gender and Racial Discrimination*, Report of the Expert Group Meeting, 21–24 November 2000, Zagreb, Croatia. www.un.org/womenwatch/daw/csw/genrac/report.htm.
UN (United Nations). (2011). *The Map of Kenya*. www.un.org/Depts/Cartographic/map/profile/kenya.pdf, accessed 8 May 2014.
Wane, N.N. (2008). Mapping the Field of Indigenous Knowledge in Anti-Colonial Discourse: A Transformative Journey in Education. *Race, Ethnicity and Education*, 11(2), 183–197.
Williams, L. (1988). *Partial Surrender: Race and Resistance in the Youth Service*. London: Falmer.
Wright, R., and Stein, M. (2005). Snowball Sampling. In K. Kempf-Leonard (ed.), Encyclopedia of Social Measurement, New York: Elsevier, pp. 495–500.

4 Socio-cultural background of the Maasai women in Kenya

Introduction

Following a summary of relevant postcolonial feminist theory and current understandings of the discourses of women's literacy and development in the previous two chapters, this chapter conceptualises this research by illustrating Maasai women's situation in Narok County in Kenya. The experiences of the Maasai in Kenya are inevitably linked to global policies and the implementation of women's development programmes and literacy in their society, therefore it is important to examine the economic, political and cultural aspects of the region in recent decades. From a postcolonial feminist perspective, to gain a view of local women's well-being in Narok County, one needs a brief understanding of the background of their subordinated situation in Maasai tradition and culture.

Historical background of Kenya after independence from Britain

The Republic of Kenya is located in East Africa on the Indian Ocean, sharing its borders with Ethiopia, Somalia, Sudan, Tanzania and Uganda; it gained independence from Britain in 1963. The capital city is Nairobi. Kenya has a large number of wild reserves, which especially attract foreign tourists; however, the economy is largely dependent on agriculture, and the main products are coffee, tea, cotton and maize (Sobania 2003).

In an area of 580,000 km^2, there is a population of 47 million with about 40 ethnic groups (28 Too Many 2016, p. 22). Kenyan people are Christian, Muslim or traditional believers (Sobania 2003). There are numerous indigenous languages in Kenya, with English as the official language and Swahili as the national language.

It is important to understand how Kenya was historically constructed as a postcolonial state since the attainment of its independence from Britain in 1963. Before the arrival of foreigners and Arab traders in the coastal region, the Maasai had been the major tribe in Kenya. Along with the nomadic pastoralists of the Maasai, the Kikuyu lived by agriculture. Then, after incursions by Germany and Britain, the British East Africa Company was established in 1888 when Kenya became a formal British colonial state for about 75 years. The proclamation of the colonisation of Africa was issued by two conferences in Germany and Belgium known as the 'scramble for Africa' (Alam 2007). European countries divided African land among themselves to implement their colonial power (Alam 2007). Farmers not only from Britain but also of other European origins were encouraged to settle in Kenya, and established large plantation farms with forced indigenous labour. European plantation owners employed African people at a low wage with strict work regulations (Alam 2007). Due to land registration indigenous people were deprived of their land and were restricted to protected areas as ownership of fertile land was offered to European settlers (Sobania 2003).

In October 1952, a rebellion organised by the Kikuyu called the Mau Mau movement broke out in Kenya. It led an independence and nationalistic movement. Although Jomo Kenyatta, the leader of a political group named the Kikuyu Central Association, was sentenced to imprisonment, he was eventually elected to be the first Prime Minister to form a newly independent country, the Republic of Kenya in 1963 (Sobania 2003).

As a republic, Kenya experienced an era of strong patriarchal leadership under the first Prime Minister, Jomo Kenyatta. Subsequently, women's equality was ignored. The country also has undergone periods of economic growth, capitalism and an increase in basic education aimed at nation building.

In the Human Development Index, Kenya was ranked at 142nd out of 189 countries and territories (UNDP 2018, p. 2), highlighting that 26.8 per cent of the working population was living on less than US$3.10 a day (UNDP 2018, p. 1).

Currently, following enactment of a new constitution in August 2010, replacing the 1969 constitution, the country has 47 counties. Decentralisation of administration is being implemented, where each county has an autonomous government body.

Therefore, this historical context is significant in exploring Maasai village women's subordinated situations affected by tradition and British incursions, and their efforts to improve the well-being of their families and communities.

Government initiatives to improve education and people's well-being

The government of Kenya has set "Kenya Vision 2030" for the country to become socio-economically and politically developed by 2030. In its national planning strategy between 2008 and 2030, Kenya aims to achieve an average GDP growth rate of 10 per cent annually (Government of the Republic of Kenya 2007, p. 5). The social pillar of the state of Kenya involves "building a just and cohesive society, enjoying equitable social development in a clean and secure environment" through "eight key sectors; Education and Training,

Health, Water and Sanitation, the Environment, Housing and Urbanisation, Gender, Youth, Sports and Culture" (Government of the Republic of Kenya 2007, p. 11). In particular, the government of Kenya, echoing *Kenya Vision 2030*, also commits to achieve an 80 per cent adult literacy rate by the year 2030. In addition, the political pillar states "a democratic political system that is issue-based, people-centred, result-oriented and accountable to the public" (Government of the Republic of Kenya 2007, p. 11). Here, equality is reinforced, and gender issues are strongly recognised.

The government commitment to improve the well-being of the population can be seen in their annual expenditure increases on social sectors such as the Ministry of Education, the Ministry of Health and the Ministry of Gender, Children and Social Development. For instance, there was an approximately 20 per cent increase in the social sector expenditure from KSh197.537 million (US$1.95 million)[1] in 2008/09 to KSh236.578 million (US$2.34 million) in 2009/10 (Kenya National Bureau Statistics and ICF Macro 2010, p. 39). With an emphasis on non-formal education including adult literacy centres, the Ministry of Education recorded an increase in expenditure of 32.5 per cent from KSh13.788 million (US$0.14 million) in 2008/09 to KSh18.273 million (US$0.18 million) in 2009/10 (Kenya National Bureau Statistics and ICF Macro 2010, p. 39). The government established adult literacy centres and the number of adult learners also rose. The Kenyan government, in collaboration with donor agencies and NGOs, has taken various initiatives to reduce adult illiteracy rates and to empower women. It is therefore an appropriate time to conduct research on Maasai village women's own learning strategies and community development activities to bring about a positive social change.

Policy of adult and continuing education and women's development in Kenya

The government of Kenya is committed to achieve the goals of Sustainable Development, especially Goals 4 and 5, which are related to women's education.

Goal 4 is committed to "ensuring inclusive and equitable quality education and promote lifelong learning opportunities for all" (UN 2015).

Goal 5 is committed to "achieving gender equality and empower all women and girls" (UN 2015). To respond to the SDGs and the prior UN MDGs, Adult and Continuing Education programmes in Kenya have been supported by a variety of organisations under the advisory Board of Adult Education of the Ministry of Gender, Sports, Culture and Social Services. The actual implementing agency of the Ministry has been the Department of Adult Education, which had been responsible for providing literacy and other forms of education to adults and out-of-school youth.

With the new policy enacted in 2010, the placement of Department of Adult Education has been shifted from the Ministry of Gender, Sports,

Culture and Social Services to the Ministry of Education. While the management of adult and continuing education programmes are centralised at the Ministry, there are field offices at provincial and district levels to monitor and evaluate the programmes.

The Ministry of Gender, Sports, Culture and Social Services and the Ministry of Education allocate funds to adult learning and continued education and the funds are used for the development of learning/teaching materials, training of staff and payment of salaries. The new Adult Education Donor agencies such as UNESCO, UNDP, UNIFEM, UNICE, UNDPPA, CIDA Canada, DFID and GTZ provide both technical and financial support for the adult education programmes.

The Department of Adult Education had implemented three main programmes; basic literacy, post-literacy and non-formal education. Basic literacy programmes involve basic skills of literacy and numeracy. Post-literacy programmes aim at sustaining and improving the acquired basic literacy skills in leaners' everyday lives. Non-formal education programmes are provided mainly for the youth who have no access to primary school education or those who had dropped out of school (Wanyama 2014).

Although the government had been attempting to improve adult and continuing education in Kenya, some challenges remained, for instance a shortage of adult literacy instructors and low funding allocation devoted to adult and continuing education programmes were reported (Wanyama 2014).

Currently, with the new adult and continuing education policy under the Ministry of Education, the Ministry of Education of Kenya has established three main programmes: literacy, continuing education, community education and extension (Republic of Kenya 2010, pp. 13–14). The literacy programme aims at providing the basic skills of reading, writing and arithmetic to illiterate adults and out-of-school youth (Republic of Kenya 2010). The continuing education programme targets semi-literate adult and youth to be integrated into the formal education system. They can learn the school-based curriculum in a non-formal setting (Republic of Kenya 2010). The community education and extension programme aims at providing knowledge about agriculture, health issues including HIV-AIDS, and gender education. In addition, it also includes vocational training for business management and crafts (Republic of Kenya 2010). Gender in education is one of the four main emerging issues addressed clearly in the policy statement (Republic of Kenya 2010, p. 26).

Under the national adult and continuing education policy described above, the Kenyan government is preparing for a new adult education curriculum aimed at certificate-oriented learning.

The government literacy centres will most likely be primary school education for adult learners to sit for the Kenyan Certificate for Primary Education (KCPE) (Republic of Kenya 2010). Income generating activity will be specifically included in literacy centres' activities.

This government shift in the adult literacy programme might create more distance between village women's actual needs and their existing practices of learning. In implementing the new and nation-wide literacy programme, the government is also concerned about how to mobilise resources to reach remote areas.

However, as the women's experiences were highlighted in the above discussion, to create their own knowledge or learning activity in their cultural context, they do not demand huge resources. Village women can manage their informal learning by themselves. They require a particular skill and knowledge at a specific time in their space to improve their everyday life. They are aware of gender disparities and/or the disadvantages of being 'illiterate', yet they create their own strategies to tackle these issues.

In addition, the Ministry of Gender, Children and Social Development had the highest increase in expenditure of 82 per cent from KSh3061 million (US$30.24 million) in 2008/09 to KSh5581 million (US$55.13 million) in 2009/10 (KNBS and ICF Macro 2010, p. 41). Gender-awareness raising or income generation programmes for women were implemented by the government.

Since independence, many efforts have been made to accelerate the country's development. Economic development has been the Kenyan government's main focus. The policy affirms that there should be women's empowerment programmes, concentrating on the productive and reproductive roles of women (Government of the Republic of Kenya 2007).

However, the government's welfare policies addressing the needs of the poor and vulnerable people have not been successful (Chuma and Okungu 2011). Social protection programmes for vulnerable people have been inadequate and crucial needs of the poor have been left out (Mwenzwa and Misati 2014). There is a gap between the government's policies and its implementations in Kenya.

Maasai women's situation in Narok County

While men act as bread-winners, herding cattle and protecting their households, women often carry out all household tasks (Saitoti and Beckwith 1988).

Cultural, social and economic measures of women's status are low in Maasai culture and this negatively affects all aspects of their lives. Because of this obvious gender inequality, women's access to resources as well as even basic education is limited. It is important to note that marriage systems as they apply to women and women's ownership rights differ considerably across Kenya.

Narok County in the Rift Valley Province is situated in the Southern part of Kenya and northern central Tanzania along the Great Rift Valley. The area of the district covers as much as 4662.7 square kilometres (Republic of Kenya 2010b, p. 27).

82 Socio-cultural background of the Maasai

The population of the Rift Valley Province was recorded at 10,006,803 in 2010 (Republic of Kenya 2010c, p. 128) and the population of Narok County was 258,544 (Republic of Kenya 2010c, p. 162). The population is also very scattered, with the exception of the area far away from the Main road, the so-called 'inland' or 'interior'. The Maasai speak Maa (the Maasai language), and most people can communicate in Swahili and/or English. It is important to note that 91.8 per cent of women in Nairobi (the capital city of Kenya) are (officially) literate while only 73.2 per cent of women in the Rift Valley Province are literate (Central Bureau of Statistics 2004, p. 45). For men, the corresponding figures for Nairobi and the Rift Valley Province are 94.2 per cent and 83.9 per cent respectively (Central Bureau of Statistics 2004, p. 45). Literacy is defined by the Kenyan government, for persons over the age of 15, as being that one can read and write. These people are regarded as being literate (Bunyi 2006). The statistics rely on a self-responding system (Bunyi 2006). There is an absence of a written or oral examination to examine the adult literacy level.

Traditionally, Maasai people consume meat, milk and blood from cattle; however, currently, they also eat maize, potatoes, cabbage and rice. As Maasai are originally semi-nomadic people, hunting and grazing cattle and goats were the most important activities. Due to a communal land system, they graze their animals on surrounding lands, but because of the privatisation of land, Maasai people have had difficulty in accessing land, which has influenced their cattle herding and food production. The pastoral Maasai have been forced to cultivate land to meet their basic needs. According to tradition, utilising the land for crop cultivation is an offence against nature. For the Maasai, everyone should have free access to land and water sources.

When wearing traditional clothes, Maasai people wear a one-piece colourful garment wrapped around their body, along with hand-made beaded accessories and ornaments. Maasai women can make these accessories at home, and some sell the hand-made beaded accessories at the local market. They are traditionally semi-nomadic, relying on livestock such as cows, sheep and goats. Traditionally, the Maasai did not cultivate the land, nor did they rely on a cash economy. Cattle correspond to food, power and wealth. The more cattle a Maasai person has, the more influence the person has in his/her community (Saitoti and Beckwith 1988). However, this is a challenge as the inland area is very dry and people have suffered from severe drought.

Polygamy is traditionally practiced in the Maasai community. While the government of Kenya states that the minimum age for legal marriage is 16 years for women and men, it is common that younger women are married off to an old man as his second wife through her parents' arrangements (OECD 2010a). According to a 2004 United Nations report, it is estimated that 17 per cent of girls of the age between 15 and 19 were married, divorced or widowed in Kenya (OECD 2010a). The researcher has observed a Grade 6 girl running away from her forced marriage in a Maasai village. According to the OECD (2010b), Kenya established an inheritance law in 1991 that states women have an equal right to inherit as men. However, equal inheritance has sometimes been ignored.

The reproductive role of women

With regard to the reproductive role of women, they have unequal access to health services (Creighton and Yieke 2006). According to the 2008/09 Kenya Demographic and Health Survey (KDHS), on average, the fertility rate per woman is 4.6 per cent, which has declined from the rate of 4.9 per cent of the 2003 KDHS (KNBS and ICF Macro 2010, p. 43). However, there is a large difference between the rural and urban areas. While the fertility rate per woman is 5.2 per cent in the rural areas, the corresponding figure in the urban areas is 2.9 per cent (KNBS and ICF Macro 2010, p. 43). The educational levels of women are strongly linked with low fertility rates. There is a dramatic decrease in the fertility rate of 6.6 per cent for uneducated women to 3.1 per cent for some secondary educated women (KNBS and ICF Macro 2010, p. 43). Knowledge of family planning stands at 95 per cent for women and 97 per cent for men aged 15–49 (KNBS and ICF Macro 2010, p. 43). They have heard about modern contraception methods of condoms, injections and pills. In spite of the knowledge of family planning, only 46 per cent of married women actually use one of the contraception methods (KNBS and ICF Macro 2010, p. 43).

In terms of the Marriage Act of 2008 in Kenya, the minimum age of marriage is 16 years for girls and 18 years for boys with parental consent.

Traditional arranged marriages are widely practised, especially in the rural areas. For instance, adolescent girls are forced to drop out of school to marry an older man as his second wife, instead of pursuing educational opportunities in Narok (Takayanagi 2014). Moreover, adolescent mothers seem to undergo complications during pregnancy compared with other girls who postpone child bearing (Government of the Republic of Kenya 2007).

FGM and early marriages in the Maasai land

Female genital mutilation (FGM) has been practiced in the Maasai land as a ritual passage for girls to become adult women, preparing them for marriage. In actual fact, it is widely practised in Kenya. It is also likely to be associated with cultural beliefs of modesty and femininity (WHO 2012). While the prevalence of FGM varies from one community to another, it is very common among Somali, Kisii, Kuria and Maasai women (28 Too Many 2016, p. 25). The type of mutilation differs according to the ethnic groups. Type two, which is an excision of the clitoris, is generally performed on Maasai women (WHO 2012). It involves partial or total removal of the clitoris, with or without excision of the labia minora (WHO 2012). It is regarded as a harmful and violent practice to girls and women by WHO without any health benefits. Complications include pain, haemorrhage, infections and so on (WHO 2012).

In 1999, the Ministry of Health of Kenya initiated the National Plan of Action for the elimination of FGM of girls and women (GTZ 2007). The Children's Act was also enacted in 2001, which shows the importance of special protection for girls who may be in danger of FGM (GTZ 2007). The law prohibiting FGM was enacted in Kenya in the Children's Act No. 8 of 2001, and persons found guilty face one year of imprisonment and a fine of KSh50,000 (approximately US$574 as of 12 May 2015, No Peace without Justice).

During the fieldwork in the community, an education officer stated that four school-girls had become pregnant and dropped out of school in the community. Some girls say that they would be outcasts if they did not undergo circumcision. Peer-group pressure for FGM among girls has a negative impact on girls' decisions regarding FGM. Education officers say that FGM affects girls' school performance causing educational dropout, producing poor academic performance and early marriages.

One of the education officers interviewed in this study suggested that 80 per cent of school-girls still support the practice of FGM. According to interviews with education officers and teachers, fathers make a decision on girls' FGM, ignoring mothers and grandmothers (women's) opinions. Furthermore, teachers interviewed in this study who have got involved in FGM awareness raising programmes stated that there is enough sensitisation and awareness of FGM in the community, yet FGM is organised quietly in the mountains. One teacher said she had seen a slight positive change in people's behaviour and thinking about the practice of FGM. A female teacher said:

> Only authorities can help. We can only educate people, at the end, it is up to them to decide if they want to do FGM or not. Old people cannot advise because they went through FGM. A man decides FGM for his daughters. A mother can help her daughter to run away from home, or take her to the authority.

She also stated that "Maasai women have no voice to speak, education only empowers women to say their opinion. The next generation of girls will not undergo FGM."

However, circumcision is an important source of income for circumcisers. In order to demolish its practice, they should be provided with an alternative business.

The international non-governmental organisation (INGO), World Vision, as well as UNIFEM, have been working to eliminate the practice in Narok. As the impact of FGM and early marriage on girls' education is severe, World Vision implemented a child sponsorship programme for several years. World Vision recruited female schoolteachers as a local resource, and trained them

Figure 4.1 School lunch and a drinking water bottle brought from home.

to play the role of facilitator among schools, girls and the office of World Vision. When a girl approached one of the 'resource persons' (trained personnel) to seek help on continuing schooling, the resource person referred the girl to the office to provide her with a school scholarship, so that she would able to study at school, avoiding FGM and early marriage (Takayanagi 2008). At the time of my research, the programme had been withdrawn from the research site, hence trained resource persons and some female teachers sought assistance on girls' protection through the government's children's office. World Vision had a project supporting girls' education, but did not implement women's groups nor adult literacy projects on the research site.

Conclusion

When considering Maasai women's subordinated situation alongside the historical background of Kenya after independence from Britain, it is evident that there is a strong patriarchy observed in various aspects of Maasai women's lives. Even though Kenya obtained independence from Britain in 1963, women's participation in social and economic spheres was given little attention by governments. By agreeing to the UN SDGs established by international donors in 2015, Kenya has attempted to improve women's literacy and development. The major Ministries responsible for women's development had a huge increase in their budgets in 2010. The Ministry of Education

86 *Socio-cultural background of the Maasai*

has essentially revised adult and continuing education policy. In order to increase adult literacy rates and to cooperate with the national certificate for primary education, certificate-based learning at adult literacy centres is more established nowadays. Literacy with which the village women engage in their everyday life, based on their needs and space, conflicts with what the formal adult literacy programme offers to literacy learners.

By illustrating Maasai women's situation in the Maasai land, it is certain that they have triple roles to play in their society: reproductive, productive and communal. In their reproductive role, women are influenced by traditional practices of FGM and early marriages. While the government implemented the Children's Act of 2001, the process to eliminate these practices completely is very slow. These practices also affect girls' educational advancement.

However, based on my research, women do not act like victims of gender inequality. Women attempt to find their own way to overcome social issues and to bring about positive change in their communities. To explore women's views on their situation and community and their activities for community development, this study adopts an ethnographic research method. The next chapter will report on the analysis of the village women's narratives and responses relating to notions of literacy and development and the key themes that emerged during the data collection period.

Figure 4.2 Playing with a ball in the school grounds.

Figure 4.3 A school classroom can be used for adult education classes.

Note

1 1 US$ = KSh101.216 as of 1 September 2016. www.xe.com/currency/kes-kenyan-shilling#.

References

Alam, M.S. (2007). *Rethinking Mau Mau in Colonial Kenya*. New York: Palgrave Macmillan.
Bunyi, W.G. (2006). *Real Options for Literacy Policy and Practice in Kenya*. Background paper prepared for the Education for All Global Monitoring Report 2006. Literacy for Life. Paris: UNESCO.
Central Bureau of Statistics. (2004). *Economic Survey 2004*. Nairobi: Central Bureau of Statistics.
Chuma, J., and Okungu, V. (2011). Viewing the Kenyan Health System through an Equity Lens: Implications for Universal Coverage. *International Journal of Equity Health*, 10(22), 1–14.
Coast, E. (2002). Maasai Socioeconomic Conditions: A Cross-Border Comparison. *Human Ecology*, 30(1), 79–105.
Creighton, C., and Yieke, F. (2006). *Gender Inequalities in Kenya*. Paris: UNESCO.
Government of the Republic of Kenya. (2007). *Kenya Vision 2030: A Globally Competitive and Prosperous Kenya*. Nairobi: Government of Kenya.
GTZ (2007). *Female Genital Mutilation in Kenya*. www.gtz.de/en/dokumente/en-fgm-countrieskenya.pdf, accessed 12 September 2016.
KNBS (Kenya National Bureau of Statistics) and ICF Macro. (2010). *Kenya Demographic and Health Survey 2008–09*. Calverton, Maryland: KNBS and ICF Macro.
Mwenzwa, E.M., and Misati, J.A. (2014). Kenya's Social Development Proposals and Challenges: Review of Kenya Vision 2030. First Medium-Term Plan, 2008–2012. *American International Journal of Contemporary Research*, 4(1), 246–253.
No Peace Without Justice. (2018). *Status of African Legislations on FGM Legislation*. www.npwj.org/FGM/Status-african-legislations-FGM.html, accessed 24 October 2018.
OECD. (2010a). *Atlas of Gender and Development. How Social Norms Affect Gender Equality in Non-OECD Countries*. Paris: OECD.
OECD. (2010b). *Gender Equality and Social Institutions in Kenya*. http://genderindex.org/country/kenya, accessed 2 November 2010.
Republic of Kenya. (2001). *Children Act, No. 8 of 2001*. Nairobi: National Council for Law Reporting with the Authority of the Attorney-General.
Republic of Kenya (2010a). *The Constitution of the Republic of Kenya*. Nairobi: Government Printer.
Republic of Kenya (2010b). *2009 Kenya Population and Housing Census, Volume I A*. Nairobi: Kenya National Bureau of Statistics.
Republic of Kenya (2010c). *2009 Kenya Population and Housing Census, Volume I C*. Nairobi: Kenya National Bureau of Statistics.
Saitoti, T.O., and Beckwith, C. (1988). *Maasai*. London: Elm Tree Books.
Sobania, N.W. (2003). *Culture and Customs of Kenya*. Westport, CT: Greenwood Press.
Takayanagi, T. (2008). Indigenous Approach to Community Development in Kenya: Experiences of a Female School Teacher. *Journal of International Cooperation in Education*, 11(2), 161–172.

Takayanagi, T. (2014). The Complexity of Literacy in Kenya: Narrative Analysis of Maasai Women's Experiences. *Compare: A Journal of Comparative and International Education*, 44(5), 826–844.

28 Too Many. (2016). *FGM in Kenya*. County Profile Update. www.refworld.org/pdfid/58bd4e2a4.pdf, accessed 13 March 2019.

UN (United Nations). (2015). *Transforming our World: The 2030 Agenda for Sustainable Development*. New York: UN.

UNDP. (2018). Human Development Report 2018. *The Rise of the South: Human Progress in a Diverse World*. New York: Oxford University Press.

UNESCO. (2010). *EFA Global Monitoring Report 2010: Reaching the Marginalized*. Paris: UNESCO.

Wanyama, I.K. (2014). Challenges Facing the Sustainability of Adult and Continuing Education Programmes in Kenya. *Mediterranean Journal of Social Sciences*, 5(5), 159–166.

WHO (World Health Organisation). (2012). *Addressing the Challenge of Women's Health in Africa. Report of the Commission on Women's Health in the African Region*. Geneva: WHO.

5 Narratives and process observation of village women

Introduction

Drawing on the key literature on postcolonial feminist theory, this study complements a growing field of scholarship on the notion of informal learning/literacy and women's empowerment in the context of development. As discussed in the previous chapters, village women have their own learning and community development strategies and mechanisms. However, as previous research focus has mostly been on formal literacy rates conducted in large quantitative studies, women's perspectives on informal learning/literacy and its effectiveness have not been explored in great depth.

This chapter reports mainly on two sets of data from the field, the narratives of the research participants drawn from interviews and the data from process observation. Complementing the data collected from the interviews, the observational data provided a means of understanding informal learning in action, aspects that research participants did not state and/or explain during the interviews. Process observation is a process of observing "the behavioral patterns or human processes of a group" (Conole 1978, p. 11). It is a means of recording the processes of events and incidents. By attending the meetings of women's groups, school committees, church services, the reconstruction of a house and microfinance groups, I observed the process of these incidents, placing myself as a researcher to listen to the research participants' voices. In addition, in the process of analysing the data, a number of themes generated by the data formed a useful means of understanding the process of informal education in the village context.

In this chapter, I present the first level of data analysis through a presentation of participant profiles. The profiles for each participant's story are organised according to the following six categories:

1   Response to Self-introduction and learning experiences in relation to schooling and/or adult literacy classes
2   Response to household resource management
3   Response to women's group activities
4   Response to learning processes

5   Response to the impact of women's group activities and learning for improving well-being
6   Perceptions on the future for the community.

I constructed the profiles from the voices of the women in their individual interviews. The profiles are presented so as to include the voices of each participant prior to imposing a narrative analysis on the data.

This chapter also examines the notion of informal literacy/learning from the research participants' perspectives, outlining how each of them undertakes to bring about positive changes in their community. The women's voices are the key forms of evidence highlighting informal learning, which strengthens knowledge production and conscientisation (Freire 1970). This research presents women's issues as multidimensional, demonstrating how socio-cultural, traditional and economic factors influence their status. In this respect, the chapter examines whether positive changes that improve gender-based issues can emerge from women's informal learning in the process of self-empowerment.

It is important to note that as the researcher I positioned myself as a listener to the research participants, hence I have illustrated how the information I obtained from the Maasai village contributes to building my knowledge of current development and literacy discourses present in the Kenyan context. More closely, I also sought to show what I learnt from local people about informal learning and literacy, in relation to community development and gender inequality.

Background of the research site: the village where I stayed

I stayed at my Kenyan mother's (Agnes)[1] house located in the Amu Division, Narok County, Rift Valley Province, Kenya between April and September 2011. People travelled by 'matatu' (a public bus) between the village and main cities like Nairobi. Within the village, there were a few 'bike taxes', which people occasionally used. Otherwise, they travelled by foot to visit homes, markets and attend other occasions. While some people lived in iron-sheeted wood houses, most people still lived in traditional Maasai houses of timber poles with small branches plastered by cow dung, sticks and mud.

In the Division, when this study was conducted in 2011, there were 20 primary schools, one government education office, and one health clinic owned by an NGO. Village people purchased food, clothes and other necessary goods at the local markets. People took cows, goats and sheep to different markets. Hence, on market days, the village was very lively. On Sundays, most people went to church to attend services. Many Maasai people had converted to Christianity. Men and women in the village were wrapped in colourful pieces of clothes with colourful bead-ornaments. Red was the favoured colour.

Agnes was the head-teacher of a primary school. Two of her children were boarding at a secondary school in the city and the other two were living at home with their own family. Apart from during school holidays, Agnes was very busy, engaged with various kinds of schoolwork and meetings. Agnes's house was modern, made from concrete, with two bedrooms and a kitchen and washroom outside the house. Each of us slept in a simple single bed with a mosquito net. The house had electricity, and the radio was on in the morning. Occasionally, we went to watch television at a neighbour's house. Agnes and I had bread or chapatti and sweet milk tea for breakfast. Agnes had fresh milk delivered each morning. We took bananas, oranges and a few slices of biscuits for lunch when time allowed. We had a dinner of green vegetables, beans, and rice or ugali. Ugali is a staple food of maize flour cooked with water with the appearance of dough. A chicken was slaughtered by Agnes to welcome guests and served for lunch or dinner. We normally ended our dinner with sweet milky tea. In the early mornings, Agnes boiled water for us to wash in. We took a bucket of warm water to the wash room outside. It was rainwater captured from the roof. However, during my fieldwork in the village, there was a severe drought that resulted in the loss of livestock and crops. Due to the scarcity of rain, water had become a valuable commodity, and schools and some villagers bought water from commercial water companies. Otherwise, women had to walk a long way to fetch water. We obtained water from our neighbours and the local dispensary. Near the end of my stay, we had water delivered by a water company. For drinking water, I bought bottles of mineral water from larger towns.

While I was on a visit to other places away from Agnes, we communicated by mobile phone. Friends of Agnes came to her house to recharge their mobile phone batteries. When I visited other homes, sweet milky tea was served to me as a guest. The next section reports on 11 village women's narratives followed by analyses of the narratives.

Narratives of village women

This section opens up a space for the voices of the village women's experiences in informal learning and literacy and community development through a narrative form of what they revealed in interviews. Out of 15 women's interviews from a settled Maasai community, 11 are presented, as the other four women's interviews had insufficient responses to construct a profile and story. Through individual narratives told by each woman, each participant is depicted as separate, demonstrating their different qualities and experiences. This research does not assume that any women from the village share the same experiences; rather I borrow from Spivak's (1988) notion of strategic essentialism to find commonalities among women in order to support a group of individuals. I entered into my research with the assumption, developed through the literature review and my own research experiences, that the research participants have may have certain collective experiences that are reflective of the Maasai culture.

In the following section there is an introduction to each research participant, highlighting her background and the activities she conducts in a women's group. The first questions put to the participants were: How long have you been participating in a women's group? What activities are conducted in your women's group? What kind of informal literacy activities were you engaged in through the group? It was also aimed at understanding the roles the women played in improving well-being in their community.

The 11 narratives highlight village women's learning processes. They also explained how they obtained information and skills based on their needs to improve well-being. The women demonstrated that through their participation in women's group activities, they brought about a positive change in their lifestyle. Lastly, women's views on the future of Narok County were also indicated in each narrative. It is important to note at this stage that any information that might have enabled identification of the research participants, such as school and office names or the location of the literacy centres, has been strictly eliminated.

Each narrative was drawn from field notes, and had come via a local interpreter who spoke English, Swahili and Maa. The language reflects the women's cultural and social ways of positioning themselves. Each woman was free to speak whichever language she was comfortable with to express her opinion to the researcher. Four major themes that emerged from the narratives of the village women are explained later in the chapter.

This analysis clarifies the understanding of informal learning/literacy and the outcomes from the analysis, which enables ideas to be put forward for a community-based development approach. The narratives reveal that women without formal education are aware of gender inequality and patriarchy and that a community-based women's group offered access to knowledge and skills that consequently brought about social change. Life-long informal learning has been a key process in seeking solutions and increasing the capacity of women to fight against poverty in the Kenyan context.

This level of understanding challenges current discourses of development and literacy. It was also evident that the women did not regard themselves as poor village people in their community. For them, literacy acquisition, and economic and social development, were interlinked processes of self-improvement, and were not seen as a short-term process of achievement.

The postcolonial feminist perspective provides a lens to reveal how often invisible, taken-for-granted processes structure life and educational opportunities and experiences. In turn, women's social positioning in the social structure might be a great disadvantage to their formal learning and their ability to manage community development and other related issues.

Cultural influences were viewed as being helpful or unhelpful depending on the participants' learning experiences. A postcolonial feminist perspective informed my exploration of how social injustices and unequal social relations affect women's access to learning resources. It also recognises the need for knowledge construction from the women's point of view, and that their voices have traditionally been silenced in the production of that knowledge (Kirkham and Anderson 2002).

Narrative 1: Mary's story

I do not know my age, maybe around 44 years old. I did not go to school. I have not attended an adult literacy centre. I have eight children and all of my children went to school. I milk cows and manage farming. I work at other people's *shamba* and the school's *shamba*. My husband drinks excessively and becomes violent at home. He does not do anything. I have been a member of a traditional birth attendance (TBA) group for six years. I attended a TBA certificate course and I memorised what I was taught during the course. I was given gloves, a razor blade, threads, plastic sheets and a bag. I also learnt about HIV–AIDS infections through contact with a pregnant mother's blood. I have attended childbirths many times in the community. I am not paid for the delivery, but I receive a piece of slaughtered meat. When a local NGO provided me with sunflower seeds, I rented two acres of the land to plant the seed. After returning some seeds from a harvest, I sold some of the crop and replanted some of the seeds again. I learn from learnt [educated] people. My mother taught me how to build a *manyatta* [house]. For example, we sit down and make bead ornaments together. I changed after participating in the group. I learnt how to attend a child and a mother. How to live without contracting HIV–AIDS was taught on the TBA course. I learnt how to prepare well-balanced foods for my children, not one kind of dish for the whole day. I can teach other women. I feel I am in a better position than other women. I hope in the future in Narok that all the Maasai girls are to be taken to school. Tell men not to exchange girls for cows or blankets. Education will change a family, an individual, Narok Maasai community as a whole. I am positive about education and have seen how people benefit from education. For example, educated people were employed. I think female teachers also set a good example and that educated children would be able to use correct medicines, fertilizers and seeds.

Narrative 2: Maria's Story

I am 39 years old. I dropped out of school in Year 3 because of an early marriage. I have never attended an adult literacy centre, but I can write my name. I can read a few words in the Bible but due to eye problems, I cannot read letters clearly. I manage a large farm of maize, beans and potatoes. I also help my husband in taking care of livestock. Land and livestock belong to my husband, hence, I am not allowed to sell an animal in the market. My four children are educated, including the girls. I also take care of an orphaned girl, sending her to school. I have been a treasurer of a women's group for four years. Meeting weekly, each of the 15 members contributes a certain amount of money to be given to a member in what we call a 'merry-go-round' as members draw lots to decide the order of the receiving the merry-go-round money each time. I collect money, and take some to the bank for saving or receiving a loan. When I received the merry-go-round money last time, I spent it on farming and paying children's school fees. I also run a small business, buying clothes and oil in Nairobi and selling them in the local market. A formally educated member taught me how to keep records, hence I can undertake bookkeeping for the group. My mother in law showed me how to make a manyatta. I ask my children or go to the group and ask educated women [to gain knowledge and advice]. I was living in the manyatta, I have improved my house of iron-sheets roof. The house improved. I even hire a few men to look after cattle, weed my farm. My family is clean. I can see my house is clean, organised. I planted trees. I know which medicine to give to animals, what dosage I should give. [I hope that in the future of Narok that] people educate their children and have sufficient supply of water. Maasai keep a small number of animals to get more milk (good breeding livestock).

Towards the end of our conversation, her daughters called out to Maria to say that two men had come to discuss her farm. Maria wanted to employ the men to weed her farm, hence they were negotiating wages and areas to be weeded. Maria had learnt from her husband how to manage casual workers' employment.

Narrative 3: Naserian's story

I am 59 years old. I did not go to school. My father did not know the need for education. I have participated in an adult literacy centre for one month held at church, but the centre was not stable, so I stopped going to the class. The class was held once a week, I attended for a total of four times, so could not grasp anything. I am the first wife among five wives. When my husband passed away, his property was shared among his five wives. I look after cattle, do house chores, and fetch water from the dam and firewood. I joined the first women's group for five years. Every woman contributed one sheep worth around Ksh1000. The women asked men to go to the market to buy calves. The women of the group brought up the calves, sold them to get money and shared the money between themselves. After sharing the money, sometimes, we hired a field for farming. Every woman made sure that one built a kitchen with an iron-sheeted [corrugated iron] roof. I also joined another women's group for two years. Each woman contributed Ks3000 to the group, but the chair woman ran away with the money, I got nothing from the group. All of the women just went off from the group. I know everything, I know how to weed, how to cook and plant. My mother and husband taught me how to count money. Otherwise, I gain knowledge and information from the radio and my children. [After participating in the group] I was changing my life, [I am] happier. [I hope in the future of Narok] there will be more development of farming and livestock. People will build houses or improve their house. Every year, after harvesting, people buy materials and construct good houses as we keep repairing a manyatta during the rainy seasons. Modern houses cannot be rained on. We no longer smear cow dung.

Narrative 4: Namunyak's story

I am 40 years old. I have eight children. I did not go to school. At the time, parents never took their children to school. I came to know Swahili at the literacy centre. I attended the literacy centre for two years. I gained knowledge and can interact with any other tribes of Kenya though the literacy centre. We teach each other. When I did not know how to communicate in the language (Swahili), I hired someone to go to Nairobi for my small business. Now I can go to Nairobi by myself. Through business, I also knew Swahili. I established the small-scale business through the literacy class. I buy fat in Nairobi and sell it in the village to make a profit. I also buy maize and sell it to gain a profit at the market. In a class, I copy what I have been taught. We teach each other. I can read time on the mobile phone. [After participating in the group] I changed my clothes, started business. My children are getting food. Other people say, what is this woman getting from the class? [I hope in the future of Narok] I would be a role model for those who have never been to school. I could advise adults to come to the class. More farming in Narok would be good.

Narrative 5: Resson's story

I am 27 years old. I have four children. I do farming, milk cows and sell milk. I did not go to school because my father did not take me to school. I have not attended an adult literacy class. My husband is in charge of finance, he sells a goat, brings a kilo of sugar, tea, a packet of two kilograms of maize flour. About the rest of money, I do not know. I use money generated by selling milk to pay school fees. I participated in a women's group for one year. The group members contributed money and helped each other to weed a field. We discuss development. I get advice from educated people, listen to the radio.

[After participating in the group] the group members bought seeds for me, came to my field and worked together. The house used to be a manyatta, but now it is an iron-sheeted house. I used to eat one type of food, now I eat different foods. I know the importance of education and send my children to school. [I hope in the future of Narok] people take their children to school because it will bring a change to the district.

Narrative 6: Namelok's story

I am 36 years old. I attended Year 1 at school in another district. My father removed me from school and when I was 12, I got married off. I have never attended adult education. I have nine children. I look after animals and do farming. The animals belong to us, so if my husband is not here, I can sell the animals. But my husband is in charge of finance. I have joined a women's group for two years. There are 12 members. To join the group, one has to pay Ksh100. we help each other and work with each other. We plant, harvest plants and share money. We hired one acre of shamba to plant maize. We do merry-go-round and we buy cups with the merry-go-round money. A mother lacks school fees, so a mother borrows money from the group. A mother can borrow money from the group for medical treatment. We want to open a bank account to keep the money of the group. I ask teachers or the group members who have learnt for advice. I learnt how to build a house from my mother. I saw her doing it, I was always near her and assisted her. I want to go to an adult literacy class. [After participating in the group] my husband is happy, women are happy. [I hope in the future of Narok] children go to school. Adults go to adult literacy centres.

Narrative 7: Nahiegu's story

I do not know my age, maybe around 42–45. I did not go to school because my father did not take me. I attended an adult literacy centre for a short while, but cannot read or write. I am one of three wives. I have ten children. Two did not go to school. The others went to school. I milk cattle and cultivate my husband's farm. I sell a bottle of milk to her [the researcher's interpreter] every day. I have participated in a women's group for a long time. There is a meeting every two weeks. I learnt bead-work from fellow women in the group. I make Maasai bead ornaments and sell them to buy food, clothes and shoes. I also constructed a latrine at home, based on the group's advice. I get new information from my children; for instance, my children told me about the necessity of using soap for hygiene. I got advice from the group. I rent a piece of land at different places, do farming without

Mzee's [her husband] knowledge. I harvest, sell, keep money, I am not relying on him, I make maize flour from maize, Mzee does not know where the maize flour comes from. There should be food at home. If I have ten bags of maize, I make sure to keep the half of the harvest for the next year, I hide it from Mzee, use my common sense. Mzee cultivates maize, he provides us little. [After participating in the group] the way of eating changed, before, it was only white things like ugari, and milk. They drink clean water. I am not looking at Mzee to give us food, I learnt self-reliance from the group. [I hope in the future of Narok] I advise all Narok people to do some work with their hands, make sure they have the kitchen garden at home, greens for children, take their children to school.

When the interview was almost completed, her husband appeared, and told Nashiegu to go and milk because it was getting late. Nashiegu rushed to the cow and started milking immediately. He was just watching her milking. The children were also waiting for her and to be fed inside the Maasai house.

Narrative 8: Rhoda's story

During the interview Rhoda was collecting beans from shelves outside while her husband was looking after their animals with their children. After that activity she made oil from milk cream by boiling it for a long time. The younger children took a spoonful of the oil to be healthy.

I do not know my age. I have seven children. Two daughters are married. One son is at a local secondary school. I did not go to school. During my father's time, no one went to school, hence my brother and sisters did not go to school. I attended an adult literacy class for two weeks, then a teacher left. I sell milk and work for other farms to earn income. My husband is in charge of finance. Money generated from milk and a harvest is mine. I can sell a goat or sheep if there is a problem at home, but not cows. I have participated in a women's group for one year with ten other women. We cultivate each other's farms together in turn. We plant maize and beans. After harvesting, each one contributes money on a weekly basis. Every week, the group members visit one member. Each member should bring two cups, two plates and 220 shillings. In total, at the end, everyone gets 20 cups, 20 plates and KSh2200. The group members continue this process of visiting each member in turn. We talk about our children, we help ourselves. Children are in our hands. I take my children to school with that KSh2200. I can buy school uniforms. I learnt how to build a traditional Maasai house from my grandmother. I was living with my grandmother. When my grandmother was constructing a house, she was telling me to observe the house construction. She said, "When you are someone's wife, you will make it [a house] for your husband". I learn from others, from the church, learnt people. [After participating in the group] my husband is appreciative, a house has cups and plates for a visitor. I use that money [generated from a harvest] to feed my family. [I hope in the future of Narok] both boys and girls are at school. Stop marrying off girls. Maasai people will put all their children into school.

Narrative 9: Agnes's story

I am 48 years old, I am the second wife among three wives. I did not go to school. My father did not take me to school. I attended an adult literacy centre for one month. The teacher was not present sometimes. I learnt how to write my name, but I forgot. I do farming, keep poultry, look after cattle, take the cows to the field, sell milk. My husband strolls around home. He is in charge of finance. I control money generated by selling milk and two acres of shamba. I cannot sell cows and sheep. I have been a member of three women's groups for many years. In the first group, we had a shamba, sold the harvested plants, bought a mill. After some years, we sold the mill and shared the money. The second group is TBA[traditional birth attendance]. There are 20 members. The members taught me about TBA, I assisted at a lot of children's births. I learnt a healthy way of handling a baby, cutting an umbilical code. I remember everything. The third one is a merry-go-round, there are 13 members. Each member puts KSh100 every day after selling milk. We gave one woman the saved money, and another woman to assist in her house. I learn from educated people, other members and from the TBA group. My mother taught me how to build a manyatta. I am very curious about seminars to educate mothers and the groups. So I attend seminars if there are any. I want to attend an adult literacy class. I could have read some sentences on the question sheet [of the researcher] if I had been to school. [After participating in the group], many changes [occurred]; how to wash a body properly, spray insecticides on cows, take children to school. I used to take one type of food [ugali: porridge, mixture of water, milk and flour], but now I use food full of necessary nutrients for my family. [I hope in the future of Narok] parents will take children to school, specially girls, let their girls complete education, get [girls] married later.

Narrative 10: Estha's story

I am 50 years old. I did not go to school. My father did not take me to school. I have attended the literacy class since 2010 [at the time of the research, one year previously]. I can write my name and count numbers, but it is still very difficult for me to copy what is written on a blackboard to my notebook. I am a divorced mother with two children.

100   *Narratives of the village women*

Both children are married. I have sheep, goats, chicken, cows and a shamba [a field]. I have a small-scale business, buy sugar, soap and tea leaves in the local markets, sell them at home to make a small profit. Through discussion and casual conversations among the literacy centre peers, I have learnt how to manage my business and how to write things down. [I hope in the future of Narok] good farming of maize and beans.

Narrative 11: Luisa's story

I am 52. I have eight children. My husband is blind. I did not go to school. My father did not take me to school. My father told me to look after animals at home. I attended an adult literacy centre for one month, but I got busy looking after animals, so I stopped going. I grow maize, look after animals, sell milk and construct my house. My husband is in charge of finance. After selling goats, the money goes to him. Small business money is mine. My husband and boy go to the market to sell [animals], they get money for school fees. I participate in three women's groups. First group is about HIV-AIDS. I have been a member for one year, attended a seminar and had a certificate framed on the wall. We were taught about HIV-AIDS. I tell people not to get involved in unsafe sex, use a condom. I told my daughters about it. The second one is TBA, and I have been a member for five to six years. I attended a training course on TBA. When a mother in the community is about to deliver, I am called to assist a mother's delivery. I go with equipment and attend the childbirth. I have also joined another group for one year. I was taught to put (water-purifying) medicines into water for clearing. At church, ladies came and talked about water. They were from an NGO, they gave us medicine. I visit neighbours to tell them how to treat water and put medicine in for safe drinking water. The medicine is finished. I am waiting for the ladies to come back. I get information and advice from church, educated people. They update us. For instance, global warming was taught at church. When I attended a ceremony at church, I heard a lot of things about child development. [After participating in the group], my husband and family are happy. I was drinking dirty water, now I put medicine into water, let it settle and drink directly. I am happy because I have told my neighbours about water. [I hope in the future of Narok] education will be first for all families.

All eleven women indicated some form of activities in informal learning and literacy learning. However, overall it was evident that literacy classes provided in the community were haphazard and were provided inconsistently – with the women often not being able to complete the course. Therefore, it was the informal processes of learning and gaining literacy that appeared most consistent for the women.

In the process of learning, the women raised their critical awareness of social issues and gender inequality and attempted to improve the situation through collaborative learning. It is evident that they assessed needs independently and conducted various kinds of activities to improve the well-being of their families and the community. The interviewed women conveyed the view that collective action and solidarity bring about a positive change at the pace of their choosing. As Tamale (2006) emphasised, the form of activity should be linked to political structure, if individuals strongly demand to have a more equitable and democratic society.

Analysis and discussions of the village women's narratives

This section focuses on the findings and discussion of the outcomes and challenges that village women have experienced when implementing activities in an informal group. Group activities and peer support appeared to have equipped the village women for resistance to and prevention of poverty, resulting in their families improved well-being.

Through a hand-coding process, five major themes emerged from the women's narratives: (1) women's learning processes; (2) resource management of the household; (3) women's group activities; (4) impact of women's group activities and learning on improving well-being; and (5) perceptions of the future. I respond to the research questions through the key themes.

Key theme 1: Women's learning processes as informal learning/literacy

The women's voices are valued, respected and addressed through recognising that their everyday experiences are a form of knowledge production. From a feminist perspective the aim is not only to explore and prioritise village women's perspectives about their experiences but also to communicate new knowledge to support changes to aspects of the oppressive conditions in which they live. Feminist research is politically undertaken, in that it challenges the dominant group of people who influence women's lives and seeks answers on how to address issues and find solutions (Anderson 2002). The process of building an empowerment element to knowledge production is through open dialogue in order to develop a critical insight into one's own oppressed situation, creating potential to become an active agent to change one's life. According to Freire (1970) empowerment approaches are significant as they enable women to gain understanding of their situation through self-reflection.

Lack of 'formal education' was reported by all the 11 interviewed women. While nine women reported no education, two had some level of primary education. The women reported that their fathers did not enrol their daughters in school, or withdrew them from schooling due to an early marriage.

102 *Narratives of the village women*

The perceived gender roles from a cultural and traditional perspective influenced how girls were socialised in the home and school.

Collins and Andersen (2001) state that work, family, educational institutions and government are all institutions where race, class and gender divisions emerge. There is an historical legacy of Maasai women being excluded from or encountering barriers in gaining access to institutions of formal education. Working in alignment with Spivak's concern about the double colonisation of women, the evidence suggests that girls and women are significantly less likely to have access to or complete literacy education.

For example, although Maria was familiar with alphabetical literacy, as she had attended formal schooling for a few years and she learned bookkeeping. However, looking after the group members' money through participation in the women's group was a practical method of learning by doing was a way to gain skills. Maria also made an effort to generate income for her children's education. Bown (1990) and LeVine *et al.* (2012) reported that literate mothers tended to send their children to school, yet, although Maria herself is not highly educated, she recognised the importance of education. She educated her children, including an adopted orphaned girl. Maria was confident that the future of educated people would be different to that of uneducated people. Resson, Namelok, Nahiegu, Rhoda, Agnes and Luisa made the point that educated people are knowledgeable and informed, hence the women would approach educated people to seek new knowledge.

The practice of early marriage (child brides) was also highlighted in Maria and Namelok's narratives as early marriage had terminated their schooling. Traditionally, a woman (girl child) is married off to a man as a gift or for an exchange of cows, a practice that is still widely undertaken. As Maria and Namelok reported, it the patriarch of a family who decides and arranges his daughter's marriage.

While four of the women did not attend an adult literacy centre, seven women participated in an adult literacy centre for periods between two weeks and two years. Mary, Maria, Namelok, Rhoda and Agnes reported that they learnt about traditional house construction through observation of their mothers or grandmothers.

While all the interviewed women explained that they asked for advice or obtained new information from educated people, Maria, Naserian and Nashiegu expressed the usefulness of their children's advice from their schooling. Namunyak noted that she learnt Swahili through a literacy centre and she was able to communicate with other tribes of Kenya.

Significantly, self-learning appeared to have empowered Nashiegu to be independent from her husband to some extent, although she seemed to fear her husband's orders to carry out house duties. Despite her compliance with her husband's orders, she was able to convey many positive aspects of women's self-empowerment through learning in her narrative, which is often an aim of aid agencies' literacy and development programmes (UNESCO 2003, 2005, 2014). However, again, in the case of Nahiegu, it was her own motivation and learning processes that resulted in personal empowerment, not programmes introduced by outsiders.

Nashiegu had created her own space to access information and advice from the group to seek a possible solution, utilising 'praxis', 'the inseparable unity of reflection and action' (Freire, 1970). It is evident that some women critically looked at and analysed their social situation in their cultural setting, found a solution and then acted to solve the problem. Nashiegu recognised that she should reserve some maize in case of drought. She did not wait for an outsider's aid to provide empowerment or agricultural training programmes. Instead of being reliant on outsiders, she identified a problem and aimed to improve her family's well-being by herself. Dependency on men, or the traditionally strong patriarchal system, had, to some extent, become manageable for some women in cooperation with fellow women. This is a fundamental social aspect of what literacy offers. What is most significant, however, is that as a subaltern woman, Nashiegu found the means, for example, informal learning activities, to speak and be heard without the need to transform her position in society but rather strengthen it through solidarity with other women in her village.

Western feminist movements have had a history of viewing women as "an already constituted and coherent group with identical interests and desires" with no viewed differences between race, class, ethnicity, or any other identity community (Mohanty 1991, p. 197).

The informal learning approach and related group activities that the village women went through helped women to create a space and the position for their culture (Freire 1970). The ethnographic approach opens up spaces for advocacy, alliance and political action on the part of the researcher by inserting her as a collaborative learner. The model developed here worked to engage with the enhancement of multiple literacies and can contribute to a challenge to representations, and resist gender inequality.

Mary highlighted her method of recording knowledge; she attempted to memorise information that she gathered from the oral communication by her mother, friends, educated people, children and church. She learnt from other people and applied what she had learnt in her daily life, for instance, traditional birth attendance (TBA) skills. This learning also raised her self-confidence. As Carmen argues, "we all remain orates under the (literate) skin – literacy cannot fully replace the pre-existing oral order" (1996, p. 100). Through "orality", the traditional African way of recording knowledge and communication, people, like Mary, transfer knowledge on traditional, cultural and modern practices such as HIV–AIDS.

Being a widow, Esta managed all of the household activities, including the care of livestock. She seemed to recognise the impact of literacy on livelihood, yet she attended the class for another purpose, which was to gain small-scale business skills during discussions at the literacy centre. This is a significant aspect of literacy supported by Clodomir Santos de Morais (Carmen and Sobrado 2000, p. 17). He criticises the functional literacy approach and argues that poor people need another type of literacy, "entrepreneurial literacy, which will allow them to develop self-managing organisations based on the division of labour" (Carmen and Sobrado, 2000, p. 17). He argued that the root cause of poverty is not the fact that illiterate people need to be functionally literate in order to gain the basic ability to acquire a job, but rather the fact that there is a large unemployment issue in poor countries. Hence, gaining literacy skills should be a process that people go through, a 'capacitation (learning)' process, and by organising groups, people can create jobs by themselves. In Brazil, for example, a successful landless people's movement (Movimento dos Trabalhadores Rurais sem Terra; MST) has been established which occupies disused lands (Carmen and Sobrado 2000).

Using orality or verbal communication with the teacher and literacy class participants, Esta acquired practical knowledge and skills connected with small-scale business. The first priority or motivation for her to come to the centre was to learn more about business management and to exchange ideas with peers. Moreover, there was space available for her to voice her opinions and be heard or contribute to discussions at the centre (Spivak 1985).

Gathering new information and knowledge through three women's groups, Luisa shared her expertise with her neighbours comfortably. Luisa seemed to consider not only her own family but also her community members' well-being. This highlights people's cooperative learning and the togetherness of the community (Pradervand 1989). This has been the major method of learning in a communal society like many in Africa. While it is still regarded as a difficult topic to discuss contraceptive methods or HIV transmissions through sexual intercourse, Luisa is confident enough to bring up the issue with her neighbours and her own daughters. Luisa encouraged other women to challenge gender inequality, as women have no say in sexual activities traditionally. It is evident that Luisa has gone through the process of developing a critical consciousness (Freire 1976), from which she has developed her critical awareness on social issues and has understood the risk of being HIV positive. This led Luisa to move into the process of 'Praxis', the act of applying knowledge (Freire 1976). Social and cultural factors may prevent people from using condoms as a method of birth control in the traditional Maasai community, yet Luisa has comprehended condom use, which was introduced by outsiders. As Bhabha (1994) explained about hybrid cultures in the previous chapter, from Luisa's observation, modern and traditional cultures are interacting with each other in the village around the modern intrusion of the disease of HIV–AIDS.

It is evident that the participants of this study challenged structural barriers by speaking out and wanting to bring attention to their possible social injustices and the unequal social relations of their individual experiences.

They wanted to contribute to improving their families' well-being and how care is provided for women in the traditional community. This process provided a way of bringing an emancipatory element to knowledge building; one that recognises social injustices and unequal social relations that disempower the women, and identifies marginalised voices (Freire 1970; Spivak 1985). Some participants also gained transformative knowledge; that is new knowledge constructed to support them from being a passive vulnerable woman to one that actively advocated for women who are struggling with family issues.

The research participants also articulated their appreciation for being protected from domestic issues, such as male-dominant resources control and lack of school fees, and being offered opportunities to move forward in a positive direction. Through the support received in collaborative learning through women's groups the women learned that they do have choices and they don't have to live with poverty.

Mary and Nashiegu had many domestic troubles but they received the support and information they needed to cope and manage with their household issues by pursuing different avenues for mutual support and assistance.

By taking part in the women's group activity, Nashiegu was empowered to be self-reliant and self-confident, trying to manage farming and generating income for her family behind her husband's back. Her experience is consistent with Haraway's (1991) observation that subordinated people can act on bringing about a positive change to improve their status through togetherness and collectively, as occurred among village women. Nashiegu's narrative indicated that she was aware of the traditional patriarchal system, that men control resources and make decisions on the utilisation of the resources; however, her narrative also reflects a form of resistance against the male-dominant social system.

The research participants are empowered to discuss, take an initiative to improve their well-being. In this way, a non-traditional learning environment becomes a space for participatory democracy (Freire 1970; Alexander and Mohanty 1997), and empathy is created through the 'dialogic' encounters in the groups rather than just through the consumption of new information, skills and knowledge (Freire 1970).

As noted by Rogers (2004), the informal learning space offers small-scale knowledge that can examine specific problems under particular situations. The values of communalism and collectiveness were promoted through cooperative learning. Also collaborative informal learning and literacy strengthened the tradition of community collaboration (Trutko *et al.* 2014). Moreover, needs-based learning and improved skills were viewed as a means to obtain information to be able to make more informed decisions, and offer better life opportunities.

The women's narratives also suggested that their learning is collaborative, localised and action-oriented. The research participants shared knowledge that can inform specific problems and specific situations. In this way, all involved women's group members, regardless of class and age, together become part of the learning process, actively working on analysing their own issues, how these are challenged, and how new insights result through try and error.

Key theme 2: Resource management of household; how does gender appear in the women's narratives?

The literature on women's development in Africa widely recognises that men control resources, including domestic animals and household finance, while women do all the household chores (Robeyns 2010; USAID 2010). The literature also suggests that women are restricted from access to resource management and land ownership (Robeyns 2010; USAID 2010; Hodgson 2011; Sen and Östlin 2011). This section presents an analysis of responses to interview questions such as: 'Who is in charge of finance?'

A postcolonial perspective informed my exploration of how social injustices and unequal social relations affect the research participants' access to and ownership of resources. Throughout the individual interviews, the participants spoke about the person of the household responsible for finance and resources. Participant narratives often illustrated their husbands' role in resource management of their household.

While Mary's husband was described as an alcoholic and she was busy managing farming and working in other people's fields, there was no clear indication of who controlled household resources. Maria was responsible for the farm, employing a few men to weed and harvest. Although Maria's husband controlled their land and livestock, she negotiated the casual workers' wages and made payments. This was traditionally a key male role as it relates to finance. Resson, Namelok, Nashiegu, Rhoda, Agnes and Luisa mentioned that their husbands controlled household finance and livestock. Namelok and Rhoda shared the role of trading livestock in the absence of a husband, which did not appear in other women's responses regarding household resource management. Naserian and Estha were single mothers, hence they managed household resources, including livestock. All participants spoke about using their pocket money generated from selling milk and small businesses on their children's schooling and/or food for their families.

Related to the issue of limited access to finance is the notion of patriarchy and socially and historically constructed gender roles in the village in which men are the bread winners, hence own and control resources and finance, and women maintain household chores and have access to only small amounts of money. Responses from village women described gender-based stereotypes of men's and women's needs and roles as the cause and continuation of this differential access to finance. Such a gendered understanding of the division of labour implied that men are to be the providers for and women the caregivers of the family. Therefore, men in the village in their role as providers were required to leave the house and graze animals or seek a job.

Interviewed women in the village, on the other hand, in their roles as caretakers of the family were not required to leave their home to step into the labour market and, therefore, are relegated to being an assistant to milk cows and do farming, as ordered by their husbands. A significant finding was the observation of how these factors affected the village women's ability to negotiate their status and situations with their husbands.

Gender affects the power and control men and women have in different ways over their socio-economic determinants (resource management, income, education, household chores) and their status, roles, access to resources and other treatment in society (Moser 1993; USAID 2010; Hodgson 2011; Sen and Östlin 2011). Socially constructed differences between men and women often result in discrimination and inequalities. It is therefore important to recognise that the multiple contextual factors affecting the village women's lives are related to power relations between the sexes and the structural barriers and class position of Maasai women within society (Crenshaw 1989).

Key theme 3: Women's group activities

The central aim of this work is to give an accurate account of the women's group activities and to build knowledge of the conditions of their lived experience. The postcolonial perspective recognises the need for knowledge production from the women's view, and that their voices have traditionally been silenced in the production of that knowledge (Kirkham and Anderson 2002). Throughout the individual interviews, the research participants spoke about the various ways in which they experienced women's group meetings and activities.

Research participants were asked various open-ended questions to gather information about how the women operate their informal groups and what kinds of activities the women had been engaged with.

The research participant's perspectives frequently centred on the expected responsibilities of wifehood and motherhood. Drawing on postcolonial feminist perspectives it brings into focus that some women face simultaneous difficulties such as provision of sufficient food, clean water and school fees. Lowered socio-economic status and inadequate social supports can be disempowering for village women and as a result create vulnerabilities and disadvantage.

When the interviewed women spoke about their experiences about women's group activities, they mentioned the organisation of their women's groups and major activities. Eight out of 11 interviewed women mentioned that they participated in one group, Naserian had joined two women's groups, and Agnes and Luisa were affiliated with three different women's groups. The women's groups operated as grassroots self-help groups. No women stated that their group was registered with the government. The women's groups' membership ranged from 11 to 20 members, and they were comprised of married women and widows. Membership fees also varied among the groups. Namelok said that one had to pay KSh100 as a member registration fee, yet other women did not mention the registration fees. They scheduled and conducted their own meetings.

The village women had found a way of reducing their workload through cooperation and organisation of a group and the women's groups were formed to share the workload of cultivating farms. They were aware of the large amount of work that women were expected to manage. Hence, by avoiding quarrels with their husbands, they came up with a constructive solution: they formed a group to share the workload amongst themselves. Rhoda and fellow women seemed to accommodate men's self-pride in order to live harmoniously. Togetherness in a communal society is a key aspect of African culture (Pradervand 1989). The village women were aware of gender disparity through an unequal workload and men's general expectations of women, yet they discussed a solution based on their capacity and attempted to create a better situation for women. This process reflected a praxis (Freire 1985), meaning people raised their own awareness of social issues and acted to bring about solutions. The women were not ordered or persuaded by outsiders to plan and implement a development project; instead, it was cooperative and mutual learning to change their situation. In addition, based on their everyday needs, each woman contributed a small amount of money to the group members as a whole. Each woman would indicate that she had a high expectation for education and she utilised the money to educate her children. However, again, the women's views can be overly optimistic, as Puchner (2003) emphasised that socio-economic development cannot be guaranteed by providing only an education to people.

The groups provided the members with better opportunities to network and share business ideas. The interviewed women often mentioned their unique forms of microfinance activity like the 'merry-go-round' system, and public health related activities such as TBA, HIV-AIDS and access to clean drinking water. While Mary, Agnes and Luisa mentioned TBA as the group's activity, other women declared small businesses and 'merry-go-round' to be the purpose of the group activity. While Mary and Luisa obtained a TBA certificate through a training course, Agnes gained TBA skills from her group members. The women voluntarily attended and provided childbirth care in their village.

The women illustrated how the merry-go-round activity was formed and maintained. As Maria and Namelok explained in their interviews, in their women's group meetings, each member contributed a certain amount of money to the group. The members drew lots to receive the total amount of the collected money. Numbers were written on a small piece of paper and the papers were folded. The members picked one piece of paper, opened it to see the number. The number determined the order in which the total sum of the money would be received. When Maria received the merry-go-round money from her group, she spent it on schooling fees and food. In this way, the women's group members met regularly to discuss issues affecting them and to contribute money, which they gave each other in turn to alleviate financial problems. The concept of the 'merry-go-round' was to generate wealth or capital for small business start-ups. Maria played the role of record-keeping for her group with the help of more formally educated people.

This practice illustrates solidarity among members of the women's group (Mohanty 2003). Furthermore, Maria was responsible for the farm, employing a few men to weed and harvest. She negotiated the casual workers' wages and made payments. This task was traditionally a key male role as it relates to finance. However, Maria had discussed this matter with her husband and in the absence of her husband, she carried out this task at home. Maria's skills were gained through 'doing', through the process of needs-based learning which she was able to do at her own pace. Through this process Maria acquired knowledge, and she had gained agency in order to develop a strategy to improve her life (Maslak 2008). The participants of this study indicated that, overall, they had a positive view of their experience in the women's group activities.

It may also necessitate further training in literacy and numeracy skills that could well be integrated into individual member's community development activities. The interviewed women in the village were subsistence farmers. Therefore, the women depended heavily upon farming and milking to maintain themselves and their children. Like many other marginalised people living in remoter communities in Kenya, subsistence farming offered very little certainty, because the size of the harvest is normally determined by many factors, e.g. rainfall, timing etc. Most of the women interviewed stated that they gained support of other members of groups who were also trying to reduce a heavy workload of farming. The interviewed Maasai women were still largely excluded from decision-making within the home and community, and were unrepresented in leadership roles.

It is common to find women gathering at a local kiosk in the village discussing children and issues that concern women. It was evident that there was hope to create spaces for new conversations and new connections. In relation to Spivak's notion of 'space' (1985), for individual women such as Mary, there was very little space available to negotiate with her alcoholic husband about issues at home, but she found her own space to raise her voice in the women's group. Mary's narrative indicated that she was well aware of the economic challenges confronting her family and of the extra work she needed to do to maintain her family's well-being.

As mentioned above, the groups are spaces for dialogue among women, focusing on collaborative learning and collective empowerment (Merriam *et al.* 2007; Papen 2002; Kabeer 1999). To create space for new conversations and new connections, feminist postcolonial concerns brought to attention in Chapter 1 can be applied. How might this methodology specifically move away from 'one-story-of-Africa' toward multivocal narratives and a disruption of postcolonial power dynamics? Consider the assisting skills of childbirth (TBA) in the village as favourable help that would be necessary in the traditional community, where some village women still give birth at home. Mary, Agnes and Luisa have obtained a TBA certificate from an unknown NGO and appeared to be happy with helping pregnant women with their deliveries in the village. This implies that they cooperate and help each other when in response to specific needs and are bound together in a lasting community relationship, reflecting a sense of solidarity and togetherness.

The groups of women became a 'space' where village women interact with other women around family, community and social issues. They also share their cultural and political vision, concerns, and seek support for individual problems. The importance of the women's group as a place of belonging exceeds the necessity of functional and material support for education, health, finance, agriculture and security. Friedman's (1992) and Spivak's (1988) discussions of the power of exclusion and how it can produce agency suggest that in order to confront the oppressive reality the women face, they have extended their resistance in their created spaces. However, the engagement does not go beyond the local and into public spaces by actively engaging with policy-makers, non-governmental organisations, local and national governments to create awareness of the social issues faced by local women.

Women's groups have become a distinct space for village women to engender agency towards securing social justice and to reflect their sociocultural life. I would argue that, in this context, the women have been empowered through group networking and engagement with various activities. The women's groups also sought to develop individual and collective capacities for critical analysis, to resist patriarchy and to mobilize for change. The localised women's groups are owned and controlled by women themselves, hence a participatory methodology was appropriately used. Development of capacity to claim financial and livelihood issues in individual situations and organise collectively to manage small-scale projects is one successful example of collective empowerment (Allen 1998; Phillips 2015).

Mary and Luisa mentioned that external NGOs as programme facilitators provided skills development seminars for women's group members, which contributed to TBA and cleanness of water. There is also a hint of collective empowerment in the village, where regular meetings were held to discuss problems and seek suggestions. Earning money gave some women some power in making family decisions. Nashiegu's comment indicates that men are not sharing in the costs of care as much as they ought to, leaving women to bear the costs. In addition, women are represented as efficient and responsible financial managers when compared with men, especially due to their primary caretaking role (Voola 2013).

In contrast to the theme of women's responsibility, what emerged from the responses in both contexts was the notion of men's irresponsibility towards the costs of care, often leading to 'wasteful expenditure' such as inappropriate consumption of alcohol. The theme of men wasting money on alcohol appears in the women's narratives. Due to women's limited access to finances as compared to men, it can be argued that women are constrained in their ability to spend on items beyond the necessities, such as alcohol. This could also mean that men enjoy the power provided by being in control of finances, which they can utilise in a manner suited to their individual needs and interest, rather than the needs of the family (Voola 2013).

In the hierarchy of household needs, Mary, Maria, Namunyak, Nashiegu and Luisa explained that a man's needs are addressed first, and those of the children. In this particular example, there is no space for women's needs, highlighting the power balance in interpersonal relationships between men and women.

Some women did not relate any actions towards gender inequality. As Tamale (2006) emphasises, the form of activity should be linked to a political structure, if individuals seek to demand to have a more equitable and democratic society. In keeping with African 'womanism', the women accommodated men's self-pride and seeking to live harmoniously (Tamale 2006). Togetherness in a communal society is a key aspect of African culture (Pradervand 1989). However, the women were aware of gender disparity through unequal workloads and men's general expectations of women, yet they discuss a solution based on their capacity and attempt to create a better situation for women. This process reflects a form of praxis (Freire 1985), meaning people raise their own awareness of social issues and act to bring about a solution. The women were not ordered or persuaded by outsiders to plan and implement a development project; instead, it was cooperative and mutual learning to change their situation. The women expressed high expectations for education and utilised their money to educate their children. However, again, the women's views can be overly optimistic as Puchner (2003) emphasised, socioeconomic development cannot be guaranteed by providing only an education to people.

While Mohanty (2003) and Haraway (1991) suggest that solidarity and togetherness among subordinated women can help them bring about positive changes in society, the women have rarely engaged in political initiatives to challenge gender inequality. However, while Mohanty (2003) and Haraway (1991) also raised the significance of solidarity and togetherness that marginalised women need to have in order to bring about a positive change in society, the women in this case rarely attended political initiatives to challenge discrimination and prejudice. Their voices were heard and have an impact on implementation of their projects observable only within their created spaces.

Key theme 4: The impact of women's group activities and informal learning/literacy on their well-being

When questioned about the significance changes in their lives since joining a grassroots women's group, the research participants spoke about attitudinal shift, that is, a shift in how they viewed themselves, their abilities and their families' well-being. Based on their narratives, it was evident that this was not a one-off event but rather sustainable informal learning which was promoted as a result of participating in a women's group. For instance, by reflecting on positive life changes since joining in women's groups, Mary Maria, Nashiegu and Agnes reported behavioural changes towards a healthy diet and hygiene and cleanliness to improve overall health, and the capacity to pay school fees. Moreover, they had achieved improved housing conditions, such as iron roof sheeting and newly built kitchens.

Tangible changes through the women's group activities were also noticed by friends and family. Maria and Luisa also reflected on how their husbands and neighbours noticed the positive improvement after their participation in the women's groups. The new attitude towards community development activities and collaborative learning had made a difference to how the women perceived themselves. Mary was confident that she could assist many mothers in her village through her practices and experiences. Mary seems to value communal society and cooperation of her village (Pradervand 1989).

Similar observations were made about new approaches and skills gained through learning. In the process of learning, the women raised their critical awareness of social issues and gender inequality and attempted to improve the situation through collaborative learning. They also gained empowerment via the process of learning literacy and informal learning. The village-based literacy centre created a forum for the women. The women considered not only benefits to themselves and family but also to their relatives, friends and neighbours. They demonstrated collective action and solidarity to bring about a positive change at the pace of their choosing (Mohanty 2003).

In the case of this study informal learning to strengthen capacity to manage to stay out of poverty was observed. The research participants in this study also got involved in village-based microfinance or small business programmes. These village women create an opportunity to increase their income by building links among women and cooperating with each other. This discussion is supported by Huiskamp and Hartmann-Mahmud's (2007) study, in which social spending helped to secure gender-specific forms of insurance and maintain solidarity within the society, in a manner consistent with social and religious norms concerning generosity and humanism. It could be said that women taking part in collective action have increased their control over equipment, or decision-making over some farm revenues, either systematically or significantly (Sally 2013).

Kabeer (1999) observed that the process of empowerment is completed with an exercise of agency while acknowledging the importance of access to resources, including employment, and its impact on well-being. According to Kabeer (1999), a key aspect of women's empowerment is whether one has power and ability to make choices. Rhoda and Teresa appear to be empowered as they have managed to independently implement a micro development project. Relating Kabeer's (1999) point to the purpose of this study, the interviewed women also illustrated that they have the ability to act within their communities as agents of change for community development.

Self-empowerment and poverty alleviation were highlighted in the research participants' comments. Egbo (2000) looked at the personal impact of literacy on women and she suggested that it resulted in an increase in one's self-esteem to bring about a better life. This was supported by the instructor's comment on the impact of literacy on one's well-being. However, Maddox (2005) reports that some marginalised women can be reluctant to demonstrate acquired literacy skills due to culturally restricted gender roles. This implies that the level of one's self-confidence developed in the process of learning, therefore the village women's perspectives on literacy/learning and well-being were explored in interviews. As Knowles observed, adults learn and gain knowledge based on their needs and experiences while children learn mostly in a classroom setting. Adult informal learning is distinct from formal learning. Knowles (1973) clearly showed that adult learning is all about self-directed and problem-based learning, bringing in life experiences. Critical reflection on learning and outcomes are key aspects of adult informal learning. While formal learning takes place at institutions based on planned curriculum, adults learn spontaneously, leading to immediate solutions through practice and solidarity. This process of learning also recognises the production of knowledge. In the process of collaborative learning subordinated women raise their voices in a created space among women and, by sharing each other's issues and ways of solving the issues, women learn and act upon solutions together. The women have become subjects to the process of community development (Sen and Östlin 2011). They have owned and controlled small development projects within their capacity (Carmen 1996).

The women gained the various opportunities for informal lifelong learning through women's group activities. Their individual struggles to overcome oppression and marginalisation are directly connected to development of agency and self-empowerment.

Key theme 5: Future

At the close of the interview, I asked participants about their future. Many women had survived with gender inequality and it was a proud moment not only sharing what they had learned but how they had gained control of their lives, thus creating a hopeful future for themselves.

Nine of the interviewed women highlighted the importance of education for their children. Mary, Maria and Rhoda showed particular concern about girls' education in Narok and they stated that girls should be sent to school, not married while young. In addition, Mary and Resson highlighted the impact of education on better farming and employment opportunities.

Village women's voices on learning/literacy and well-being

As the impact of informal literacy learning on community development was discussed in Chapter 2, village women's perspectives on literacy and well-being was a focus in the interview. Adult informal learning is distinct from formal learning and Knowles (1973) clearly showed that 'andragogy' is all about self-directed and problem-based learning, based on life experiences. Critical reflection on learning and outcomes are key aspects of adult informal learning. While formal learning takes place in institutions based on planned curriculum, adults learn spontaneously, leading to immediate solutions through practice and solidarity. This process of learning also recognises the production of knowledge. In the process of collaborative learning subaltern women raise their voice in a space created among women and by sharing each other's issues and ways of solving the issues, women learn and act upon solutions together.

The interviewed women were eager to speak about their experiences to the researcher. Just as Spivak (1985, 1988) suggests that women have been silenced socio-culturally and politically for many years, the village women in this study have also been given less opportunity to raise their voice in public. However, the village women showed that they had created a space within women' groups, from which they speak and raise their opinions on possible solutions to overcome domestic and community issues. It is certain that Maria, Nashiegu and Mary were powerful in raising their voices and acting upon bringing about changes through women's groups. However, the village women occupy two different spheres according to their gendered status. On the one hand, the women are powerful in own their projects through women's groups by cooperating and learning together, on the other hand, the women seem to comply with gendered stereotypes in a male-dominated community. The women know strong resistance to patriarchy in public creates complications, therefore, the women have their own way of solving problems within their capacity. The women understand their expected role in their male-dominated community, yet they look at their surroundings and analyse the issues by themselves (Narayan and Harding 1998).

In the forum created by the self-help group through learning activities, village women raised their voices and became more active, getting involved in community development projects. The interviewed women actually moved into action and implemented a small-scale business and primary health care project. The participant in the process of gaining new knowledge and literacy skills built a collaborative relationship with others.

The following section describes the process observation data. To explore the village women's everyday lives, during the fieldwork, the researcher wrote a diary of her routine activities. Also the researcher took notes when she observed and experienced gender and community issues in the village. The data is organised by key themes of activity that formed the basis of women's distinctive informal learning and community development programmes.

Process observation

The researcher documented the processes of events and incidents within the village that contributed to informal learning and literacy, and community development activities through women's groups.

The first thing I took note of was the microfinance conducted within the women's groups. While the interviewed women had discussed the microfinance activity called merry-go-round during interviews, the researcher had another opportunity to participate in a microfinance-aimed group facilitated by a local NGO. All of the women in the group showed concerns about generating income to help their family and all of the groups had similar small microfinance projects. Further, the reproductive role that village women are expected to carry out was observed and the gendered ownership and management of resources in the village were explored. These areas provided insight into gender roles and inequality in the village. Some casual conversations contributed to the process observation data below. As a whole, this section of reporting on observations seeks to construct a complex picture of literacy practiced by village women in Narok County, Kenya.

A Maasai woman possesses a variety of skills and competencies to improve the well-being of individuals and community members. A Maasai woman in Narok County plays significant roles in community development through collaborative informal learning and solidarity. The women understand risks to basic household security, and also seek to protect their own security from male dominance through women's networks. Women use their own strategies of microfinance and managing male-dominated resources management.

It was broadly observed that the village women acquire their own literacies to manage life skills that formal literacy/schooling does not offer in a timely way. Moreover, women have cultivated the capacities of life skills that are used in the process of acquiring their own literacies. Key themes that emerged as informal learning and literacies included: (1) microfinance, (2) basic household chores, (3) production and protection from male dominance, (4) resource management and (5) conservation of culture. Other types of literacy such as health promotion, communication skills and long-term development activities leading to sustainable development were mentioned by women's leaders and will be described in Chapter 6.

Theme 1: Microfinance

To overcome the social exclusion of the poor, microfinance has been widely practised, especially in poor countries. Microfinance is expected to create financial opportunities for vulnerable people. Microfinance is defined as "a credit methodology that employs effective collateral substitutes to deliver and recover short-term, working capital loans to micro entrepreneurs" (Consultative Group to Assist the Poor 2003). It includes the services of credit, savings, insurance, loans and so on. This model was applied in Narok County. The group was established on 12 March 2011 and had been registered to a domestic NGO located in Nairobi City. The registration fee for this NGO cost KSh1000. A chairperson, vice chairperson, secretary and treasurer were nominated within the group. The group's microfinance was for a joint liability loan and a group meeting took place for loan payments, savings and other contributions. The members were responsible for all expenses and opportunity costs. Each member had to buy a KSh150 book of records to record their cash flow.

While some village-based women's groups had their own informal microfinance activity, formal microfinance as a women's group based on process observation is introduced below. This is because it was hard to get information on times and venues of meetings of informal women's groups in the field, and the researcher was able to participate in meetings of this formally registered women's group. The group meeting was planned on Saturdays fortnightly and the members of the group communicated via mobile phone to reconfirm a time and venue for the meeting. The meeting was held in the living room of one of the members' houses. Inside the house was very hot. All the participants sat on chairs in a circle.

One Saturday afternoon, a meeting of the women's group was organised, consisting of 12 female and three male members. There were two teachers, one policeman, the others were businessmen and women. The members' educational backgrounds varied from no schooling to higher education. All of the members helped each other in reading and writing down the information, written in English on the passbook. Whenever one had a question on group management or microfinance, s/he raised a hand to ask. There was a local young man who was interested in joining the group. All the members had a discussion on the protocol to recruit new members and the members raised concerns about the young man on the basis of his reputation in the community. The members gave his/her opinion freely. A young male instructor with a secondary education background attended the group meeting. He was a programme coordinator of the NGO and monitored about 100 village-based microfinance groups in Narok County. He checked on the monthly performance of the group. The instructor wrote down the attendees' names and checked the ID cards of the members, and he and the treasurer calculated the total amount of money and the balance. It took them about 30 minutes while others watched them. The instructor took KSh5000 to the bank as savings.

A member of the group could get a loan with 1 per cent interest for the duration of a three-month repayment. Otherwise, if the loan was larger, the member would have to make the fixed monthly payment for a loan with 10 per cent interest. Depending on the amount of savings a member has, a member can take out a loan from the NGO. For instance, if a member has saved up to KSh500, the member is entitled to borrow KSh2500. The members don't check for what purpose a loan is used. Basically, members have a high level of trust in each other and the members visit a borrower if s/he needs assistance for repayments. A monthly KSh2200 merry-go-around amount was given to a woman after she beat one female and one male in a lottery. Eventually, accumulated interest on savings become a bonus to the members.

The village-based microfinance activity offered women a chance to help themselves in becoming 'literate' through collaborative informal learning. All of the members of the group helped each other to write down the sum of money, the date and other information. A space to raise one's opinion was also created so that every member was able to raise her voice freely and could discuss financial matters. The regular meetings of the microfinance group contributed to the development of financial literacy for its members.

The implications of this norm reconfiguration was that the village women, who had been hitherto confined to private spaces as 'home makers' with limited financial exposure, were now offered a new subject position, microfinance group member, which extended and expanded their interactions in public as well as in financial spaces. Nevertheless their role as primary carers remained unchanged. While women were directly accessing and 'controlling' the small finances, they were doing so from their position as primary carers to meeting carer needs. In other words, the design of the activity was not emancipatory for women. Therefore, the gendered need of household maintenance by women was met, but the norm underpinning this need, i.e. the gender norm of women's responsibility for the private sphere remained intact.

Theme 2: Women's household chores

Wangui (2003) observed that work for pastoral women and girls had been increasing due to drought and land tenure, resulting in the restriction of pastoral livelihood systems. Although caring for a family's health needs, women also look after domestic animals. In addition to the production of household food, women also help men grow cash crops.

Women are concerned about basic household security as they play a significant role in reproduction to maintain their household. The role includes childbearing, housework and caring for old and sick family members, comprising, generally, of the unpaid work of women at home (Moser 1993). Hence, two cases of women's and men's daily activities are detailed below. Many women have a large family due to the absence of effective family planning.

Takayanagi (2008) observed that a Maasai woman managed all the housework by herself; preparation of meals, milking, fetching water and firewood, washing clothes, taking care of her children. In addition to the housework, a Maasai woman cultivated vegetables with her husband. To understand women's reproductive role in their village, I observed and had casual conversations with women about their daily activities.

Case 1: A woman's activities from Monday to Friday

Namelok is the first wife among three wives. She has five children. Namelok wakes up at 5 a.m., and prepares her children to send them to school. After the children have left for school, she milks cows, cleans the house, washes utensils and takes cows out for grazing. When children come home from school, she feeds them lunch. After the children go back to school again, Namelok goes to fetch firewood and water. She washes clothes. Before dinner, she milks cows again. She cooks dinner at 8 p.m. After all of her family members have dinner, Namelok washes utensils and washes the children. She then goes to bed at 10 p.m.

HER HUSBAND'S ACTIVITIES FROM MONDAY TO FRIDAY

He wakes up at 5 am, washes his face and goes to town for socialising. He comes home in the evening. He has dinner and goes to bed. When he is not with his first wife, he is with his second or third wife. He does not look after livestock.

Case 2: A woman's activities from Monday to Friday

Namunyak is the second wife, and has eight children. Namunyak wakes up at 6 a.m. and sweeps the house. She makes a fire to warm a little water for washing her face. She prepares tea for her family. She milks cows and boils milk. She wakes the children up and all of them have tea. Namunyak assists her children to get ready for school by 7 a.m. She cooks lunch and has a morning meal and takes animals for grazing. She looks after cattle, goats and sheep. After school, when the children stay at home, Namunyak goes home to do other house duties and children look after the cows. Otherwise, She stays until 5 p.m. with the animals. Then she goes to collect firewood and fetches water from the dam. During her free-time, Namunyak makes beaded items until the animals have returned. She milks the cows again, cooks and has dinner. She washes her body and goes to bed at 9 p.m.

HER HUSBAND'S ACTIVITIES FROM MONDAY TO FRIDAY

He wakes up at 8 a.m. After taking breakfast or early lunch, he leaves home. He goes socialising at the local market or visiting his friends. He comes home for dinner. When he arrives at the house late, he wakes the wife up, and he is always fed by his wife. He generally goes to bed before his wife, perhaps around 8 p.m.

Based on case studies above, it is confirmed that women carry out demanding household tasks from dawn to dusk, yet reward for this level of work is absent. One Maasai woman said there used to be a saying about women in the community: women never get ill. When a woman is pregnant, Namunyak does extra work of fetching water and firewood to save some for after the delivery. Neighbours and her female friends also help with household duties during and after the delivery of a baby.

According to a Maasai female teacher, a Maasai woman has more duties than in the past. Men used to graze cattle far away from home and women were left with the children. In the recent context, if there are three wives, each wife is poor and each is responsible for taking care of her own children. A woman also looks after animals at home. If a woman employs a casual worker to look after the vegetable field and cattle, it will be another added responsibility on top of her daily duties. The woman has a business role to play at home.

Gender hierarchies within the family context may be played out as power, domination and control over women. This can create unequal social relations between men and women, and place women in a socially disadvantaged position. As a result unequal power relationships may affect the family through economic roles and challenges.

A common pattern of a day for many women is to manage family responsibilities, and uphold the cultural and traditional norms of the Maasai. It is well known that female gender roles frequently require women to be responsible for a disproportionate amount of domestic and paid work, as well as balancing childcare and housework (Chege and Sifuna 2006; Puchner 2003; Rao and Robinson-Pant 2006; Hodgson 2011; Voola 2013). However, multiple roles could make women more vulnerable to gender issues. As a result, gender roles and statuses together with embedded power relations within the family may also influence a woman's access to formal education and learning opportunities (Puchner 2003; Rao and Robinson-Pant 2006; Hodgson 2011). Traditional gender roles increase vulnerability by stressing submissiveness and imposing a duty to take on the care of others (Voola 2013).

Figure 5.1 A woman taking care of a wounded goat.

Namelok and Namunyak had the increased responsibility for the stability of the family and retaining the care-giving role. The women in their primary role as carers were unable to fully participate in the labour market. On the other hand, men in the primary role as providers provided their families with minimal to no conditions on their contribution to care work and household maintenance.

Production and protection from male dominance

Both men and women played a productive role, which includes paid work and producing cash crops or livestock. Both men and women looked after domestic animals and cultivated crops such as maize and potatoes. However, in almost all cases, the ownership of livestock resided with men. Women were engaged with agricultural work, especially, in producing food for their family. Many women expressed in casual conversations the belief that women could not own livestock such as cows, sheep and goats. These animals are the husband's property. Land including crop fields often also belonged to a man and he gave his wife permission to farm. In a typical Maasai family, a wife was also her husband's property, the same as his children. This was evident when a husband called a wife *Mutoto* (the word for 'child' in Swahili). It also meant she was under the care and protection of her husband, with a similar status to his child.

I observed in the local Maasai market that mostly men traded animals. On the market day, men were busy. Some men took animals to the market on foot, some transported animals to the market by car. Other tribes or people from Nairobi came to the Maasai local market to purchase animals. Alongside the animal market, women sold vegetables, fruits, sour milk, clothes, drinks and so on. I had casual conversations with two women who were trading cows in the market. They were widows. The women said that they had bought cows, goats and sheep, reared the animals and sold them in the animal market to make a profit. Their sons helped the women in transporting the animals between the market and their house. One of the women said that she bought a cow for around KSh14,000–15,000 and was eager to sell it at a price of KSh18,000–20,000. This woman never went to school, but she was able to calculate for trading. Her children had all been sent to school.

Because a cow is the most important product in their society, men eat the tastiest part of its meat and women are given the leftovers. When a woman gives birth, she is provided with the red part of meat for post-natal recovery. Even meat consumption reflects gender issues and the male dominant cultural aspect of the Maasai.

Women also make Maasai traditional beaded ornaments and crafts at home and sell them at the local market or shops in town. Women have the knowledge and skills to make complicated artistic bead ornaments. Selling vegetables and ornaments are the main source of their income, generating activity within an informal economy. While men trade in a bigger economy or the formal economic sector, women's production seems to be regarded as less valuable.

According to USAID's (2010) gender analysis in East Africa, including Kenya, ownership of livestock and usage rights differ from region to a region. In some communities, men have entire exchange rights over the whole stock, yet they own only larger stock in some places.

In addition, when the commercial value of women's goods grows, control over the products shifts from women to men. This is also the case observed in certain Massai communities in Kenya. Since women also looked after cattle at home, Maasai women managed milk production. Women could decide to sell milk products or exchange it as gifts to enhance social networks. However, to increase milk products for the market, control over the products from women to men has been changing slightly (Mitzlaff 1994). Women could gain access to local markets on foot, but they required additional transport such as a bicycle or car to sell milk products in larger markets, which could be managed by men in Narok County.

Maasai women milk cows and sell milk to other people such as teachers and shopkeepers. It was possible to sell two to three bottles of milk (1–1.5 litres of milk) a day resulting in KSh40–60 income. The income generated from milk was a Maasai woman's pocket money. Because this income was very small, a husband did not control this income. Women in the village stated that their husbands were in charge of home finances. For example, when a family needs money for school fees, a man can decide to sell an animal at the local market. Otherwise, a mother saves her pocket money from selling milk to pay school fees. Some women are involved in the cash economy. Women ensure their children's schooling by protecting a small income from their male counterpart, usually their husband.

Resource management

During the six months period of fieldwork in the village in Narok, I had the opportunity to observe many women fetching water from water dams and ponds on daily basis. On local school visits, there were students drawing buckets full of water from a water tank. A water tank to collect rainwater had been set up at some residences in the village and some women and children were taking water out of the tank. Due to it being a drought-stricken area in 2011, the issue of rainfall had appeared in everyday conversations. While I was staying in Naserian's house in the village, I became involved in securement of water for my host family, as water was essential for the survival of people and domestic animals.

Securing water

It was a woman's primary role to fetch water from the dammed water reservoir, from which animals also drank. A few houses had 500–1500 litre water

122 Narratives of the village women

tanks to harvest rainwater, but because a traditional Maasai house is not constructed with a roof gutter, a water tank cannot be used next to it. According to a few village women, when water tanks or dams are dried up due to a drought, women would look for water by walking as far as ten kilometres. For instance, a woman would leave home at 6 a.m. and return home at 3 p.m. with 20 litres of water. This task was hard physical labour and she was responsible for this duty every day.

During my stay in the village, I encountered a water management issue controlled by men. In the compound where I stayed, there was a large concrete-made water tank owned by a local dispensary. All the families in the compound were entitled to have access to the water tank when they had inadequate water. However, the tap of the water tank was normally locked. Hence if a family needed water, they had to ask permission for the tap key, which was administered by a local elderly man. When I went to collect the key to unlock the water tank, he gave me the key with permission to fill four water containers of 20 litres. One of the neighbours suggested we take more water than the man ordered, as the number of my host family members was large at the time. Each water container was heavy, hence my host mother arranged a young man to carry the water containers to our house. When my host mother was drawing water from the tap into a water container to pass it to the young man, the elderly man suddenly appeared, shouting "Give me the key, I told you, 40 litres!", and then the key was snatched by the elderly man. Later it was found that a male friend of his was watching our water work and rang him up quickly to stop us from fetching water. Water had become a valuable commodity during a severe drought in the small compound. Women were primary users of the water, but they were excluded

Figure 5.2 A village dispensary in Narok.

from any power over water management. Women's central role in water could have been recognised in the community.

Conserving culture

To conserve the culture, women were also engaged with various community services and events. This was observed at funerals, wedding ceremonies and other events, such as church services or school events and meetings.

When there was an event in the community, such as fund raising for school fees or a house opening ceremony at someone's house, women gathered at a venue and prepared traditional foods of sweet milky tea, sour milk and roasted meat for guests. On the event day, women dressed up in full traditional garments. Women cooked food and cleaned up the venue at the end of each event. This work was conducted voluntarily. Men played a leadership role and they often contributed some cash to event organisers. Observations made during a church service are described below. In addition, I received an invitation to participate in two local school events in the village; one was to receive a British pastor at the school and the other was to celebrate the opening of the school dormitory. These two full-day observations provided me with a chance to participate in the local events to see how gender roles were played out in community events. These incidents are illustrated in the discussion below.

For example, women were involved in school management. School management committees elected by parents were usually male, with a few female members. Yet, during a meeting, female members generally kept quiet. When there was a function at school such as a school dormitory opening ceremony or receiving a foreign visitor, the school management committee organised its programme with senior teachers. Men gave instructions and orders to females to conduct an event. Most of the time mothers, female teachers and senior girl students prepared food. Roasted meat was served for men first and a small piece of roasted meat was served to the women. As affirmed by Spear and Waller (1993), culturally, men are regarded as leaders and superior to women and hence they are provided with roasted meat before women.

Second, when there was a function at the church, women cooked meals outside the church. Pastors and church leaders were also mostly men. Men stayed in the church service. A few men also appointed young women to meal preparation duties. When the church service had finished, all the men lined up in front of the church entrance. As stated previously, women and children passed by each man, greeting him with their heads by bowing. The man placed his hand on their heads. Women and children were regarded as possessing the same status. Although there were a few female church leaders, a young woman sometimes faced a communication issue with a senior Maasai man. When she raised her opinion on a certain issue in front of elderly men, she would be told to be quiet. In this case, she asked her fellow younger men to discuss the issue with the older men. For example, when the roof was to be repaired or there were functions at church, each man contributed 2000. On the other hand, each woman contributed KSh1000. Church members discussed the amount of the contribution and decided it in accordance with gender.

Religion also plays a significant role in certain male and female relationships and plays a part in formulating gender codes and social norms. A gender-based hierarchy of Christianity has excluded women from church leadership roles and historically has placed women under men's authority (Hall 1992). For many girls and women, religion is used as a way to reinforce certain rules and norms. This data shows that it is as an oppression of local women that has been supported through colonial institutions such as Christianity that has persisted as a patriarchal construct. The Christian influence of imposing a patriarchal authority through the church is evident, women's formal role in the church business is secondary. It is also an example of how the Church, via its missionary participation in the British colonisation of Kenya, has assured women's subaltern status in the postcolonial period.

Gender is an important determinant of social inequality and influence on women's status and situation. This raises important questions about gender disparities across power, roles and responsibilities in the community. As noted in the literature review, coupled with being emotionally and financially dependent on their male counterparts this status may leave women extremely vulnerable and disadvantaged in terms of protecting themselves and seeking appropriate assistance.

Productive role of women in the village

While women produce some crops and ornaments for generating income under the productive role, the task of house construction is emphasised as a theme in this section. Unlike the contexts in many other countries, house construction is a women's task in Maasai communities. This is because the work of house construction generally represents the male's responsibility to provide for a family in many countries (Moser 1993). However, this task has traditionally been conducted by Maasai women, and it should be noted as a featured task under the productive role of women. The traditional round Maasai house was designed for nomadic people as the house could be easily built and broken down with locally available resources during grazing trips. On my house visits there were two occasions to observe Maasai women constructing a house in the village. I watched one young woman who was drawing a plan for a house on the ground with sticks, and she explained to me about the collected house materials of wood, branches and mud. The young woman proudly showed the current house and described that she needed one more house for her extended family members. Her husband praised his wife's competent work and looked proud of her. According to her, building a house has been one of the women's core tasks traditionally and women generally learn about house construction from their mothers. On another occasion, I had a chance to observe an elderly woman renovating her house. The elderly woman was changing wall sticks inside the house. The elderly woman described how traditional house renovation was very important work for Maasai women.

House construction

Constructing a traditional Maasai house was also a wife's responsibility. When a woman got married, she built a house for her husband. Women also helped each other to construct a house. Some women said that when they sensed rain, they collected cow dung and smeared it on the roof to prevent damage from rain. A husband would wake a wife up at night when it started raining. She went up to the roof, applied cow dung and came back inside. She set a fire to warm herself, changed *shuka* (Maasai clothes) and went back to sleep again. There are a few houses with a corrugated iron roof in the village. This modern house construction reduced women's duties. One of the women said, "men are superior, so women do a small jobs, but small jobs are many and daily …".

Documentation of activities such as women's role in house construction indicates the domesticity and feminisation of women's work. Their economic activity such as beadwork can also be seen as an extension of their family roles.

The above observations show that women in the village work longer hours than men, being responsible for various tasks in and around the house. Some men graze cattle, goats and sheep and trade the livestock in the market. There are some men who share household chores with women, yet it was clearly observable that the community still expects women to take the primary responsibility for unpaid domestic tasks. While women are responsible for the household's maintenance, major decisions are being made by the men of the house. Men are responsible for functions in the community, including rituals and protecting the community from other threats by tribes and animals, reflecting the highly patriarchal traditions of the Maasai. Moreover, because women play the productive role, in the case of natural disasters such as drought, their workload, such as collecting water and firewood, increases. Also, women are expected to work even harder to preserve natural resources during pregnancy and baby rearing. Women rely less on male partners' assistance or other basic services.

Although women strictly follow the patriarchal community rules, they were observed expressing sentiments of resistance in songs and dances. My observations support Spear and Waller's (1993) view that women also attempt to emphasise that they are counterparts of men.

From my observations, there was clear gender inequality and clear structures of patriarchy in the community, yet women played different roles simultaneously to prevent poverty. Men and women had different needs in accordance with their gender roles in the community. However, women's voices were seldom presented in the decision-making process in the community. Empowering women and the participation of women in the community and government policies are necessary to bring about more positive development.

House construction is considered to be one of the hardest physical jobs in village life, along with the collection of water and firewood. The exclusion of men from these roles also reflects men's dominant social position in the Maasai lands (Hodgson 1999, 2011). While women played central roles in house management and caring for children, men were responsible for protecting their settlements and pasturing livestock (Hodgson 1999, 2011).

The way of passing on knowledge and techniques of house construction from a mother to a daughter echoes what Hodgson (1999, 2011) discussed as women being also part of the (re)production of masculinities. Maasai culture seems to dictate the leadership and domination of men in the village and men are considered superior to women in the village. By controlling men's self-pride in the community, however, women in Kenya make efforts to maintain life from daily food production for the long-term investment of the future for their children by paying school fees (Tamale 2006). This can be seen as an example of African feminism (womanism), where women aim to live harmoniously with men (Tamale 2006). Moreover, as Oyewumi (2003) noted, a woman in Africa is part of a communitarian affair including the care of men and the whole community, hence, she just accepts the task of building a house as one of her traditional core responsibilities.

Conclusion

This chapter has presented the sets of data derived from observations and interviews. Both data collection methods were necessary in order to gather the research participants' views on informal learning/literacy and women's group activities to improve their well-being. A combination of these methodologies gave the researcher access to more of the reality of living in the research site.

For some participants there is a central belief that they are responsible for the stability of the family and having the care-giving role. With limited resources and access, the village women made efforts to maintain their families. However, the traditional role is so powerful that it affects the choices the women make. The key observation based on the data is that the village women have gained skills and knowledge through collaborative informal learning and cooperation to prevent poverty. Also women have become collectively empowered to challenge gender issues.

The analysis above suggests that the narrative of each woman's experience of informal learning/literacy and community development was the most powerful tool for building my knowledge on how the Narok village women improved their well-being.

Overall, the reflective comments by all village women indicated that despite being formally illiterate, interaction and cooperative informal learning

Figure 5.3 Adult education classes in Narok.

with fellow women helped to alleviate fears of poverty and gender inequality and built their collective empowerment and self-reliance. The women enhanced their capacity to assess needs and solve issues. They also improved their problem solving and learning skills through observing and interacting with fellow women via the key sites for informal learning.

In discussing aspects of women's informal learning activities this chapter has reflected on the various meanings of literacy. The data from the process observation indicated that village women played significant reproductive and productive roles in their village. The women were conscious of male dominant decision-making processes in which women's opinions in the community were often silenced. Therefore, the women were keen to ensure women's expected roles in their society and maintain their families' well-being.

It is evident that women have many tasks on a daily basis, but clearly manage all of their responsibilities. In addition, in order to raise a household income, village women participated in small economic activities, such as selling milk and marketing traditional ornaments. Plus, when they need a certain amount of money, especially for school fees, they use a microfinance system in the group or organise a fund raising event in the community.

The chapter has addressed the key research questions for this study, including questions related to village women's perceptions of the role of education in Narok; the nature of informal learning activities; the impact of women's community development activities on improving their status and well-being in Narok; and the power structure played out in the decision-making process. While development policy tends to be an "instrumental view of policy as rational problem solving" favouring literacy as an instrument (Robinson-Pant 2008, p. 780), the chapter has demonstrated that there is an alternative to the top-down literacy and development approach, which is self-directed informal learning (Smith 2008; Rogers 2004) or women's solidarity (Mohanty 2003). Women practice literacy and numeracy skills in environments such as the market and small-scale businesses. This can be counted as 'everyday literacies' (Gebre *et al.* 2009). Supporting Freire's (1970) and Allen's (2008) view, this chapter has demonstrated that village women go through empowerment in which women have become a change agent to make a positive change in their life.

This study also clearly shows that non-literate village women generate knowledge and skills through solidarity and cooperative learning. As Tamale (2006), however, pointed out, their struggle to promote women's rights is barely engaged with a political agenda. To achieve a more gender balanced society, they need to have a strong will and continuous movement in a harmonious way.

While Udvardy's (1998) study concluded that the needs of women's groups in Kenya are based on material resources, information and income generation, women's groups in Narok County also included peer cooperation and building networks among participants. The interviewed women reported that the collective power of local women was widely observed in the village.

Reflecting on the women's comments on resource and financial management, gender inequality or rather patriarchy was highly dominant in their community. Brydon and Chant (1989) noted that cultural constraints restricted women's participation in development. This is observed in the above interview and observation data, which means the progress of gender development programmes had been slow and ineffective. Furthermore, this chapter revealed the concept of 'being poor' from a woman's point of view. Supporting Saitoti and Beckwith's (1988) view, it was apparent that the more cattle a Maasai person has, the more influence the person has in one's community. Cattle are central to Maasai food, power and wealth.

The following chapter reports on significant voices and opinions on gender, education and development. The comments of women's leaders and bureaucrats were relevant to my study to enhance my understandings of education and gender development, by comparing them with perceptions of the village women.

Note

1 Naserian is not her real name. The researcher was treated like her own daughter by Naserian and called Naserian "mother".

References

Alexander, M.J., and Mohanty, T.C. (eds). (1997). *Feminist Genealogies, Colonial Legacies, Democratic Futures.* New York: Routledge.
Allen, A. (1998). Rethinking Power. *Hypatia*, 13(1), 21–40.
Allen, A. (2008). *Power and the Politics of Difference: Oppression, Empowerment and Transnational Justice.* Hypatia, 23(3), 156–172.
Anderson, J. (2002). Toward a Post-Colonial Feminist Methodology in Nursing Research: Exploring the Convergence of Post-Colonial and Black Feminist Scholarship. *Nurse Researcher*, 9(3), 7–27.
Bhabha, H.K. (1994). *The Location of Culture.* London: Routledge.
Bown, L. (1990). *Preparing the Future: Women, Literacy and Development. Action Aid, Report No. 4.* London: Action Aid.
Brydon, L., and Chant, S. (1989). *Women in the Third World: Gender Issues in Rural and Urban Areas.* New Brunswick, NJ: Rutgers University Press.
Carmen, R. (1996). *Autonomous Development: Humanizing the Landscape. An Excursion into Radical Thinking and Practice.* London: Zed Books.
Carmen, R., and Sobrado, M. (2000). *A Future for the Excluded: Job Creation and Income Generation by the Poor: Clodomir Santos de Morais and the Organization Workshop.* London: Zed Books.
Chege, F.N., and Sifuna, D.N. (2006). *Girls and Women's Education in Kenya.* Nairobi: UNESCO.
Collins, M., and Anderson, H. (2001). *Race, Class and Gender.* Wadsworth.
Conole, L. (1978). Process Observation. *Asia Pacific Journal of Human Resources*, 16(2), 11–17.
Consultative Group to Assist the Poor. (2003). *Annual Report 2003.* Washington, DC: Consultative Group to Assist the Poor.
Crenshaw, K. (1989). Demarginalizing the Intersection of Race and Sex: A Black Feminist Critique of Antidiscrimination Doctrine, Feminist Theory and Antiracist Politics. *University of Chicago Legal Forum*, 1989: 139–167.
Egbo, B. (2000). *Gender, Literacy and Life Chances in Sub-Saharan Africa.* Clevedon: Multilingual Matters.
Freire, P. (1970). *Pedagogy of the Oppressed.* New York: Continuum.
Freire, P. (1973). *Education for Critical Consciousness.* London: Sheed and Ward.
Freire, P. (1976). *Education: The Practice of Freedom.* London: Writers and Readers Cooperative.
Freire, P. (1985). *The Politics of Education: Culture, Power and Liberation.* New York: Bergin and Garvey.
Friedmann, J. (1992). *Empowerment: The Politics of an Alternative Development.* New York: John Wiley & Sons.
Gebre, A., Openjuru, G., Rogers, A., and Street, B. (2009). *Everyday Literacies in Africa: Ethnographic Studies of Literacy and Numeracy Practices in Ethiopia.* Addis Ababa: Fountain Publishers.
Hall, S. (1992). The West and the Rest: Discourse and Power. In S. Hall and B. Gieben (eds), *Formations of Modernity*, Cambridge: Polity Press, pp. 275–331.

130 Narratives of the village women

Haraway, D. (1991). *Simians, Cyborgs, and Women: The Reinvention of Nature*. New York: Routledge.

Hodgson, L.D. (1999). Pastoralism, Patriarchy and History: Changing Gender Relations among Maasai in Tanganyika, 1890–1940. *Journal of African History*, 40(1), 41–65.

Hodgson, L.D. (2011). *Gender and Culture at the Limit of Rights*. Studies in Human Rights Series. Philadelphia: University of Pennsylvania Press.

Huiskamp, G., and Hartmann-Mahmud, L. (2007). As Development Seeks to Empower: Women from Mexico and Niger Challenge Theoretical Categories. *Journal of Poverty*, 10(4), 1–26.

Kabeer, N. (1999). Resources, Agency, Achievements: Reflections on the Measurement of Women's Empowerment. *Development and Change*, 30(3), 435–464.

Kirkham, S., and Anderson, J. (2002). Postcolonial Nursing Scholarship: From Epistemology to Method. *Advances in Nursing Science*, 25(1), 1–17.

Knowles, M.S. (1973). *The Adult Learner: A Neglected Species*. Houston: Gulf Publishing Company.

LeVine, R.A., LeVine, S., Schnell-Anzola, B., Rowe, M., and Dexter, E. (2012). *Literacy and Mothering: How Women's Schooling Changes the Lives of the World's Children (Child Development in Cultural Context)*. New York: Oxford University Press.

Maddox, B. (2005). Assessing the Impact of Women's Literacies in Bangladesh: An Ethnographic Inquiry. *International Journal of Educational Development*, 25(2), 123–132.

Maslak, M.A. (ed.). (2008). *The Structure and Agency of Women's Education*. Albany: State University of New York Press.

Merriam, S.B., Caffarella, R.S., and Baumgartner, L.M. (2007). *Learning in Adulthood: A Comprehensive Guide* (3rd edn). San Francisco, CA: Jossey-Bass.

Mitzlaff, U.V. (1994). *Maasai Women: Life in a Patriarchal Society: Field Research among the Parakuyo, Tanzania*. C. Groethuysen and T. Dibdin (trans.). Dar es Salaam: Tanzania Publishing House.

Mohanty, C.T. (1991). Under Western Eyes: Feminist Scholarship and Colonial Discourses. In C.T.R. Mohanty, Ann Russo, and L. Torres (eds), *Third World Women and the Politics of Feminism*, Bloomington: Indiana University Press.

Mohanty, C.T. (2003). *Feminism without Borders: Decolonizing Theory, Practicing Solidarity*. Durham and London: Duke University Press.

Moser, C. (1993). *Gender Planning and Development: Theory, Practice and Training*. London: Routledge.

Narayan, U., and Harding, S. (1998). Introduction. Border Crossing: Multicultural and Postcolonial Feminist Challenges to Philosophy (Part 1). *Hypatia*, 13(2), 1–6.

Oyewumi, O. (2003). *African Women and Feminism: Reflecting on the Politics of Sisterhood*. Trenton, NJ: Africa World Press.

Papen, U. (2002). *TVs, Textbooks and Tour Guides: Uses and Meanings of Literacy in Namibia*, unpublished PhD thesis, King's College, London.

Phillips, R. (2015). How 'Empowerment' May Miss Its Mark: Gender Equality Policies and how They Are Understood in Women's NGOs. *Voluntas: International Journal of Voluntary and Nonprofit Organizations*, 26(4), 1122–1142.

Pradervand, P. (1989). *Listening to Africa: Developing Africa from the Grassroots*. New York: Praeger.

Puchner, L. (2003). Women and Literacy in Rural Mali: A Study of the Socio-Economic Impact of Participating in Literacy Programmes in Four Villages. *International Journal of Educational Development*, 23(4), 439–458.

Rao, N., and Robinson-Pant., A. (2006). Adult Education and Indigenous People: Addressing Gender in Policy and Practice. *International Journal of Educational Development*, 26(2), 209–223.

Robeyns, I. (2010). Gender and the Metric of Justice. In: H. Brighouse and I. Robeyns (eds), *Measuring Justice: Primary Goods and Capabilities*, Cambridge: Cambridge University Press, pp. 215–236.

Robinson-Pant, A. (2008). Why Literacy Matters: Exploring Policy Perspective on Literacies, Identities and Social Change. *Journal of Development Studies*, 44(6), 779–796.

Rogers, A. (2004). Looking Again at Non-Formal and Informal Education: Towards a New Paradigm. In *Encyclopedia of Informal Education*. www.infed.org/biblio/non_formal_paradigm.htm.

Saitoti, T.O., and Beckwith, C. (1988). *Maasai*. London: Elm Tree Books.

Sally, B. (2013). *Women's Collective Action*. Oxford: Oxfam.

Sen, G., and Östlin, P. (2011). Gender Inequality in Health. In WHO, *Improving Equity in Health by Addressing Social Determinants*, Geneva: WHO, pp. 59–87.

Smith, M.K. (2008). Informal Learning. In *Encyclopedia of Informal Education*. http://infed.org/mobi/informal-learning-theory-practice-and-experience, accessed 15 March 2016.

Spear, T., and Waller, R. (1993). *Being Maasai: Ethnicity and Identity in East Africa*. London: James Currey.

Spivak, G.C. (1985). Can the Subaltern Speak? Speculations on Widow Sacrifice. *Wedge*, 7/8(Winter/Spring), 120–130.

Spivak, G.C. (1988). Can the Subaltern Speak? In C. Nelson and L. Grossberg (eds), *Marxism and the Interpretation of Culture*, Basingstoke: Macmillan Education, pp. 271–313.

Spivak, G.C. (1999). *A Critique of Postcolonial Reason: Toward a History of the Vanishing Present*. Cambridge, MA: Harvard University Press.

Takayanagi, T. (2008). Indigenous Approach to Community Development in Kenya: Experiences of a Female School Teacher. *Journal of International Cooperation in Education*, 11(2), 161–172.

Tamale, S. (2006). African Feminism: How Should *We* Change? *Development*, 49, 38–41.

Trutko, J., O'Brien, C., Wandner, S., and Barnow, B. (2014). *Formative evaluation of job clubs operated by faith and community-based organizations: Findings from site visits and options for future evaluation* (Final report submitted to the Chief Evaluation Office, U.S. Department of Labor). Washington, DC: Capital Research Corporation, Inc. and George Washington University.

Udvardy, M.L. (1998). Theorizing Past and Present Women's Organizations in Kenya. *World Development*, 26(9), 1749–1761.

UNESCO. (2003). *Gender and Education for All: The Leap to Equality. EFA Global Monitoring Report 2003/4*. Paris: UNESCO.

UNESCO. (2005). *Literacy for Life. EFA Global Monitoring Report 2006*. Paris: UNESCO.

UNESCO. (2006). *Gender Inequalities in Kenya*. Nairobi: UNESCO.

UNESCO. (2014). *Education for All Global Monitoring Report 2013, Teaching and Learning: Achieving Quality for All*. Paris: UNESCO.

USAID. (2010). *Gender, Agriculture, and Climate Change: An Analysis for USAID/East Africa*. Washington, DC: USAID.

Voola, P.A. (2013). *Beyond the Economics of Gender Inequalities in Microfinance: Comparing Problem Representations in India and Australia*, unpublished PhD thesis, University of Sydney.

Wangui, E.E. (2003). *Links between Gendered Division of Labour and Land Uses in Kajiado District, Kenya.* LUCID Working Paper, No. 23. Nairobi: International Livestock Research Institute.

6 Interview analysis of women's group leaders and bureaucrats

Introduction

As established in the previous chapter, the village women of Narok face complex resource and reproductive demands to ensure well-being. Their voices reveal many strategies and forms of resistance that have emerged from self-organised informal learning and literacy. In contrast, this chapter explores more formal educational relationships with village life through the views of the women's group leaders and bureaucrats.

This chapter reports the views of women's group leaders and bureaucrats (government officers) derived from interviews about women's informal learning/literacy and community development. Through interviews with women's group leaders, the chapter examines gender issues that they have observed in the village and how, as leaders in the community, they have tried to motivate fellow women and possibly challenge men to bring about a social change.

This chapter also examines the notion of informal literacy/learning from the perspectives of the women's group leaders and bureaucrats, outlining what each of them undertakes to bring about positive changes in their community. The women's group leaders' voices highlighted the processes in which informal literacy learning strengthened knowledge production and critical awareness of fellow women. The data includes narratives of women's group leaders, all of whom held leadership positions at the time of the interviews. Bureaucrats' comments also reveal how they perceive and manage women's literacy and development programmes to induce improvement in the daily lives of the local women. The data was gathered from women's group leaders during their involvement in the women's group meetings and/or specifically arranged interviews.

In this chapter, first, I present the first level of data analysis through a presentation of women's group leaders' voices. Each participant's narrative is organised according to the following three categories:

1 Response to self-introduction, education background and work role
2 Response to women's group activities and a leadership role to play
3 Perceptions on the future of their community.

First, the chapter illustrates women's group leaders' involvement in women's groups, which enhanced gender status and the well-being of their community. Various types of women's group activities were evident. All of the women reported the importance of girls' education and women's literacy through cooperative learning and solidarity. Second, the chapter shows two government officials who were involved in literacy and gender development programmes and one literacy class instructor. As will be noted in this chapter, the interview data demonstrated that all of the bureaucrats adhered to the conventional meaning of literacy, which was the standard Western definition of the ability to read and write, a form of literacy that is seen to contribute to and improves one's income, health and the political process.

Narratives of women's group leaders

This section provides the space for listening to the voices of the women's group leaders' experiences in women's group activities and to hear of the role they played in their groups through a narrative form of what the women leaders revealed in interviews. Like Chapter 5, through the individual narrative of each woman, I hope that their voices depict their own distinct self and demonstrate their different qualities and experiences.

In the following section there is an introduction to each research participant, highlighting her background and the activities she conducts in a women's group. The first questions put to the participants were: How long have you been participating in a women's group? What activities are conducted in your women's group? What is your role in a women's group? It was also aimed at understanding the roles the women played in improving the well-being of their community. Lastly, women's views on the future of Narok County were also voiced in each narrative.

Each narrative was drawn from field notes, and had come via a local interpreter who spoke English, Swahili and Maa. Each woman was free to speak in a language they were comfortable with to express their opinion to the researcher. While school teachers spoke to the researcher in English, other women spoke to the researcher in Swahili and/or Maa. Again, any information that might have enabled identification of the research participants such as the specific school or office names or the location of the church has been strictly eliminated. Three major themes that emerged from the narratives of the village women are explored later in the chapter.

A postcolonial feminist perspective provides a lens to reveal how often invisible taken-for-granted processes structure life and educational opportunities and experiences. Also it allows recognition of women's social positioning in the social structure and how it might be a great disadvantage to their formal learning and their ability to manage community development and other related issues. A postcolonial feminist perspective shifts the analysis beyond such structures to illuminate the lived experience of each of the research participants. In some instances, cultural influences were viewed as

Narratives of women's leaders and bureaucrats 135

being helpful or unhelpful depending on the participants' group activities. The postcolonial perspective informed my exploration of how the village had been influenced by prior or recent colonial practices related to women's educational attainment.

Narrative 1: Joan's story

I am 48 years old and am a school teacher. All of my four children are educated. I participate in four women's groups. One of the groups is about TBA (Traditional Birth Attendance). I am a secretary and have been in the group for five years. Most members are illiterate. The group members were invited for a seminar by a local NGO at school and were trained for a week as TBA, assisting mothers' delivery. Some women in the villages are hesitant to go to the hospital, or some of their houses are very far from the hospital. Each member of the women's group is given a bottle of zinc, soap, threads, a cutting blade, gloves, and table size sheets during the seminar. I once attended a child-birth on a public bus. The group members made some red ribbons to raise awareness on HIV-AIDS and sent them to people in the USA. We were told to wait for the payment of the ribbons, but we have never received any payment. In another initiative, the group members were provided with sunflower seeds and beans to plant and harvest. For instance, with a 2 kg packet of beans, each member had a harvest of 4–6 kg of beans and returned the original beans of 2 kg to the organisation. However, I did not harvest any crops in 2011 due to a severe drought. The NGO also regularly organised seminars on cleanliness or health issues. There are 18 female members in the group. Members hold irregular meetings. I did not attend meetings for a while, yet I received updates of meetings from other members. I also joined another group for the promotion of girls' education and the eradication of FGM. I have been a member of the group for seven years and am a treasurer of the group. There are four male and 18 female members in the group. The group members visit schools to empower girls. We teach both boys and girls about harmful cultural practices such as FGM, early sexual activities, early pregnancy, and early marriages. The group also aims to create awareness of the effects of HIV-AIDS. The members also visit churches. I ask male members to discuss issues of girls' education and FGM with men in the community. The negative aspects of FGM and early marriages are explained to women to promote girls' education. When the group received funding from the National AIDS council, we travelled to the interior region to talk about HIV-AIDS. The group described the benefits of empowering women at churches and schools, showing female members as a role model for the impact of girls' education. The group has worked closely with an international NGO, World Vision, previously, yet the NGO has disappeared from the region. I am well known in the community for rescuing girls who had decided to run away from FGM. When a girl escapes from her own house to my place, I coordinate with other members to transfer the girl to the District Education Office or Children's Office for the girl's safety. I would dress the girl in boy's clothes and would travel with her to the district offices by bus in the very early morning so that no-one in the community would see them. I hope to develop a grant proposal to establish a post-secondary education programme for young people in the future. I expect that her fellow women in the community, especially those who are not educated, to change their attitude and to be self-reliant. I also hope that mothers can negotiate educational opportunities and early marriages with fathers, on behalf of their daughters. Moreover, I hope that fathers retain their daughters in school, and men do not marry off their daughters. I also hope that girls will be empowered to be able to say no to FGM, early sex and marriages. Girls can stand firm and run away to a teacher, a rescue centre, or the District Children's Office. I also expect that people are united and work together for a better future and I also note an improvement in women's empowerment and girls' education.

Narrative 2: Rose's story

I am 56 years old and a mother of six children. I am a school teacher. All of my children are educated. I participate in three women's groups and am a chairperson of one of the groups, which promotes girls' education. The group has been in existence since 2001and registered with the division of Social Services at the local District Office. With members, I have organised seminars at schools and churches to raise awareness of the issues of FGM and HIV-AIDS. Collaborating closely with Joan, I have also supported girls to escape from forced FGM practices that has resulted in them dropping out of school. By discussing and coordinating with the district offices, I assist Joan in moving rescued girls to the District Office safely. I focus on psychosocial support and empowerment of girls and women.

The second group is a women's self-help group aimed at improving the standard of living for women. I am the secretary of the group. The group has been in existence since 2009 and registered with the Division of Social Services at the local District Office. There are 33 women in the group. The group's major activities are planting trees in order to improve the environment, and also improve members' livelihood, and providing households with a system for storage of rainwater. The members plant 50,000 seeds in the forest to provide a nursery/young forest for local schools. Female members make bead ornaments and sell them in the market for income generation. I advise members to plant 25 fruit trees and another 25 ordinary trees at home.

The fruit trees are essential to improve the nutrition of families. People know the needs in their community best, hence, they can work together to improve education, the economy and their livelihoods. About colonisation. village people have a distinct culture and dignity, but are colonised because they are illiterate, outsiders came and the village people saw the outsiders as good, and they adopted everything from the outsiders. The outsiders left, and village people lost culture as a consequence. I hope and think economic empowerment is the only way for a woman to raise her status, as with this a woman begins to have a say. A woman sells vegetables at the market, buys food for her family, her husband notices that his wife contributes something for the home.

Narrative 3: Ruth's story

I am 47 years old and am a primary school teacher. I have a small grocery shop in the local market, and have hired a young man to assist me. I have been in a women's group for five years and I am the secretary of the group. The group aims at improving women's daily needs and economic situation. Women are updated with new information or technology constantly through the meetings. The group conducts a 'merry-go-around' microfinance activity (each member contributed a certain amount of money to be given to a member as members draw lots to decide the order of the receiving the merry-go-round money each time). Meeting twice a month, each member contributes a sum of 500 shillings for the 'merry-go-around' activity. On top of this money, each woman contributes 50 shillings for buying utensils for a member's house. One of the members in turn receives this money to purchase utensils for her house. In addition, 50 shillings is also collected from each member to save in case of an emergency experienced by a group member. When there is a death in a member's family, everyone contributes 200 shillings to organise a funeral. I expect that the women will become independent and learn not to depend on their husbands, or to beg from other people.

Narrative 4: Sara's story

I am around 55 years old. I have not gone to school. However, I have attended an adult literacy class for a few months. [At the time of the interview, Sara was engaged with building a new Maasai house for her family, whilst still carrying out all the household tasks.] I also look after the domestic animals. I make traditional Maasai ornaments to sell in the village. As some women do not know how to produce ornaments, they contract me to make special ornaments and accessories, especially for weddings.

I have been the chairperson of a local church committee for ten years. I organised a water project with a local NGO. The church women's group collected 2000 shillings from each woman for the project, and the NGO contributed some funds to the project. A water tank was distributed to every family in the church to harvest rainwater. When one of the female church members has a problem, or a woman gives birth, fellow women from the group fetch water and firewood for the woman. Fellow women purchase new clothes and utensils for newborn babies. Women of the church also contribute some money and milk for the mother. After services, women remain to discuss issues at church. Women actively participate in church activities. I actively encourage village women to attend church. There are two types of meetings at church that I organise: (1) meetings of senior women to act as role models for young women by teaching them about social rules, (2) meetings of young women to encourage them to love their husband and children, and to be hard working. People do not abuse other people and they become good people after attending church activities. I hope to have a peaceful community where all children are taken to school.

Narrative 5: Teresa's story

I am a pastor and farmer. I have never been to school. I have nine children. The first-born child completed secondary education, and I hope that the child will continue to higher education. I have a small business, making and selling Maasai ornaments in the market. I also go to Nairobi city to purchase animal fat, which I boil to produce oil at home, and sell by retail in the market. When I was young, my mother taught me how to make Maasai ornaments at home. It is a Maasai tradition for women to make ornaments. I also have a certificate in pastorship ministry. I went to pastorship lectures, which were conducted for two groups, one for those who were formally 'literate' and one for those who were formally 'illiterate'. 'Illiterates' were taught in their mother tongue. In my heart, I could hear, catch what was taught, and follow the Bible. A teacher explained about the Bible in lectures, and participants discussed it. I caught the contents of lectures, and remembered them. As a pastor, I oversee the church participants' behaviour, teaching the value of Christian life and working hard at home. I advise church members to build a toilet at home within hygiene and cleanliness education. I also encourage the women's group of the church to contribute 40 shillings every Friday to assist those who are less fortunate. I am keen for people to become more active in daily work. I am also concerned about the sustainability of my church, and I wish to educate church members to be able to play my role so that I can go to several other churches to supervise. I want God to empower women because they are very much behind in Narok. I feel that women should be at the front-line in the community, not lagging behind men. Adult education is beneficial for women, as I am able to write my name from attending adult education classes. However, at church, I rely on other church members to read and write.

I organise women's seminars on how to improve their houses, how to approach men and husbands, and advise about women's rights. I also coordinate a women's ministry whose members have become church pastors, and encourage them to teach fellow women in my community. Despite being a woman, people welcome me to church seminars and meetings because of my status as a pastor. I also teach men how to cooperate with women, and preach to men to encourage them to provide opportunities for women to manage various tasks in the community.

Analysis and discussions of the women's group leaders' narratives

This section focuses on the findings and discussion of what women's group leaders have experienced when implementing activities in an informal group.

Through a hand-coding process, responding to the interview questions, two major themes emerged from the women leaders' narratives; (1) Women's group activities and informal learning; (2) the women's perceptions towards the future.

Their narratives highlight that gender is a factor that has affected them in many ways and that collective action against gender inequality and poverty alleviation was essential. It also is apparent that the women respect differences within their group (Crenshaw 1989).

Key theme 1: Women's group activities and informal learning

Joan, Rose and Ruth obtained higher education (teacher training collage). Sara did not receive 'formal education', but had an experience in attending an adult literacy class for a few months. Teresa also did not go to 'formal school', yet she received a certificate in pastorship through oral lectures and memorization of the contents of the Bible. Joan, Rose and Ruth each had a formal job as a school teacher. Sara and Teresa were farmers and also had small businesses selling Maasai traditional ornaments. It can be said that the beadwork aimed to help the grassroots women generate income by selling it in the market or village. The women view their families as the ones who most ensure maintenance of hegemonic womanhood for Maasai and as the space where tradition and cultural rituals are taught and enforced.

Three out of five women reported that they participated in one group. Joan, however, participated in three women's groups, and Rose was affiliated with three different women's groups. While four women did not mention their groups' formal registration, Rose stated that two of her three women's groups were registered with the division of social services of the local district office. The size of membership ranged from 18 to 33 members. The groups were comprised of women and men. They schedule and conduct their own meetings. The activities of the groups led by the women reflect both an adherence to colonial legacies of education but also a process of decolonisation and emancipation of women and girls. Processes that can be seen as decolonising and emancipatory include informal microfinancing and the protection of young girls from traditional FGM.

The interviewed women often mentioned their distinct methods of microfinance activity, such as merry-go-round, and public health-related activities, including action related to TBA, HIV-AIDS, FGM and actions towards ensuring access to clean drinking water. While Joan mentioned TBA as the group's activity, other women described tree planting, small businesses, water supply and microfinancing as the purpose of the group activity.

Joan and Rose described their involvement in promotion of girls' education through a women's group, in which they coordinate and collaborate in rescuing village girls who are to be married off or are to be forced to undergo FGM. With their high level of motivation for the promotion of girls' education and women's empowerment, Joan and Rose had also been involved in outside school activities.

In Joan's second group for promoting girls' education and the abolishment of FGM, the group partnered with another NGO to facilitate more effective programmes. As funded FGM programmes by the outside NGO, World Vision, in Narok were withdrawn from the region, NGOs of developed countries try to control with their economic resources without proper consultation with grassroots groups (Hulme and Edwards 1997; Cordonier Segger and Khalfan 2004).

By cooperating with government and non-government organisations for girls' education, Joan played a role as a local resource person. Having a connection with government officers, Rose was an effective resource person who could convey women's needs to national development strategies (Mohanty 2003).

Health and women's issues have been the major concern for the women's groups as, in their male-dominant society, men make decisions on the practice of FGM and arrangements for marriage. Research demonstrates that mothers' access to public health information and understanding health guidelines have an effect on children's health (Nutbeam 2000; LeVine et al. 2012). Nutbeam (2000) and Levine et al. (2012) suggested that community-based health education is crucial for village people to overcome structural barriers to health. Carmen (1996) also noted that for a project to be effective, it had to be owned and controlled by group members. In this case, the members took control of the direction of their projects. Joan had opened a space for girls to raise their voices via the group and within its activities produced by the group (Spivak 1985). Joan was aware of the local communication mechanisms and hindrances imported by the local patriarchal system. Hence, she asked her male peers to discuss harmful cultural practices with fathers and senior male leaders. She attempted to work harmoniously with all the members of the community (Tamale 2006). Based on the context and who she was speaking with, she applied different communication channels. Applying different communication channels, Joan was able to convey her message to her community members.

Second, being a secretary of the TBA group, Joan had established a sense of togetherness within the group (Mohanty 2003). Joan also recognised the importance of cooperation and solidarity, and had formed an effective communication mechanism that was constantly updated with the outcomes of group meetings. Joan reported that her illiterate colleagues were comfortable in discussing and exchanging ideas with her. This implied that a space for women to express themselves had been created in the group, a place from which to speak and be heard. As highlighted by Batliwala (2002), grassroots groups often feel that they are dominated and used by their counterparts from developed countries. The story of Joan's group activity making red ribbons for American citizens illustrates Batliwala's point. Living in the postcolonial country, Kenya, it seems that women's group members did not examine the red ribbon project organised by Americans critically, which resulted in a failure of the project. This also highlights the power imbalance between the local women's group and the external group in America.

Third, Rose led two other women's groups aimed at improving socio-cultural opportunities through microfinance and environmental programmes. Rose exercised her capacity of human agency, so, as noted by Alsop *et al.* (2006) and Kabeer (2000), a woman like Rose manages a development programme based on her creative knowledge. In doing this, Rose analysed issues from both inside and outside community perspectives. Rose promoted the idea that income generating activities would develop women's capacity of self-reliance.

Rose also understood and identified the fundamental factors of poverty and lack of power of women in the community. Rose recognised the value of low-cost technologies, with which village women managed small-scale businesses with locally available resources such as beadwork (Schumacher 1973; Akube 2000). Rose was also aware of the significance of cooperation and solidarity that groups created for local women (Mohanty 2003; Oyewumi 2003). By learning and working together, women could conduct a sustainable development programme. Moreover, Rose acknowledged that local women could take the initiative to manage community development programmes based on their needs, rather than being imposed upon by outsiders' interventions. As Allen suggests (2008), a collective empowerment approach to running programmes had been adopted in the village context.

Furthermore, Rose had effectively opened a space for village women to speak out about their views on community issues. Rose's activity demonstrated how a space can be opened up in order for subaltern women to be heard (Spivak 1985). By learning and working together in a group, the women had developed confidence to manage income generating activities. This was one of the aspects of adult learning highlighted by Knowles (1973) and Freire (1976), where adults can learn based on their needs and develop self-empowerment in seeking solutions. While Rose acknowledged the positive side of Maasai culture of communalism and mutual cooperation, she was concerned about the negative influence of colonisation on Maasai culture.

Fourth, in the case of Ruth, through the village women's method of microfinance, the group had developed a high level of mutual trust to run a continuous microfinance activity. Ruth also explained about how the merry-go-round activity was managed, which was also practiced by grassroots village women in Chapter 5. As the women of Ruth's group spent the merry-go-round money on utensils, this indicates that women are managers of their house and spend money on their families rather than their personal interests. Ruth encouraged fellow women to be independent through the microfinance activity, and women identified the most urgent needs to spend money on (Consultative Group to Assist the Poor 2003). This small grassroots microcredit activity was managed and controlled by the local women and was observed effective and emancipating. The small microcredit programme empowered women to work collaboratively (Malhotra *et al.* 2002; Phillips 2015). In this instance, microfinance literacy had been acquired through informal learning. Orality was the dominant mode of exchange for new information and knowledge in the group (Knowles 1973). Meeting regularly, the women could discuss issues and gained access to new information. Women had their own space in the women's group meetings to find solutions to overcome problems based on their needs. Initiatives to improve the well-being of their families had been taken by the women. Women utilised local resources and knowledge to organise their activities, they did not have to rely on outside funding. The group produced a method of saving money for emergency cases and it has become meaningful for them (Goetz and Gupta 1996). As Ruth above highlighted, self-reliance among village women had been cultivated through cooperation and solidarity, which was in keeping with her collective empowerment approach (Nyerere 1974; Maathai 2004; Allen 2008) for prevention from poverty (Carmen 1996; Huiskamp and Hartmann-Mahmud 2007).

Fifth, Sara was well aware of the severe impact of droughts on village people, and exercised her capacity to manage the water tank project in cooperation with a local NGO. This counters conventional views that illiterate people have no capacity to organise and manage development projects, and must negotiate outside expert assistance to implement projects for them. In Sara's case, the project was organised by her and her colleagues. Carmen (1996) and Pradervand (1989) strongly highlight the point that village people are critical players in evaluating urgent needs and have a capacity to implement development projects by themselves. Sara's water tank project in collaboration with an NGO highlights an effective and cooperative partnership. Both the NGO and the church-based group contributed to distributing a water tank to each member of the church. This partnership between a local women's group and an NGO was more effective than the partnership as explained by Joan because it was needs-based and initiated by village women.

Sara facilitated collaborative informal learning among women to produce ideas to solve issues (Rogers 2004; Jeffs and Smith 1997, 2005, 2011). This implied that Sara recognised the importance of solidarity and togetherness among people. She placed importance on senior women's life experiences, which reinforced Knowles's (1973) views on processes of adult learning. In addition, Sara emphasised the perseverance of tradition and values to pass down to future generations (Omolewa 2007). Literacy that supports preservation of culture was discussed and promoted at the women's meetings. Sara recognised the importance of learning from experiences, and actively supported the building of spaces for women to exchange their opinions and ideas (Spivak 1985).

Sixth, Teresa recognised the importance of education and had attended a college to gain a degree in pastorship ministry by memorising the contents of the study programme. For her, illiteracy was a very small disadvantage that she could overcome in order to acquire new knowledge and the skills of pastorship through orality (Ong 1982; Foley and Michl 1999). The significance of orality was well recognised within religious higher education. This reflects Carmen's perspective on orality, which is that "literacy cannot fully replace the pre-existing oral order" (1996, p. 100). Teresa also facilitated women's cooperative learning and solidarity in establishing self-help activities. This process demonstrated that in cases when people have an urgent need, they will take the initiative to establish cooperative activities (Carmen 1996; Pradervand 1989; Freire 1976; Daniels 2003; Maathai 2004). Communality and mutual support are key for the women for poverty prevention. It can be interpreted as collective empowerment, into which Teresa led other women (Young 1997; Allen 2008). The process of power through informal literacy and learning was reflected within the women's group. Even though Teresa experienced interruptions from men in the community, she avoided conflict with men. Teresa accepted men's pride, a position echoed by Oyewumi's (2003) theories about creating a harmonious society. Teresa respects a positive aspect of Maasai culture such as traditional ornaments and craft making. Also, Teresa discussed women's issues or their situation with men at church and encouraged men to be more accommodating to women. She used a dialogue to convey her messages towards village people. Teresa was well aware of the Maasai's strong patriarchal system, which effectively meant that women's voices were often ignored by men. Hence, she approached both men and women with different communication methods and tried to engage both men and women to bring about social change together. Here, men and women of her church worked together in accordance with their gendered roles and responsibilities (Oyewumi 2001). Cornwall (2000) identified the issue of men's problem discourse, which shows men are always problematic in promotion of gender equality, and observed that there is not enough dialogue between men and women. Teresa's point echoes Cornwall's (2000) view that emphasised a dialogue and understanding of different roles played by men and women within the church. In addition, Teresa applied role modelling as a method of empowering village men within the church with the aim of countering women's subordinate position.

On a separate occasion grassroots women's groups led by Joan, Rose and Sara collaborated with local NGOs or District Offices to advocate for FGM abolishment, girls' education and water resource issues. In each situation, the collaboration supported members' views and respected their gender and social status within society, while it strengthened their networking and collaborative informal learning and empowerment.

Similar to those in Chapter 5, the activities of women's groups are directly structured by the immediate needs. Gender not only manifested as some part of women's groups agendas, but also arose as a social issue to tackle. This was particularly clear when the women discussed their traditional practice of FGM, girls' education and the heavy household tasks during and after pregnancy. Aspects of Maasai culture and patriarchy were visible in their narratives as they told stories of their group activities.

What was also significant was the autonomy that the women had attained. The leaders held that the women's collaborative informal learning and action towards social change had empowered them to make decisions about their lives. However, Rose and Ruth reported that economic independence from men was also powerful and could empower a woman.

It was observed that collective empowerment experienced by the women was supported by how the women shared their family and community issues among themselves and attempted to find solutions by themselves. This group activity encouraged community cohesion and cooperation among the participants. Again, collaborative informal learning appeared to be an effective strategy for promoting empowerment among the women,

The leaders, especially Joan, Rose and Teresa, observed that patriarchy and cultural stereotypes are negative factors and Rose and Ruth agreed with the women that a lack of financial resources would disempower women. The leaders criticised the harmful practice of FGM, early marriages and the low level of literacy. They argued that some elements of Maasai tradition forced the women to remain under patriarchal domination.

However, the information that the women acquired from the activities taught them to reduce or completely eliminate some of these hardships. Hence, the women's group leaders emphasised skills and knowledge that allowed the women to participate in decision-making processes.

The leaders seem to see themselves as active agents responsible for cultivating collective empowerment, mutual cooperation and cooperative learning with the grassroots women. They seem to overlook the active role that the women play in the process of empowerment.

Women's leaders' responses imply that the leaders show some form of power that the village women do not have. The power can be derived from education levels, formal employment, wisdom or age. Since the women's leaders already perceive empowerment as transference of power to the village women, it implies that they already possess power that enables them to empower the women. Thus, the leaders see themselves as having power-to empower the women (Allen 1998). In addition, as their empowerment seems to be corrective through working together for improving the standard of living, power-with also is observed in which each woman works together for her fulfilment and self-empowerment (Allen 1998). These narratives imply that if the women's leaders do not have power-to, they would not be able to empower the grassroots women.

The women's leaders felt that they had opened a space, given the opportunity and taken collective action to empower themselves by advocating the abandonment of FGM, and promoting economic independence, girls' education and gender equality. Therefore, it can be said that they acted as agents of positive social change.

The group members sought transformation and emancipation as women as well as in social class and status, but they did not take a hostile attitude to men, thus practicing an African womanism approach (Ogunyemi 1985). They pursued emancipation by building networks with some NGOs or sisterhood to accomplish better conditions. In an acknowledgement of their subjectivity, the women cooperated with each other, respecting their multiple positions in society. Their actions contributed to arguments for intersectionality and postcolonial theory to promote women's equality.

Collective social actions hold promise for real social transformation within the Narok in Kenya. From the perspective of the women's leaders, they had power through collective social actions, spoke their opinion in public and acted as women's leaders in their community. Because of the women's leaders' support and collaborative informal learning, other group members could view the community and themselves in it differently. Group members seemed to understand that they were strong in their collective voices working towards change.

Women's group members together with their leaders had already demonstrated their agency by taking action in seeking a better life. Informal learning and activities through women's groups strengthened their agency. Through conscientisation members become aware of the complex social, economic and political factors and took initiatives to solve community issues. All of the women learnt from and worked to enhance agency, autonomy and self-esteem, building on a sense of empowerment. The women taught and learned from each other.

The focus was not just on one's empowerment and agency, but on their families and community. The narratives highlighted the focus on communality. For example, it was critical for women to be able to make decisions and strategic life choices for improving their families' well-being.

A postcolonial feminist approach is useful in terms of analysing these findings about socially constructed gender power relations, where women are placed in a lower position than men within the household and Maasai community. This finding also highlighted the dynamic nature of power. A single individual can be both powerful and powerless in relation to different situations and relationships.

Key theme 2: Future

At the close of the interview, I asked participants for their views about the future. Joan and Sara showed a concern about education in Narok. Joan's concern about the youth in the community suggested she was concerned about the issue of high unemployment rates of the youth in the community. Joan had observed the fundamental issue of poverty, where people have no job to earn income. This concern had been discussed by Carmen and Sobrado (2000) in relation to the need for employment to develop literacy skills. Joan was able to anticipate future directions or educational issues for the young people in the community and attempted to establish a youth programme to assist their skills development. Sara stated that children need to be sent to school.

Rose, Ruth and Teresa mentioned women's empowerment and self-independence so that empowered women could raise a voice to change their subordinated status in the community. As a church leader, Teresa foresaw the sustainability of her church. She expressed a desire to train other church members to take over her responsibilities within the church community. This can be understood as sustainable development where, using her opportunity as a pastor, she attempted to open a space from which women could speak.

The impact of women's group activities on well-being

Women's leaders, such as chairperson, secretary and pastor, demonstrated the positive impact of group activities on the livelihood of the group participants' families and their community as follows:

> Many women have now changed from a traditional way of living to a modern one, for example, how to ensure a balanced diet after they have learned about it at a seminar. Most women are fighting for the rights of children. Some women go to the District Children's Office to say, "my husband is going to marry off my girl". Women also send their girls to school.
>
> (Joan)

> FGM, girls go into hiding from FGM. Some say no to FGM. It will take time. By the time a girl is in secondary school, she is empowered, she can

say no to even her father. Year 3 girls get circumcised, don't know their rights. Four girls from my school were circumcised. I took some children to the World Vision FGM seminar last year.

(Joan)

Although a mother's education is a crucial predictor of a child's nutritional status (Abuya *et al.* 2012; LeVine *et al.* 2012), Joan's comment implies that uneducated women are also concerned about their family's health. They seek health information and some women apply new knowledge about a healthier and more nutritious diet for their family. After attending seminars, some women learnt about obstacles to girls' education, which is the consequence of a mix of factors, FGM and early marriages. With knowledge gained from informal learning among women's group activities, instead of fighting against a husband, a woman can make an informed decision and take a strategic direction (Stromquist 2005). These strategies are evidence of women's resistance to patriarchy (Mohanty 2003). Whilst Joan knows that it takes time to abolish the harmful cultural practice of FGM, she is aware of the impact of education on girls' empowerment to deny unfair decisions made by adults that affect them. Education can empower girls to make a decision for themselves (Freire 1970).

> Women are able to carry out their business from home to become traders, buy and sell shukas, beads, able to buy more beads, make more ornaments and sell.
>
> (Rose)

> Women have an improved livelihood and improve their children's lives. Women have been informed through organisations. They can make decisions based on information, they learn ideas and share experiences. They help each other, people come together, and it is about sharing.
>
> (Rose)

> Yes, a lady can buy on her own things, furnish her own house. A lady is now waking up, being responsible, getting respect from a husband, being enlightened, personal hygiene is improved so that a husband cannot run away [men use women's hygiene as an excuse to run away].
>
> (Ruth)

Rose and Ruth highlighted women's development as self-reliance, aided by conducting income generation activities. Microfinance engagement in the cash economy has shown that women can improve children's livelihoods or have been through the process of economic independence to purchase necessary commodities. Female grassroots entrepreneurs seem to have lower education, less formal business training and little capital to conduct business (Hernandez *et al.* 2012).

However, by gaining knowledge from new information through informal learning and literacy, women can also analyse problems and make a decision by themselves. Women also work in solidarity, exchanging experiences and cooperating with each other.

> Women were not allowed to speak before, they are speaking their opinion at church now, and some men are listening to women, changing slowly.
>
> (Sara)

In terms of speaking up in front of men, Sara indicated a slow change could be observed in public places. Women appeared to be able to open up a small space to give their opinion at church. The progress of development of women's confidence and empowerment to be able to speak and voice their opinion is not a fast process, but it does demonstrate how gaining a voice that is heard and can bring about change within the space in which it is heard. Gaining confidence through speaking one's opinion echoes with Freire's view on literacy in which local people raise critical consciousness and start speaking their opinions (Freire 1970, 1973). If there is an "institutionally validated agency" (in this case, it is church), the subaltern could speak in a public space (Spivak 2012).

The concept of literacy from a women's group leaders' perspective

The notion of literacy was explored by asking women's group leaders' their opinion on literacy. While two research participants were a pastor and farmer, three research participants were school-teachers, and they described their experiences about dealing with formally 'literate' and 'illiterate' parents at school. Also, the implications of formal 'literacy' during elections were mentioned. The impact of literacy on economic development in the community was also noted. First, according to Joan:

> Literacy is the one thing pulling our district down, hindering many things in the district. Primary and secondary schools, most teachers are from other districts.
>
> (Joan)

> Literacy is to transform acquired/accumulated knowledge, experience to record (writing), leave the information with the next generation. It is about improving existing knowledge, skills. Basic writing/reading with skills is literacy, we don't want to be left behind.
>
> (Rose)

> Illiteracy amongst women is very high, we encourage them to go to adult classes, but women's time is tied up. Her own bank account, she can

sign, she is encouraged, she can keep confidentiality. Illiteracy is hindering development of women.

(Ruth)

Based on the views of the literate group leaders, illiteracy is an obstacle for progress within the district generally, as well as women's development. Studies show that there is a link between literacy and privacy; literate women can have some privacy of information by, for example, signing bank account-related documents by themselves (Zubair 2001, 2004; UNESCO 2006). Also the women's group leaders noted the outcome of schooling or literacy education in producing teachers within the District.

Joan and Rose indicated a clear difference in understanding of information between literate and illiterate individuals.

> Literate can be informed, can read news, can hear the radio, understand different languages.
>
> (Joan)

> Illiterate, you may interpret wrongly, they just take what was said, this is what a politician is doing, taking advantages of illiterates.
>
> (Joan)

> [For] Illiterate, no secret ballots. A shuka, a kilo of sugar, they get things, but elect the other person who gave three shukas. They elect according to clans, tribe.
>
> (Joan)

> There is a difference between literate and illiterates, literates grasp information easily, illiterates take time to understand, illiterates have to have secondary information (translated [information]).
>
> (Rose)

These comments by the research participants highlight the disadvantages faced by illiterate people in gaining access to information, and the assistance required in translation of primary information. An issue of transparency in the political election process was also raised by the women. Literate people are likely to vote and are concerned about democratic values (Carron *et al.* 1989; Hannum and Buchmann 2003). Illiterate people (often women) have to rely on a literate election officer to vote at a polling station. This reflects a power relationship between literate people and illiterate people. It appears that illiterate people select a politician depending on the politician's donations. Even though many electoral campaigns by different parties or tribes are organised in the district, illiterate people seem to be conservative or defer to tribalism in electing a candidate from their tribe. It seems that some illiterate village women have not raised their awareness of political issues (Freire 1970).

Furthermore, Rose commented on the importance of women's learning:

> Women can go into a trade/business, keep records, budget for their home. Women are managers of home, to be literate is important.

Women manage all of the household tasks at home, from raising children to other housework. Although men control most of the resources at home according to village women, women still manage resources to maintain their family. Even if a woman is illiterate, she can generate income by trading or organising a small-scale business to help her home budget.

> A poor person is an illiterate person. You cannot manage resources if you are not literate.
>
> (Joan)

Here, Joan indicates the interrelationship between the poor/poverty and literacy. Even though village women are not literate in a formal education setting, again, through the method of informal learning and literacy by cooperating and helping each other, the women could create knowledge to control local resources by themselves (Carmen 1996). Some illiterate women have become empowered with skills to solve problems (Rogers 2004; Allen 2008). This reflects Spivak's perspective on education, which is that "my desire is to produce problem solvers rather than solve problems" (2012, p. 135). People need to acquire methods and skills to apply to addressing particular issues rather than simply memorising the solutions. Informal literacy and learning is powerful for illiterate village women to solve issues specially faced by women.

Opinions about women's situation in the community and overcoming women's inequality

As part of the research inquiry, women's group leaders were approached by the researcher to ask their frank opinion on the way to bring about a change related to women's inequality. The women responded:

> Very very difficult, and very hard. Men never accept [women], even myself, they see me as a woman, you are a great woman leader, they say.
>
> (Ruth)

> Culture dictates women.
>
> (Rose)

> In the Maasai community, women cannot say their true opinions before husbands. They are beaten by husbands, women fear husbands so much. Girls are nothing. I have two boys, so I am safe, otherwise, brothers of my [late] husband come to take everything from me. Girls are the property

of men. We are governed by culture. Even it is there in the constitution, girls do not inherit anything.

(Paula)

Men don't listen to us, women must be under men.

(Naomi)

Although there is a sense of oppression within these views, there is also an implicit understanding of how patriarchy functions as gendered power. This in itself demonstrates the potential for collective resistance to that oppression.

Four women expressed their thoughts on improving the situation of gender inequality, in the following:

By women working hard to be seen their products, products will be seen by men, men see women can do something equal to men.

(Ruth)

I try to speak nicely, sweetly to Mzee to change his opinion, tomorrow I talk to Mzee again.

(Teresa)

If women want to refuse sex, humble themselves before husbands, talk to him in a polite language, because of this and this, I cannot do sex.

(Naomi)

Economic empowerment, this is the only way for a woman to raise their status, come to have a say. She sells vegetables at the market, buys food for her family, husband notices that wife carries something for home, a husband might say "do you need my help?"

(Rose)

Voices are political.... There is no voice, they have their own way to find solutions. Women cannot be involved in the decision-making process of selling animals, it is a husband's property, a wife looks after animals, and a husband sells.

(Rose)

Education is the only way to raise awareness and economic empowerment, she [a woman] is aware of issues around her.

(Rose)

Although gender power relations are evident in everyday lives, such as partnership with men, property ownership, socio-economic factors, social support networks, and reproductive and productive roles, these statement demonstrate some strategic resistance to that powers.

From an intersectionality perspective, women's everyday experiences of class, race and sexual orientation are mutually interlinked with each other (Crenshaw 1989). These interactions of oppression are complex and influence the well-being of the Maasai women in Narok. In social conditions of inequality, and particularly with poverty, obstacles can be created to induce social change.

For example, tangible outcomes from women's work may change men's perceptions towards women's capacity for managing and producing some resources (Tamale 2006). Ruth seems to recognise visible products are more effective for men to realise women's skills than just discussing and exchanging ideals on solutions for social change.

The women highlighted certain existing cultural characteristics and the reasons why women were afraid of discussing them with men. First, traditionally women are not allowed to confront men, and the polygamy system also interferes with women's discussions with men. For instance, some women tend to believe that their husbands will not approach them or he will go to another wife if a couple has an argument at home. However, some wives attempted to have a 'sweet-talk' with their husbands when there is an issue to discuss to have a wife's opinion heard by a husband. Again, women seem to acknowledge the male-dominant decision-making process and they pay a lot of attention to culture and expectations towards ideal wives (Chege and Sifuna 2006). Women would not set a discussion agenda on household matters on an equal basis within marriage; it seems that there is a very little dialogue between men and women. Moreover, women are concerned about men's pride and put extra efforts into keeping a harmonious community (Tamale 2006).

Rose confirmed that women in the village know their needs and issues. To overcome these issues as well as gender inequality, generating income through education and economic empowerment by women themselves is recognised as important. Rose also confirmed the male-dominant decision-making processes and instead of having an argument between a couple, Rose believed a woman could find her own way to overcome an issue and could show her capacity to her husband demonstrating that a woman can become self-employed. This reflects, once again, an African womanist response to culture (Ogunyemi 1985).

Although these comments have revealed that formal education could contribute to development of women's capacity in income generation and overcoming gender inequality in the community, the overall analysis of the women leaders' experience reflects a strong emphasis on the informal processes, networks and learning that are central to the groups.

Narratives of government and NGO officers

This section demonstrates three government related officers managing education, literacy and gender development projects. Sankale, an instructor of a government-owned literacy class, was a farmer and had received a monthly allowance from the Kenya Adult Learners Association (KALA). The two officers, Moses and John, had been employed by the Kenyan government to work at the District Office. While one male literacy instructor had completed secondary education, the other two officers had studied at higher education institutions. They supervised projects of girls' education, aimed at improving women's socio-economic status.

Three narratives of the government and NGO officers are examined below to explore their understanding of literacy and gender programmes organised by the government, and their relationship to a postcolonial framework. The impact of these programmes on people's well-being and women's emancipation is also discussed.

In the following section there is an introduction to each research participant, highlighting their background and the activities they conduct. The first questions put to the participants were: How long have you been working in your current position? What activities are conducted in your role? Lastly, they were asked for their views on the future of Narok County. The responses are indicated in each narrative, which were drawn from field notes. Each participant spoke with the researcher in English. Again, the confidentiality of each participant is respected. Three major themes that emerged from the narratives of the officers are explained later in the chapter.

Cultural influences were viewed as being positive and negative depending on the participants' views towards women's literacy and development. The postcolonial perspective informed my exploration of how the traditional Maasai factors had influenced women's educational attainment and well-being.

All three officers emphasised the promotion of collaborative learning. In addition, they all had the role of supervision in community development activities such as microfinance and small-scale businesses. While Sankale did not comment on his role in promoting women's empowerment in his literacy class, Moses and John had a clear gender target in their development programmes. Sankale and Moses mentioned the significance of solidarity and togetherness of people to work towards bringing about better life development programmes, yet John did not clearly support this aspect in the interview. Key themes emerged from these narratives are: (1) a responsible programme; (2) learning approach; and (3) future.

Narrative 1: Literacy centre instructor, Sankale's story

I am 34 years old, and have been teaching at a literacy centre for four years. I am a farmer, and also graze animals. I completed secondary education, yet due to financial issues, I could not pursue higher education. My approach is to write down the Swahili alphabet and words on a blackboard and explain the words to adult learners. I also elaborate the meaning of the words in Maa so that the participants can understand the meaning correctly. Income generating activities have also been organised by participants of the centre. The participants buy and sell potatoes, maize and clothes to make a small profit in the local market. The subject of a small-scale business is integrated into the literacy programme. How to establish and where to locate a small business, and how to identify a profitable commodity are topics discussed in the classroom. These learners should know all the fundamentals of a small-scale business in order to have a successful income generating activity. The literacy participants attract customers because of their business/trade communication in the market. Also, they sell clean products and talk to customers politely. In 2010, the literacy participants organised a group farming project. Each participant contributed 200 shillings to purchase seeds, to hire one acre and a tractor to dig furrows to sow seeds and eventually harvest. However, because of inadequate rains, this project was not successful. The project of traditional ornaments making was also planned, but has not been implemented. The participants organised a self-help group with a chairperson, treasurer and secretary, two women were appointed in the chairperson and treasurer positions. I became the secretary to record discussion minutes. They discussed establishing a small business or farming, and calculated the cost of seeds and hiring fees of a tractor. KALA provided the literacy participants with small financial support to manage a small business. I give an award to hard-working learners every December to motivate their learning. During harvesting seasons or local markets days, high absenteeism is observed. I hope all to be educated in Narok.

Narrative 2: Adult education programme officer, Moses's story

I am 50 year-old Maasai, having worked at an adult education office for almost 30 years. I believe that literacy programme participants acquire literacy and numeracy skills as well as income generating abilities through literacy programmes. Also the Maasai community should know the importance of education, and education can be achieved by establishing role models of educated women and girls. Government literacy centres have a class management committee with an instructor being an advisor or secretary. This also serves as a disciplinary committee to overview the organisation of learning resources. Although it is the government's responsibility to provide teaching and learning materials to literacy centres, due to the lack of finance, the government has not been able to fulfil the requirements. The government established the new adult continuing education policy in June 2010. Its curriculum is different from the on-going curriculum, and adult learners participate in the Kenya Certificate of Primary Education, for which students sit a national examination after completing an eight-year course of primary education. The subject of income generation activities is also part of the new literacy programme, organised by each literacy centre. They learn management of small-scale businesses to implement in their own house. When adult learners of literacy centres have completed the basic adult education programme of reading, writing and numeracy, they take a proficiency test equivalent to the Year 4 exam of primary education. When they pass the exam, they will participate in a post literacy programme that involves eight subjects including agriculture, applied science and technology, basic English for adults, business education, civic social ethics, environment and health, Swahili and mathematics. Eventually, after being awarded with the KCPE, adult learners can join either vocational institutions or non-formal secondary schools to achieve the Kenya Certificate of Secondary Education (KCSE). In 2010, there is one non-formal secondary school in Narok County, where adults can study the KCSE subjects at their convenience. It will take between two and three years for a leaner to reach the point of taking the KCSE examination. The school is located at a local church and has a classroom, an office and a computer room. Two teachers are paid for their full-time work. Three volunteer teachers also assist in teaching. Each learner pays 1000 shillings per month and the school spends the collected money on teachers' salaries and stationery. Thirty-two learners between the ages 20 and 49 years old are enrolled in the school. Twenty out of 32 learners are female. Some learners are class 8 leavers, some are married, some are business owners. [Later when the researcher visited the school, there were eight learners studying in the class.] The learners are motivated to study to obtain a KCSE certificate to assist in seeking employment.

Celebrating the international year of literacy in the County, a proficiency certificate for learners, trophies for best literacy centres and gifts for successful adult learners are offered. An excursion trip to visit the best literacy centre in the County is also arranged for the successful learners to sustain their motivation for learning. The impact of literacy on learners' everyday lives is that the adult learners work collaboratively to improve their standard of living and they send their children to school. Some learners have also changed a traditional Maasai house to an iron-sheet-roofed house.

Women are managers at home, hence they should be supported in various ways. Eighty per cent of the county's economy is produced by agriculture and women manage the farming. Therefore, women should be educated more about farming as well as conservation, environment and water issues. Moreover, women should be assisted in managing small-scale businesses. Women are also responsible for raising healthy children. The policy of the government is to provide basic needs to communities by 2030, with a high priority on women's and youth development programmes. I want to see literacy rates doubled specially women. We must educate mothers. We must go gradually, we shall eradicate poverty by literacy.

Narrative 3: Gender and social development officer, John's story

I have been working as a gender equality officer for three years. I believe that the functional literacy approach is the best way for adult learners to gain literacy skills and that the demonstration of new skills and technology to adult learners can be effective. In particular, the government implements a women's empowerment programme, which is the enterprise funds allocated for community-based women's groups. First, a women's group has to be registered with the Ministry of Gender and Social Services by paying a registration fee of 1000 shillings. A women's group obtains an annual renewable certificate from the Ministry. The government partners with NGOs that train women's groups in income generating activities. A grant of 2000 shillings to establish these activities is provided to registered women's groups. The government monitors implementation of projects of the women's groups. There is a gender affirmative policy, and a training programme to develop the management capacity of women's groups. Such women's development programmes result in women's empowerment and involvement of women in social development and improvement of their standard of living. However, the term 'gender' is over-emphasised. Gender aspects and assessments are everywhere. In my view, the term 'gender' is a manipulation rather than moving toward gender equality. To motivate programme participants, tokens of appreciation are awarded and a visit to observe model projects for women's groups is arranged. Sometimes, women make a visit to female politicians to see a successful outcome of girls' education.

One impact of the gender programmes is that women get involved in socio-economic development through small-scale businesses, acquiring ownership of livestock and land, which leads to an increase in girls' education. I assume that the average of marriage age for girls has been increased from the age of 12 to the age of 14, resulting in the relative reduction of early marriages (early marriages are still unacceptable in most society). It means girls retain a little more of their schooling. Cultural resistance to social changes needs to be overcome through community sensitisation to gender equality. Empowerment is a process, and it takes a long time to have cultural changes through sensitisation. Although gender equality has not been fully achieved, men punishing women at home or domestic violence has been decreased, compared with ten years before. I expect general empowerment of women will improve their life further.

Analysis and discussions of the government and NGO officers' narratives

This section focuses on the findings and discussion of what government and NGO officers have experienced when implementing activities of adult education and women's development programmes. Through a hand-coding process, responding to the interview questions, three major themes emerged from the government and NGO officers' narratives; (1) adult education activities; (2) activities to improve women's well-being; (3) the officers' perceptions towards the future. In a general sense, their narratives highlight the recognition that culture and tradition hinder girls' and women's education and that gender inequality affects women in various ways.

Key theme 1: Learning activities

The government and NGO officers demonstrated a strong view of the positive impact of literacy on one's well-being but could see that literacy skills are linked with one's everyday life. While Sankale and Moses emphasised formal literacy learning conducted at organised literacy centres, John recognised the importance of everyday literacy and practical learning.

The literacy centre instructor, Sankale, applied a conventional method of literacy teaching in the classes, in which an instructor writes and explains words on a blackboard, and learners repeat and copy the words in their notebook. Freire (1970, 1973) and Knowles (1973) emphasised the importance of practical learning; however, in his literacy centre, Sankale and adult learners were engaged in teacher-centred learning. This is one aspect of the 'banking concept of education', in which teachers are perceived to know everything, hence teachers transfer and deposit knowledge to students (Freire 1970). Also, it appeared that a socio-political dialogue about society and gender inequality was not part of class discussion. However, Sankale emphasised the importance of income generating activities within literacy learning, thus demonstrating the importance of the relationship between daily life and any form of learning.

Sankale received a monthly allowance of KSh3000 (about $33) from KALA. He sometimes continued teaching voluntarily when the allowance payment was delayed as the learners were from his community. Sankale demonstrated he understood that there was a significant impact from learning on women's socio-economic situation linked to gaining literacy. Some women were able to write their names, or sign documents. Some women had established small businesses.

Even though Moses indicated that he was confident about the new literacy programme aiming at a primary education certificate for adult learners, such a literacy curriculum, in which adult learners learn writing and reading skills through the teacher-centred way of classroom learning, had been rejected by Freire (1978). This is because "the banking type" of education, in which a teacher deposits/transforms knowledge into a learner, minimises learners' creative power and engagement in critical thinking (Freire 1970). A certificate-aimed alphabetical literacy is counter to Knowles' view of fundamental aspects of adults' needs-based learning (Knowles, 1973). Although the new curriculum included life skills, the development of the act of knowing, in which adults become critical about their culture and society and move towards positive action, is questionable. However, Moses acknowledged that the government's commitment to literacy was low. Hence, literacy centres were expected to manage leaning materials by themselves.

As a government officer, Moses was committed to the implementation and promotion of the certificate-based alphabetical literacy programme. Yet, Moses questioned adult education becoming "an act of depositing", in which learners receive and memorise the contents of the literacy course. In a sense, Moses agreed with Freire's adult education approach and he suggested that the banking approach to adult literacy would not encourage learners to consider and analyse reality critically (Freire 1970). Moses shares Freire's view that literacy and learning have a vital role to play to create knowledge by sharing experiences and cooperating among illiterate village women (Freire 1970, p. 257).

John placed an emphasis on practical learning and acquiring literacy skills through other activities, not conventional alphabetical literacy. Observation, demonstration and discussion aspects of adult learning were highlighted in his comments. John understood the process of adult learning as gaining new skills and knowledge (Knowls 1973; Freire 1976) and promoting collaborative learning between women's groups.

Key theme 2: Activities to improve women's well-being

Sankale, Moses and John emphasised the significance of small-scale businesses conducted by women through literacy centres and reported that acquiring literacy skills helps women become empowered to be self-reliant. Sankale played the role of a facilitator to create discussions on small-scale businesses as the literacy class participants were mostly women from his community. By conducting an income generating activity, the literacy class participants discussed a development programme, and planned and implemented the programme after a literacy class. The entire process of a programme was owned and controlled by the members of the class. This is consistent with the autonomous development approach recommended by Carmen (1996). Moreover, this is an example of Fals-Borda's assertion that local people in poor countries have a capacity to organise and to produce knowledge based on their socio-cultural settings (1987). The literacy participants appeared to have a high level of trust in Sankale because he respected learners' schedule and commitments at home.

Moses highlighted the importance of education, and the positive linkage between literacy and the improvement of the standard of living in Narok through income generating activities. This is the conventional course of functional literacy, the approach recommended by UNESCO a few decades ago (UNESCO-UNDP 1976).

Moses also indicated the importance of solidarity generated by literacy learners and its impact on their family or community's well-being. Instead of individual personal achievements, the greater focus is on collectivity (Mohanty 2003; Pradervand 1989). Women's capacity in managing households and a variety of tasks are acknowledged, such as productive and reproductive roles (FAO 2011; UNWOMEN 2013). While Moses recognised that literacy was more than just writing and reading and it could contribute to women's self-reliance and empowerment, he also acknowledged women's roles in national economic development. Moses appeared to have a controversial opinion about the impact of literacy on women's development and the new adult education policy.

While there was cultural resistance to gender equality at certain levels of life in the district, a positive change in girls' education had been observed. Hence, this could suggest the significance of continuous gender awareness raising programmes in Narok. Furthermore, empowerment was recognised as the process of improving women's situation and was induced by cultural changes in the context, albeit at a slow pace, because a sudden change would not bring results nor would outside interventions, as they might degrade people-centred empowerment programmes. Although John raised the issue of a slight reduction in the age of marriage of girls from 12 to 14 years old, it should be noted that Kenyan law states that the legal marriage age is 18 years old (National Council for Law Reporting 2008, p. 6). The government's involvement in the elimination of early marriages is necessary. Thus, John's conceptualisation of literacy was similar to Moser (1993) and Freire's (1976) concepts of empowerment, in which women became active participants in programmes that had to be seen as a continuous process of self-development. However, two other issues related to gender equality movements were raised: first the degree of affirmative action within policy documents and the implication that the term 'gender' is over-stressed; and second that the concept of gender itself is ambiguous, possibly confusing practitioners within women's development programmes. Confusion around the term of gender was raised by Verloo (2005), who suggested that the clear goal of gender equality in countries is often not stated in official documents, hence the term gender is not comprehended precisely. Because of this confused and ambiguous term of gender, implementation and securing of human rights for women in Africa has been an ongoing challenge (Scully 2011, p. 19). Socio-historical perspectives have been neglected in the law as well (Scully 2011). Spivak states: "Gender is not lived sexual difference. It is a sense of the collective social negotiation of sexual differences as the basis of action" (2012, p. 431). Men and women are meant to discuss social roles and activities of everyday life. Although the government contracts NGOs for training courses for local women, it is not apparent how much women's voices are reflected in the government's needs assessments and planning of the gender programmes. Although John had a positive view on reduced domestic violence, it is not a prevailing view from some organisations working against gendered violence (Smith et al. 2003; OMCT 2009; Amnesty International 2011; COVAW 2012). According to Maisha e.V., a non-governmental organisation, one out

160 *Narratives of women's leaders and bureaucrats*

of three women has experienced domestic violence compared with one out of ten men globally (*Capital News*, 5 October 2013). Domestic violence no doubt is just as serious in the Narok community, however the issue was not raised by most research participants in this study, therefore is outside of the scope of this discussion.

Key theme 3: Future

I finished my interviews by asking about views of the future. All of the interviewed men mentioned the expectation of educational attainment by local people, especially girls and women, as women's educational level is lower than men. Moses was keen to promote women's small-scale businesses so that women become economically empowered and self-independent. John recognised that women needed to be empowered but empowerment is a process and hence it will require time for women to be fully empowered. However, there was no clear sense of what a gender-equal future might be, reflecting a contrast to the much clearer views of the future indicated by the women's group leaders.

The concept of literacy from a government officer's perspective: how do they see 'literacy'?

As discussed in the previous chapter devoted to women's informal learning and literacy and empowerment, it is significant to explore the perceptions of government officers towards women's education and literacy in Narok County. Through the interviews, government officers described their perceptions of literacy and its impact on women's development.

> To know how to read and write, manage small businesses, literacy means knowing what you don't know.
>
> (Sankale)

> People to be knowledgeable, interpret government policies, they know their rights, without literacy, they cannot know their rights. Each one has his/her own role, these roles, we must act accordingly. To see literacy rates doubled specially in women, we must educate mothers, now women's literacy rate is 55 per cent, it must grow gradually, we shall eradicate poverty by literacy.
>
> (Moses)

> Literacy means how to read and write, we read to access information. Adult women are leaders of a family unit. In order to improve their family, they should be equipped with skills and knowledge to get empowerment, even nutrition and hygiene. They may train children properly. It is important to read instructions of medicine. They help their

families a lot. To change cultural practices like FGM after reading about FGM in a book. A family of an educated woman is different from an uneducated woman; an educated woman's family have a good standard of living. There are no early marriages in a literate family. Most of the children complete their education. Good guidance/counselling by a literate woman in a family. It will end male-domination. Through literacy, the millennium development goals will be met, empowering community; right decision-making will come through literacy.

(James)

Illiterate women, most of them just agree on decisions made by men. Women are to be married, and to raise up children. Women think they should follow decisions made by men. There is no resistance, and that is why there is no divorce.

(Simaloi)

On the one hand, literacy tends to be understood as the result of alphabet acquisition through literacy learning. On the other hand, the impact of literacy on people's standard of living such as self-empowerment and poverty alleviation was highlighted in their comments. Egbo (2000) researched the personal impact of literacy on women and she suggested it resulted in an increase in one's self-esteem to bring about a better life. This was mentioned by James and Simaloi regarding the impact of literacy on one's well-being. However, Maddox (2005) reports that some marginalised women can be reluctant to demonstrate acquired literacy skills due to culturally restricted gender roles. It implies that the level of one's self-confidence developed in the process of learning is more significant than only an application of alphabetical literacy skills. In this sense, illiterate village women in Narok, who have opened up a space with the help of women's group leaders, have improved a capacity to have their voices heard. Previous research on some women's contributions to community development highlights how some literate females' facilitative role in the Maasai women's group empowers illiterate women to plan activities for promotion of girls' education and the eradication of female genital mutilation (FGM) (Takayanagi 2011). Furthermore, there is capacity within a small community for some women to challenge their lack of participation by developing their own sense of agency and contributing to development from within (Takayanagi 2011). Outside development workers and researchers should also consider the capacity and power which illiterate people already have, and how they apply their informal literacy to improve their well-being. Besides, Fals-Borda (1987) asserts that local people in the Third World have a capacity to organise and to produce knowledge based on their socio-cultural settings and values to become critical learners who can enact social change. The voices of village women and women's group leaders affirmed Fals-Borda's (1987) and Takayanagi's (2014) point that illiterate village women do build self-reliance and confidence through informal literacy and learning facilitated by literate women's colleagues. In facilitating the voice of women, networks and cooperation have been built up to conduct more effective community development programmes.

In the case of Kenya, based on these accounts of literacy, accelerating the literacy rate is expected through a new literacy curriculum. Through reading, people are expected to comprehend their rights, which the government does not have to explain to adults continuously and verbally. It is also highly anticipated that improving girls' education results in their children's education in future and their family's health (Bown 1990; LeVine et al. 2012; Robinson-Pant 2008; UNESCO 2014). Assumptions have been made that educated women can be involved in decision-making processes. Simaloi's comment demonstrates that formally 'illiterate' mothers have less opportunity to participate in household decision-making processes, hence 'illiterate' mothers are generally obedient to men. Otherwise, this echoes Quisumbing's (2003) study conducted in Asia and Africa and Alemtsehay and Kerebih's (2014) research based in Ethiopia that showed that 'literate' women participate in the final decision within households. However, some village women demonstrated that they developed some form of managerial and financial literacy at home to manage their household.

Conclusion

This chapter has addressed several of the key research questions in this study through the opinions of women's group leaders and government officers: the notion of informal learning and empowerment; perceptions and activities related to informal literacy and learning; and women's activities impacting on the improvement of the status of women.

The chapter has demonstrated that 'subaltern' (Spivak 1985) women are building collective empowerment and solidarities as a means of achieving their aims. The chapter has also examined some of the foundational literature on literacy, development and gender and concluded that the theories put forward by scholars such as Freire (1970, 1973), Spivak (1985) and Carmen (1996) provide a conceptual framework to discuss the processes of self-development in the women's empowerment observed for this study.

Overall, the interviewed women's group leaders expressed the view that the low literacy levels hinder women's empowerment and development. Women's group leaders also commented that gender inequality is apparent in the decision-making process in various situations. However, they are also aware of power and knowledge that village women have, to improve the well-being of their community. In addition, they also confirmed that the issue of illiteracy could be overcome by informal learning in which the method of cooperative learning was applied to generate necessary skills. The data illustrated that the women's group leaders play a facilitative role in inducing informal learning/literacy, and they also attempt to improve women's low status in the community by providing knowledge and raising women's economic activities.

As regard to the negative cultural practices of early marriages and FGM, women's group leaders are keen on eliminating these practices and promoting education for girls. However, all of these activities have been conducted under the method of adult learning (Knowles 1973), in which adults learn based on their needs and experiences. The comments of the women's group leaders also confirmed that orality is a dominant form of passing on information among village women. Overall, village-based women's groups take initiatives and manage projects within their capacity and resources. This is the essential aspect of continued sustainable development and informal learning.

While women's leaders expressed the view that village women's informal learning are the appropriate ways of improving their well-being, government officers are convinced of resolution of gender inequality and promotion of women's empowerment in the community through mass literacy programmes. Again, in this case, the process and contents of the literacy programmes should be relevant to the local contexts. Making use of existing local networks is more effective and efficient to the implementation of the national literacy and development programmes. The new certificate-based literacy programmes seem to be inappropriate to their socio-cultural context where the adult learning method and orality are the dominant forms of learning. The traditionally accepted forms and practices of literacy learning were questioned. Women's group leaders and government officers frequently mentioned the positive impact of literacy on health in the village. Therefore, health promotion training targeting local facilitators such as women's leaders could be useful to disseminate health related information.

The next and final chapter will provide insight into women's voices on literacy and development and further discuss their process of learning and its effect on community development. It will also make suggestions/recommendations for people-driven literacy programmes in Kenya.

References

Abuya, A.B., Ciera, J., and Kimani-Murage, E. (2012). Effect of Mother's Education on Child's Nutritional Status in the Slums of Nairobi. *BioMedCentral Pediatrics*, 12, 80–89.

Akube, A. (2000). Appropriate Technology for Socioeconomic Development in Third World Countries. *The Journal of Technology Studies*, 26(1), 33–43.

Alemtsehay, M., and Kerebih, A. (2014). Household Decision Making Status of Women in Dabat District, North West Ethiopia, 2009 Gc. *Science Journal of Public Health*, 2(2), 111–118.

Allen, A. (1998). Rethinking Power. *Hypatia*, 13(1), 21–40.

Allen, A. (2008). Power and the Politics of Difference: Oppression, Empowerment and Transnational Justice. *Hypatia*, 23(3), 156–172.

Alsop, R., Bertelsen, M., and Holland, J. (2006). *Empowerment in Practice from Analysis to Implementation*. Washington, DC: World Bank.

Amnesty International. (2011). *Kenya. Briefing to the UN Committee on the Elimination of Discrimination against Women.* London: Amnesty International Publications.

Bartlett, L. (2008). Literacy's Verb: Exploring What Literacy Is and What Literacy Does. *International Journal of Educational Development*, 28(6), 737–753.

Barton, D., Hamilton, M., and Ivanic, R. (eds). (2000). *Situated Literacies: Reading and Writing in Context.* London: Routledge.

Batliwala, S. (2002). Grassroots Movements as Transnational Actors: Implications for Global Civil Society. *Voluntas: International Journal of Voluntary and Non-profit Organisations*, 13(4), 393–409.

Bhabha, H.K. (1994). *The Location of Culture.* London: Routledge.

Bown, L. (1990). *Preparing the Future: Women, Literacy and Development. Action Aid, Report No. 4.* London: Action Aid.

Capital News. (2013). NGO Decries High Rate of Gender Violence in Kenya. 5 October 2013.

Carmen, R. (1996). *Autonomous Development: Humanizing the Landscape. An Excursion into Radical Thinking and Practice.* London: Zed Books.

Carmen, R., and Sobrado, M. (2000). *A Future for the Excluded: Job Creation and Income Generation by the Poor: Clodomir Santos de Morais and the Organization Workshop.* London: Zed Books.

Carron, G., Mwiria, K., and Righa, G. (1989). *The Functioning and Effects of the Kenyan Literacy Programme.* Research Report 76. Paris: IIEP-UNESCO.

Chege, F.N., and Sifuna, D.N. (2006). *Girls and Women's Education in Kenya.* Nairobi: UNESCO.

Consultative Group to Assist the Poor. (2003). *Annual Report 2003.* Washington, DC: Consultative Group to Assist the Poor.

Cordonier Segger, M.C., and Khalfan, A. (2004). *Sustainable Development Law: Principles, Practices and Prospects.* Oxford: Oxford University Press.

Cornwall, A. (2000). Missing Men? Reflections on men, masculinities and gender in GAD. *IDS Bulletin*, 31(2), 18–27.

COVAW (Coalition on Violence Against Women). (2012). *Fired Up: 2012 Annual Report.* Nairobi: COVAW.

Crenshaw, K. (1989). Demarginalizing the Intersection of Race and Sex: A Black Feminist Critique of Antidiscrimination Doctrine, Feminist Theory and Antiracist Politics. *University of Chicago Legal Forum*, 1989: 139–167.

Daniels, D. (2003). Learning about Community Leadership: Fusing Methodology and Pedagogy to Learn about the Lives of Settlement Women. *Adult Education Quarterly*, 53(3), 189–206.

Egbo, B. (2000). *Gender, Literacy and Life Chances in Sub-Saharan Africa.* Clevedon: Multilingual Matters.

Fals-Borda, O. (1987). The Application of Participatory Action-Research in Latin America. *International Sociology*, 2(4), 329–347.

FAO (Food and Agriculture Organization of the United Nations). (2011). *The Role of Women in Agriculture. ESA Working Paper No. 11–02.* Rome: FAO.

Foley, D.K., and Michl, T.R. (1999). *Growth and Distribution.* Cambridge: Harvard University Press.

Freire, P. (1970). *Pedagogy of the Oppressed.* New York: Continuum.

Freire, P. (1973). *Education for Critical Consciousness.* London: Sheed and Ward.

Freire, P. (1976). *Education: The Practice of Freedom.* London: Writers and Readers Cooperative.

Gandhi, L. (1998). *Postcolonial Theory: A Critical Introduction*. New York: Columbia University Press.
Goetz, A.M., and Gupta, S.R. (1996). Who Takes the Credit? Gender, Power, and Control over Loan Use in Rural Credit Programmes in Bangladesh. *World Development*, 24(1), 45–63.
Government of the Republic of Kenya. (2007). *Kenya Vision 2030: A Globally Competitive and Prosperous Kenya*. Nairobi: Government of the Republic of Kenya.
Hannum, E. and Buchman, C. (2003). *The Consequences of Global Educational Expansion*. Cambridge, Mass.: American Academy ofArts and Sciences.
Hernandez, L., Nunn, N., and Warnecke, T. (2012). Female Entrepreneurship in China: Opportunity- or Necessity-Based? *International Journal of Entrepreneurship and Small Business*, 15(4): 411–434.
Hodgson, L.D. (2001). *Once Intrepid Warriors: Gender, Ethnicity, and the Cultural Politics of Maasai Development*. Bloomington: Indiana University Press.
Huiskamp, G., and Hartmann-Mahmud, L. (2007). As Development Seeks to Empower: Women from Mexico and Niger Challenge Theoretical Categories. *Journal of Poverty*, 10(4), 1–26.
Hulme, D., and Edwards, M. (1997). *Donors and States: Too Close for Comfort*. New York: St Martin's Press.
Jeffs, T., and Smith, M.K. (1997, 2005, 2011). What is Informal Education? In *Encyclopedia of Informal Education*. http://infed.org/mobi/what-is-informal-education, accessed 12 May 2016.
Kabeer, N. (2000). Social Exclusion, Poverty and Discrimination: Towards an Analytical Framework. *IDS Bulletin*, 31(4), 83–97.
Knowles, M.S. (1973). *The Adult Learner: A Neglected Species*. Houston: Gulf Publishing Company.
LeVine, R.A., LeVine, S., Schnell-Anzola, B., Rowe, M., and Dexter, E. (2012). *Literacy and Mothering: How Women's Schooling Changes the Lives of the World's Children (Child Development in Cultural Context)*. New York: Oxford University Press.
Maathai, W. (2004). *Nobel Lecture*, Oslo, 10 December 2004. www.nobelprize.org/nobel_prizes/peace/laureates/2004/maathai-lecture-text.html.
Maddox, B. (2005). Assessing the Impact of Women's Literacies in Bangladesh: An Ethnographic Inquiry. *International Journal of Educational Development*, 25(2), 123–132.
Malhotra, A., Sidney, R.S., and Carol, B. (2002). *Measuring Women's Empowerment as a Variable in International Development*. International Centre for Research on Women and the Gender and Development Group of the World Bank, Washington, DC: World Bank.
Mohanty, C.T. (1984). Under Western Eyes. *Boundary 2*, 12(3), 338–358.
Mohanty, C.T. (2003). *Feminism without Borders: Decolonizing Theory. Practicing Solidarity*. Durham and London: Duke University Press.
Moser, C. (1993). *Gender Planning and Development: Theory, Practice and Training*. London: Routledge.
Narayan, U., and Harding, S. (1998). Introduction. Border Crossing: Multicultural and Postcolonial Feminist Challenges to Philosophy (Part1). *Hypatia*, 13(2), 1–6.
National Council for Law Reporting. (2008). *Laws of Kenya. The Marriage Act. CHAPTER 150*. Nairobi: National Council for Law Reporting.
Nutbeam, D. (2000). Health Literacy as a Public Health Goal: A Challenge for Contemporary Health Education and Communication Strategies into the 21st Century. *Health Promotion International*, 15, 259–267.

Nyerere, J. (1974). *Freedom and Development, Uhuru Na Maendeleo*. Dar es Salaam: Oxford University Press.

Ogunyemi, C.O. (1985). Womanism: The Dynamics of the Contemporary Black Female Novel in English. *Signs*, 11(1), 63–80.

Omolewa, M. (2007). Traditional African Modes of Education: Their Relevance in the Modern World. *International Review of Education*, 53(5/6), 593–612.

Ong, W.J. (1982). *Orality and Literacy: The Technologizing of the Word*. London: Routledge.

Organisation Mondiale Contre la Torture (OMCT; World Organisation Against Torture). (2009). *Situation of Violence against Women and Children in Kenya: Implementation of the UN Convention against Torture and Other Cruel, Inhuman or Degrading Treatment or Punishment*. Alternative Report to the UN Committee against Torture. Geneva: OMCT.

Oyewumi, O. (2001). Ties that (Un)Bind: Feminism, Sisterhood and Other Foreign Relations. *A Journal of Culture and African Women Studies*, 1(1), 1–18.

Oyewumi, O. (2003). *African Women and Feminism: Reflecting on the Politics of Sisterhood*. Trenton, NJ: Africa World Press.

Phillips, R. (2015). How 'Empowerment' May Miss Its Mark: Gender Equality Policies and how They Are Understood in Women's NGOs. *Voluntas: International Journal of Voluntary and Nonprofit Organizations*, 26(4), 1122–1142.

Pradervand, P. (1989). *Listening to Africa: Developing Africa from the Grassroots*. New York: Praeger.

Quisumbing, A.R. (2003). *Household Decisions, Gender, and Development: A Synthesis of Recent Research*. Washington, DC: International Food Policy Research Institute.

Robinson-Pant, A. (2008). Why Literacy Matters: Exploring Policy Perspective on Literacies, Identities and Social Change. *Journal of Development Studies*, 44(6), 779–796.

Rogers, A. (2004). Looking Again at Non-Formal and Informal Education: Towards a New Paradigm. In *Encyclopedia of Informal Education*. www.infed.org/biblio/non_formal_paradigm.htm.

Said, E. (1978). *Orientalism*. London: Routledge & Kegan Paul.

Said, E. (1989). Representing the Colonized: Anthropology's Interlocutors. *Critical Inquiry*, 15(2), 205–225.

Schumacher, E.F. (1973). *Small is Beautiful: Economics as if People Mattered*. New York: Harper & Row.

Scully, P. (2011). Gender, History, and Human Rights. In D. Hodgson (ed.), *Gender and Culture at the Limit of Rights*, Philadelphia: University of Pennsylvania Press, pp. 17–31.

Smith, C.L., Ramakrishnan, U., Ndiaye, A., Haddad, L., and Martorell, R. (2003). *The Importance of Women's Status for Child Nutrition in Developing Countries*. Washington, DC: International Food Research Institute.

Spivak, G.C. (1985). Can the Subaltern Speak? Speculations on Widow Sacrifice. *Wedge*, 7/8(Winter/Spring), 120–130.

Spivak, G.C. (1988). Can the Subaltern Speak? In C. Nelson and L. Grossberg (eds), *Marxism and the Interpretation of Culture*, Basingstoke: Macmillan Education, pp. 271–313.

Spivak, C.G. (2012). *An Aesthetic Education in the Era of Globalization*. Cambridge: Harvard University Press.

Stromquist, N. (2002). *Education in a Globalized World: The Connectivity of Economic Power, Technology, and Knowledge*. New York: Rowman & Littlefield.

Stromquist, N. (2005). *The Political Benefits of Adult Literacy*. Paris: UNESCO.
Takayanagi, T. (2011). More Than a Teacher: Community Work of a Female Maasai Teacher in Kenya Analysed Through Postcolonial Theory. In: M. Campbell, C. Michelle, and R. Simon-Kumar (eds). *Connecting Women, Respecting Differences: Proceedings of the Women's Studies Association of New Zealand Conference, 19–21 November 2010*, Hamilton, New Zealand, pp. 55–63.
Takayanagi, T. (2014). The Complexity of Literacy in Kenya: Narrative Analysis of Maasai Women's Experiences. *Compare: A Journal of Comparative and International Education*, 44(5), 826–844.
Tamale, S. (2006). African Feminism: How Should *We* Change? *Development*, 49, 38–41.
UNESCO. (2003). *Education for All: Is the World on Track? EFA Global Monitoring Report 2002*. Paris: UNESCO.
UNESCO. (2003). *Gender and Education for All: The Leap to Equality. EFA Global Monitoring Report 2003/4*. Paris: UNESCO.
UNESCO. (2006). *Gender Inequalities in Kenya*. Nairobi: UNESCO.
UNESCO. (2014). *Education for All. Global Monitoring Report 2013, Teaching and Learning: Achieving Quality for All*. Paris: UNESCO.
UNESCO-UNDP. (1976). *The Experimental World Literacy Programme: Critical Evaluation*. Joint UNESCO-UNDP Report. Paris: UNESCO.
UNWOMEN. (2013). *A Transformative Stand-Alone Goal on Achieving Gender Equality, Women's Rights and Women's Empowerment: Imperatives and Key Components*. New York: UNWOMEN.
Verloo, M. (2005). Displacement and Empowerment: Reflections on the Concept and Practice of the Council of Europe Approach to Gender Mainstreaming and Gender Equality. *Social Politics*, 12(3), 344–365.
Young, I.M. (1997). Unruly Categories: A Critique of Nancy Fraser's Dual Systems Theory. *New Left Review*, 222, 147–160.
Young, R.J.C. (2001). *Postcolonialism: An Historical Introduction*. Oxford: Wiley-Blackwell.
Zubair, S. (2001). Literacies, Gender and Power in Rural Pakistan. In B. Street (eds), *Literacy and Development: Ethnographic Perspectives*, London: Routledge, pp. 188–204.
Zubair, S. (2004). Qualitative Methods in Researching Women's Literacy: A Case Study. In A. Robinson-Pant (ed.), *Women, Literacy and Development: Alternative Perspectives*, London: Routledge.

7 Conclusion

Introduction

The purpose of this study was to explore the notion of informal learning/literacy in the context of international development from the perspectives of village women in Narok County in Kenya and to examine how the village women developed strategies to resist traditional patriarchy for improving their well-being. As an applied study, the aim is that the accumulation of such knowledge will be made available and contribute to future strategic responses to women's roles and self-determined needs where women live in specific, culturally distinct subaltern spaces within poor countries.

Analyses and interpretations of the research findings have led to conclusions outlined in this chapter. Through a careful examination and reflection of the findings, recommendations for educators, international development practitioners and researchers who are interested in culturally relevant feminist literature are made, and finally implications for further research are suggested. The discussion that follows is grounded in conceptual and theoretical literature that analyses and reflects on culturally relevant literature and informal learning and literacy in the context of development.

In conjunction with theoretical aspects of informal learning/literacy and development, key ideas of *conscientisation* promoted by Freire (1970) and women's collective empowerment by Young (1997) and Allen (2008) were highlighted as possible practical and sustainable approaches in this context. Dialogic reflection and cooperative and informal learning were facilitated by women's group leaders in exploring alternative approaches to development and new perspectives literacy. Clearly, informal learning and literacy applied by the village women was a powerful tool for sharing and creating knowledge.

This research has demonstrated that the complexities and scope of literacy and development require village-centred organisations to manage in order to combat social issues and protect and improve well-being of village people. The research has revealed that adult education and development programmes are significantly effective when implemented in cooperative learning through women's solidarity. It has also shown the need for African feminist thinking for supporting harmonious societies in strategies to overcome gender inequality in Kenya.

This final chapter presents the key contributions that this research may make to the literature that brings together postcolonial feminist theory and women's literacy and development. The chapter summarises major findings from the research, including the contribution of women's voices about their informal learning and literacy, and in improving their well-being. The chapter concludes with a discussion of the implications of these findings and offers suggestions/recommendations for more effective people-centred sustainable literacy and development programmes to Kenya. It then identifies the avenues for future research on women's literacy and development in Kenya.

Postcolonial feminist analysis: the significance of women's voices

To ensure a compatible lens for this research, postcolonial feminist theory was the key theoretical framework for informing the study. It was utilised as a framework and a methodology to ensure that women research participants' voices were highly valued and clearly heard. This allowed an analysis of the relationship between the Maasai village women and nation, and their self-defined identities and the complexities of their gender in Maasai culture. Postcolonial feminist theory has also provided an opportunity to examine how grassroots women's informal networks function effectively to prevent and address poverty, in a space created by the women's groups. Through an examination of the voices, insights and experiences of village women, women's leaders and bureaucrats in informal learning/literacy, this research has built new knowledge about the definition of literacy and development with a consideration of culture and values. Evidence for this was revealed through processes that can be seen as the personal growth of the women's sense of agency and capacities to bring about a positive change through the process of empowerment, and the development of wider critical thinking for raising awareness on important social issues in Kenya.

Supporting prior scholarship, this study found that postcolonial feminist theory is a significant framework for having people's voices heard (Said 1978; Bhabha 1994; Spivak 1985). The significance of postcolonial feminist theory's application to this study was described in detail in Chapter 1. Said's theorisation of Orientalism (1978) illuminated the colonial relationships between the West and East and how Europe had constructed images of non-Western (Oriental) countries. He also criticised how the West maintains power over the 'Orient'. Following Said, Spivak (1988) argued that subaltern, subordinate and oppressed people, especially women, have been silenced by dominant groups, hence subalterns should be supported to establish a space to raise their voices and be heard. Spivak (1985) also noted that postcolonial cultural struggles observed in colonised states, and cultures, have been consistently marginalised by colonisers. Bhabha (1994) explains that postcoloniality is a constant cultural movement between coloniser and colonised, and moreover, colonised states experienced a greater cultural influence from colonisers. He argued that consequently there is no genuine homogeneous culture but rather a state of 'cultural hybridity', thus transforming or hybridising cultures (Bhabha 1994). Concerned about absence of the speech of feminist views in postcolonial theory, Spivak contributed significantly to postcolonial feminist theory by focusing on subaltern women's voices, especially women in poor countries. The categorisation of all women from poor countries is, however, of concern as Gandhi points out:

> representation of the average third world woman as ignorant, poor, uneducated, tradition-bound, domesticated, family-oriented, victimized, facilitates and privileges the self-representation of Western women as educated, modern, as having control over their own bodies and sexualities, and the freedom to make their own decisions.
>
> (1998, p. 86)

Supporting this view, Mohanty (1984) suggested that we should understand different experiences in struggles against subordination and domination among women of colour. From the previous discussion on African womanism, as was suggested by Ogunyemi (1985) and Tamale (2006), African womanism stresses that African women should seek to create a harmonious society, accommodating men's self-pride and the root of African womanism is found in the ideology of communal community rather than the individual (Tamale 2006; Wane 2008).

Showing a similar feminist standpoint, narratives of village women, women leaders and government officials in Narok County, Kenya, were analysed in Chapters 5 and 6. This was a unique study that set out to listen to village women's experiences on literacy and its impact on their well-being in Narok. The women who participated in the study expressed interest in informal conversations about their learning and everyday life with the researcher. Almost all of them invited the researcher to their house for tea, and appeared excited about speaking of their opinions to the researcher. This research has demonstrated that despite obstacles for women to raising their voices in public, the research participants themselves provided an opportunity for the village women to speak about their lives and experiences on learning, thus opening up a space that contributed to building knowledge about informal learning and literacy, and its impact on their well-being.

Literacy and development experts provided village people with technical and material resources, expertise on microfinance, small-scale businesses, gender issues and health. Village women were able to share certain resources and knowledge with their fellow women in order to sustain their community development activities. This research has demonstrated that a power imbalance lay in the decision-making processes between men and women.

However, village women have managed to position themselves to continuously improve their families' well-being.

Representing the local people's point of view, one of the women leaders, Rose, commented that "Voices are political …". Her statement reflected the position that it is difficult for women to have access to decision-making bodies and ensure their needs and opinions are taken into account. A government-related officer, Duncan, commented that "sensitization meetings for women and men for the rights of children and women" are required. He also stated:

> Leaders are born, never made. Women are also born leaders. Women are corruption free, are seen to be loyal to a job and employers. Women are peaceful. It is time to listen to women, listening is part of tackling a problem…. Men delegate to women and men taste women's capacity.

Here, it is recognised that listening to women's opinion is one of the fundamental strategies to create a gender equal society.

The interview results also demonstrated how women made an effort in order to undertake community work for oppressed girls and women within their network and cooperation. Nyerere (1968) suggested that Africans were manipulated to believe that indigenous knowledge and values and the existing traditional organisational structure were inferior to imperial countries. However, by utilising the existing traditional sense of communality and togetherness, people took initiatives to improve girls' and women's well-being. Education barriers, lower socio-economic status, cultural influence and inadequate social support seem simultaneously to cause many women in the village to be more vulnerable.

Gender influence is particularly relevant in the research of women of the Maasai because of policies that may create partiality against women, and the cultural conflict of gendered roles and expectations (Hodgson 2001) that influences the women's learning and community development activities to maintain their families' well-being.

As Maasai women, women leaders well understood which communication channels worked effectively, and how information and knowledge were passed down through the community. For instance, they did not challenge elders or parents to stop the practice of FGM or early marriages immediately. Rather, they took time to explain the negative effects on parents and the advantages for girls' education/learning to her family. While this study provided women an opportunity to speak about their actual views on development, the data also demonstrated that they had created a space for girls to have their voices heard. By liberating and decolonising their minds, women leaders enabled access to marginalized girls' opinions. As a Maasai female, a woman leader played the different roles of mediator, facilitator, counsellor and mentor to different audiences: girls, their parents and assistance agencies.

Postcolonial feminist theory and informal learning and literacy in the context of international development

Chapter 2 of this book explained that little evidence of prior documentation of the viewpoints of women in strong traditional Maasai communities in Kenya exists. Therefore, the study of informal learning/literacy and women's empowerment through a postcolonial feminist framework in Kenya has contributed to knowledge of informal learning and literacy from both theoretical and practical perspectives. How informal learning and literacy work to empower women is not well understood in the context of the Maasai in Kenya and this study has shown that women's voices on learning experiences could become a resource for more effective approaches to development and other poverty prevention measures. The findings of this study contribute to knowledge about literacy from the perspective of informal learning and this is particularly important for women in the poor world as most development theory and strategies assert only formal education processes as a means of attaining literacy and therefore economic power.

The recognition of women's empowerment processes has added to current scholarship by exploring women's informal learning and literacy mechanisms and its impact on the general well-being of village ethnographic communities. Through presenting data that articulates the lived experiences of the village women, this research also highlights the gap between national development strategies that tend to be entirely focused on formal education and the local implementation of people-centred autonomous development strategies and programmes.

Following on from the discussion of the theoretical background to informal learning and literacy in Chapter 2, it is concluded that the general failure of a functional literacy approach appears to be due to a clear top-down model, including, in particular, pre-packaged and pre-printed primers, which do not take into account people's ability to take their own initiative in learning processes. Poor village people tend to lack money, food and resources; however, according to the Italian dictum 'Prima mangiare', poor people first need to eat before they can see benefits in learning literacy (Carmen and Sobrado 2000). In contexts such as the Maasai villages in Narok, literacy teachers and organisers tend to be obsessed and sometimes blinded by the alphabet and letters, and fail to acknowledge that those who are learning to read and write are engaged in a daily struggle for food security. Carmen and Sobrado (2000) emphasises that the first priority should not be letters but food and sustainable standards of living. This perspective is borne out in this study, where the village women have developed literacy strategies primarily driven by the need to ensure basics such as food security but also capacity to improve their whole family's standard of living.

Some scholars have also examined how literacy is practised in different contexts of work, educational and religious institutions, houses, everyday life and what literacy means in these settings (Barton *et al.* 2000; Bartlett 2008).

In the case of the Narok research participants, the learning experiences of the women in the Maasai land are complex and the process of literacy learning is often achieved based on their needs and at their self-determined pace. The data presented in Chapter 5 demonstrated how formally uneducated village women can become change agents through the process of empowerment and autonomously find solutions to community problems by informal learning/literacy that occurs in their collective efforts to form groups and support each other.

Discussion and implications of the findings

As stated above, this study aimed to explore, from a postcolonial feminist perspective, the role of informal learning and literacy as a key means for village women to prevent and move out of poverty. It found that a key process was how the women facilitated becoming change agents and empowered in their community through mutual support and critical consciousness building. The book has examined primary links between informal learning/literacy, human development and gender inequality in the Narok District in Kenya via local women's and wider institutional perspectives. This study also explored how power structures played out in decision-making processes in Narok, particularly in relation to gender, given the highly patriarchal traditions of Maasai society. The six-month fieldwork research was carried out through an ethnographic approach of process observation and the use of qualitative narrative interviews. The key research questions that drove this research are addressed in the following sections.

Collectively the interviewed women were aware of the many challenges, including gender inequality, they faced in their everyday lives. These challenges were identified as being deeply rooted in the larger context of colonisation. Despite the challenges the women faced, through women's group activities, the richness of their Maasai culture was also recognised (for example, producing traditional ornaments). By reclaiming their indigenous knowledge, traditions and values, the women seem to show their resistance to the effects of colonisation.

Women's informal learning/literacy and its impact on improving their well-being

This study demonstrated that the village women have developed strategies that resulted in resisting gender inequality and the creation of cooperatives to help each other's life improvement. It was observable that the women could raise their opinion and discuss issues in the community-based women's groups, within the community spaces in churches and in literacy centres. The spaces where women raised their voices to be heard were created in cooperation with external agents such as the church, government programmes and community-based organisations. The women took advantage of these spaces to communicate and learn from each other. Some women created a space to exchange their opinions through their community-based women's informal groups. It was evident that the village women understood their own position and status in the village, hence they were opening up spaces from which to raise their voices within a self-determined capacity within their village. From a postcolonial feminist perspective, it is important to note that the women were not setting out to move out of their subaltern status or their traditional culture, rather to strengthen their sense of security within it. This does not suggest a lack of aspiration as they often imparted a sense of transformation onto their children and their futures by seeking to secure good nutrition and school education for them. In these contexts, the women gained skills and information to prevent their family and community from experiencing poverty. The women highlighted their means and ways of accessing new information, knowledge and skills through cooperation and self-learning. While they had been either educated or excluded from being educated in formal settings, and faced culturally entrenched difficulties in raising their voices, they had found a way to speak out freely, from a space that was self-determined.

This is an important point because of the need to understand the different ways that some women in Kenya may conceptualise, describe and report their learning experiences. Attention must be paid to other types of learning processes. This is critical to understand because it affects how we provide more culturally sensitive adult and continuing education programmes and also how we could ensure that the adult education services are delivered with more accessibility and appropriateness which enables the women to better manage and cope with their life issues.

Social inequalities that result from racism, sexism and class relations influence the ways women experience development and affect how these problems are understood and treated by adult education programme officers in society.

Consistent with a postcolonial feminist perspective and informal learning/ literacy and one's empowerment in the context of international development theory, there is a drive to understand the relationship between power, thought and actual situations, and an effort to uncover systemic societal practices that have marginalised people.

However, instead of focusing on the possible negative consequences of a non-education background or experiences of gender discrimination, the village women presented positive views on their current learning processes and the impact this had on improving their lives in the future. For example, cultural issues exerted both positive and negative influences that affect how women perceive and make choices in experiencing learning and community development activities. It was evident form this research that cultural beliefs can serve in positive and protective ways when women participate in women's groups and traditional customs that bolster the women's support networks.

It was found that the government officials and staff of adult education programmes believed that a certificate-based literacy programme was a primary outcome of adult education. This meant that officers had less opportunity to conduct needs assessments for literacy programmes and to consider the views of adult learners. In addition, it appeared that the system of office-based (rather than grassroots) programme development minimised officers' time and ability to listen to women's views on women's organisations and literacy centres in Kenya. The findings of this research affirmed that village women do not have to be changed; rather the findings pointed to a need for the 'outsiders' (development officers and education policy-makers) to change their perceptions on delivering effective and sustainable development programmes.

It is an unquestionable principle that we all need to have access to learning activities as a basic human right (UNESCO 2002, 2003). A person, regardless of age or gender, continues to learn in whatever place or opportunity is available. One of the major opportunities for learning that arises from field-based research studies is that ways of learning differ vastly from people to people and culture to culture. The women represented in this research clearly demonstrate that their learning approach is different from formal literacy programmes, where expected learning outcomes with a teaching methodology are designed beforehand. Village women are often too busy to attend the scheduled adult literacy classes conducted by an instructor to 'study' a set of adult literacy curriculum of Swahili, English, mathematics and small-scale business that is either offered or imposed by the Kenyan government. Therefore such strategies for development appear incompatible and unsustainable.

As Freire (1970) states, literacy is about 'reading the world'. The interviewed women appeared to read the world very clearly. They 'read' their environment, tradition, and the role they play in the community. Within conventional measures of literacy and poverty, the village women would be regarded as illiterate-uneducated poor women, strongly characteristic of the subaltern. However, in their world (community), the village women have wealth in the animals grazing at home, and are aware of their daily life issues. Based on needs, women seek knowledge/solutions and develop strategies to overcome problems and limitations. The women in this study recognised the importance of education and they sent their children to school. They are not in the modern mass-production oriented world, yet they maximise their life experience and knowledge to stay in their culture, improving their well-being little by little at their own pace. Utilising Freire's conscientisation approach (1970), the women looked critically at and analysed their social situation in their cultural setting and found solutions, then acted to implement solutions. Village women continued this conscientisation process at their own pace or speed within resources that they had. Through this process, women could become more critical about their reality and continually raise their own critical awareness. This was a fundamental aspect of what literacy is supposed to offer. Albeit on a very local scale, the village women were also able to overcome socio-economic, geographic and generational boundaries in order to facilitate mutual learning.

Perhaps, the Maasai women themselves did not create necessary knowledge itself, yet the women transformed knowledge and skills acquired from their fellow women into practice. The life skills gave the women more power in the existing social infrastructures. Moreover, the village women have now seen the positive change that has occurred through their actions. They recognised that education was a way for their children to improve the standard of living with possible employment in the future. However, an analysis of their actions suggests that women did not have a well-developed strategy for the next generation. It is arguable that young girls need to have both formal and informal education to have a sustainable life in the current age. While young Maasai girls acquired literacy and numeracy skills to access certain types of information, they also needed to be rooted in their culture and tradition through informal learning and learn about the solidarity of their mothers as a form of culture.

A conclusion that can be drawn from this finding is that educators should not expect that all the women in Narok have the same life experiences, in fact, the village women could have entirely different lives at home, in the community and at their associated women's groups. In reflecting on the interconnected influences of race, class, gender and other social relations, it has allowed the researcher to examine the complexities of how such influences may be played out simultaneously in the village women's lives in Narok, Kenya. A postcolonial feminist perspective has illuminated the examination of the Maasai women's particular circumstances from a perspective of a larger social context and directed the researcher to recognise that structural inequalities and oppressive situations affect the Maasai women's learning and community development experiences.

Women's roles in improving well-being in their community

This research confirmed that the effects of cultural practices such as child brides, polygamy and FGM continued to widely affect women's situations in the Maasai lands. Women still suffer from gender inequality resulting in various socio-economic and educational challenges. Moreover, the traditional patriarchal family system remains extremely strong and women tend to be excluded from the decision-making processes.

While external NGOs seem to implement women's needs-based projects with the village women such as TBA training, red ribbon making, HIV-AIDS seminars and child sponsorship, postcolonial impositions were widely reflected in their programme implementation. Therefore, it is suggested that when the external NGOs terminate their programmes, there will be no local people prepared or trained to take over the programmes and manage to continue helping marginalised people. Consequently, although postcolonial feminists encourage reflexivity, recognition of differences and reciprocity, such characteristics were not evident in the women's narratives. Connections to material and professional assets with ownership of development programmes that community women do not have should be eventually transferred to local people. Ensuring constant dialogue between all participants in development programmes is important.

While women play traditional roles in Maasai society as care-givers and home-makers, they are also active agents in the improvement of their family and community. Women exercise agency as capacity in needs assessment and implementing development programmes through cooperation and solidarity in the village, in order to improve their families economic and food security. This study affirmed that women have an important role in the eradication of poverty, and as agents towards social change and human development. Nationally, Kenya has focused on achieving a gender equal society (Government of the Republic of Kenya 2007), however, women have more profound needs for adequate help and appropriate support to become more self-reliant.

Therefore, solidarity, togetherness and cooperation are crucial components of effective development strategies. For village women's solidarity, a focus on mutuality and connection among women is a basis for resistance to the male-dominant Maasai society. Women's networks clearly resist patriarchal dominance. As a number of the research participants highlighted, women or mothers are the managers of a household, hence they will always prioritise their family's well-being. This is especially focused on having healthy and educated children. In doing so mothers constantly seek information and knowledge from other women and apply what they have acquired to their own family's improvement. They are on the frontline for bringing about a positive change in their family and community, and are aware of critical needs and issues. Even if their husbands are not cooperative in maintaining a healthy family life, mothers have developed strategies to generate income to feed their family members. Informal learning/literacy created in informal women's groups has framed capacity amongst the village women to ensure food security and children's access to school.

However, inherited colonial religion, Christianity, still plays a vital role in maintaining traditional patriarchy in the community as many people now have been converted to Christianity and attend religious services on Sundays.

As the women in this research have informed us, a wife would not quarrel or make an argument with her husband, yet, by resisting the incorporative atmosphere of the male-centred household, she finds a solution. Creating self-defined spaces outside of the view of their husbands is also a mechanism for how women resist patriarchy. This was evident in the women's capacity to maintain their own small development projects, protecting them and their families from poverty. The research confirmed a specific African feminism in regard to gender relations, where women attempted to work harmoniously with the men in their communities and families (Tamale 2006). Overall, this research has demonstrated that successful networking and collaboration among women also contributed to breaking down barriers of illiteracy.

Women in Narok: changes in agency through the process of empowerment

A major aim in reporting the women's stories was to illustrate both their struggles and their strengths. Feminists posit that analysis begins in everyday experiences and should be framed within a voice from their perspective. These perspectives are created through dialogue and multiple locations. Thus there is a commitment to listen and value the voices of all women (Mohanty 2003). Further, this study has revealed the intricate relationship of race, class and gender and the significant impact that these factors have in the lives of the marginalised village women. In addition, this study showed the contributions of the Maasai women to their own advancement and to the improvement of their village.

It is a strong feminist view that not all women share the same experiences and struggles; postcolonial feminists theorise that historical positioning, racialisation, class relations, or forces intersect at the same time within their experiences. The aim in feminist research is to expose these sources of oppression (Spivak 1985; Crenshaw 1989; Mohanty 2003). Further, it is important to not represent the women as 'other', as having been positioned through patriarchal beliefs as different from the mainstream or often looked upon as subordinate, with their experiences being dismissed or insignificant and thus reproducing and reinforcing positions of domination over uneducated women. Stereotyping discourses have regarded uneducated/illiterate women as being passive and without agency. Therefore this research sought to report their values, opinions and positive qualities. The participants in this study spoke of what kept them strong and also what enabled them to cope with the diverse challenges and complexities of their circumstances. Being responsible for their families' maintenance, collaborative learning, collective empowerment and a sense of hope for the future was expressed as ways to promote positive well-being. Despite facing numerous difficulties and challenges many women described their resilience in adapting to their difficult circumstances. They took an initiative to cope with the stressful events and as a result experienced emancipation and a stronger sense of control over their situation. Through informal support networks (in this case women's groups) some women found meaningful resources and strategies to cope with family and social issues. Experiencing some difficulties, some women found that a new sense of agency was created and that they had more meaning and purpose in their life after having struggled with everyday circumstances and related gender issues.

In some discourses about empowerment, Alsop *et al.* (2006) regarded one's empowerment as an explanation of agency and Kabeer (1999) highlighted the significance of access to resources, including employment, and its impact on well-being in spite of socio-cultural restrictions on women's participation in households' decision-making processes (World Bank 2012). The interviewed women showed collective empowerment in which the village women collaboratively worked in finding solutions to their family and social issues that transformed their lives effectively. Chapters 5 and 6 in this book reported the ways that the women and leaders' experiences through learning and group activities were intrinsically related to how these women viewed life itself and relations in their community and culture.

This was an apt way of describing the village women's experience. For instance, in the case of Maria, only familiar with alphabetical literacy from attending formal schooling for a few years, she learnt bookkeeping, looking after the group members' money. Furthermore, Maria was responsible for farms, employing a few men to weed and harvest. She negotiated casual workers' wages and made payments. This task was traditionally an exclusive male role as it dealt with finance. However, Maria discussed this matter with her husband and in the absence of her husband, she carried out this task at home. Another example was Nashiegu's production management skills, with which, based on her fellow women's advice, she rented and managed her own cultivation without her husband's knowledge. As she strongly claimed in her interview, she had become self-reliant in supplying food for her family. She also knew she should reserve some maize in case of a drought, not waiting for outsider aid to provide empowerment or agricultural training programmes. Instead of being imposed upon by outsiders, she identified a problem and improved well-being by herself. Dependency on men, or a traditional strong patriarchy, had become manageable for the village women to some extent. Both Maria and Nashiegu had been in a disadvantaged situation in terms of access to 'literacy', however, they found their own ways of overcoming this difficulty. They had an organic sense of where to access knowledge, advice or skills in their community.

As Freire (1970) claimed, people need to become aware of social and political injustice through the continuous process of critical thinking and acting upon solving community problems. The village women seemed to be engaged in this process. For Freire (1970), literacy ought to encourage learners to be critical thinkers, and it should be part of problem solving education.

Second, the interviewed women all raised the issues of water, food, health and education. Because women themselves identified issues and needs in their community, they organise small-scale development projects without being manipulated or guided by external organisations. The village women wielded a strong sense of agency in their shared and individual determination. Women had power (more than "being empowered") in maintaining family and community work.

The data from this study confirmed that the motivation for the village women helping themselves and the community came from village women as well as women's leaders' own internal values. It was an ordinal process for them to act upon solutions to tackle community issues, such as water and food that are indispensable human needs to survive. Since their childhood, they had observed that cooperation between people is a very important aspect of human life. As mentioned previously, Carmen (1996) argued that interviewed women in Narok are a model of a human agency in the community; they act to solve problems autonomously. It is important to recognise this knowledge and the implications it has for adult education officers and how adult education programmes are offered to village women in Kenya.

Recommendations to the government, aid agencies, NGOs and future researchers

The central research inquiry in this study sought to examine notions of literacy and development from the village women's perspectives seeking knowledge that could possibly shape the nature of future external development agencies' aid policies. Taking into account local people's views, and having a government's stated commitment to promote equal representation for women from national and local levels, are crucial mechanisms in a struggle for gender equality. Raising male awareness about women's participation is also important. Data from this study showed that resistance to women's public involvement means that even when women do gain access to local participatory bodies, they may feel uncomfortable speaking their opinions or may even be prevented from doing so. As *Kenya Vision 2030* declares, the centrality of gender in the nation building of Kenya is indispensable (Government of the Republic of Kenya 2007, p. 5).

A consideration of how broader determinants of one's well-being, such as gender inequality, poverty, economic status and discrimination, may affect individual lives is necessary in seeking social change. Only through listening to the women's voices can we deepen our understanding about the ways in which social determinants affect women's and their families' well-being. By listening to their actual stories, we can understand their thoughts and views in the context of their lives rather than regarding them as uneducated or illiterate.

It is important to understand the factors that cause women to feel powerless, dependent or isolated, and other multiple forms of oppression. A shift is required away from understanding culture as a social characteristic of the Maasai women to one that recognises culture as a dynamic process, that is important to the everyday situation of the Maasai village women. Understanding the ways culture can shape the women's responses to their families' well-being will help education and development practitioners implement their programmes in more relevant and effective ways to the Maasai women. Women's contributions can no longer be ignored, but instead should serve as a valued insight for change and for the democratisation of education. Researchers in education, particularly in adult education and women's studies, and international development scholars need to listen to the voices of women in subordinated situations. Researchers need to listen as well as take action to conduct field-based research, document their findings, and challenge those responsible for the education of adult learners to be more accountable in order to induce positive changes. While listening to the voices of the marginalised, they should offer constructive suggestions that would benefit and empower marginalised people.

According to Narayan and Harding (1998), governments seem to be in confusion or contradiction about how they place 'women' in a male-dominant society. This statement is evident in the government officers' use of the terms 'gender' and 'women' that were used interchangeably without adequate explanation. Without training in implementing women-centred gender and development programmes, government officers cannot be expected to organise coherent and effective gender programmes. Also, non-hierarchical management skills associated with teamwork and networking are necessary for government officials (Mohanty 2003, p. 247). There is clear evidence that informal women's groups function effectively under a postcolonial feminist framework. The village women know how to manage and control women's group activities at their own pace. It is these apparently simple procedures that should be recognised as informal learning and literacy and women's empowerment in the context of local development.

The Kenyan government's shift in the adult literacy programme will create a distance from actual village women's needs and their existing practices of learning. In implementing the new, nation-wide literacy programme, the government is also concerned about how to mobilise resources to reach remote areas (Kenya National Bureau of Statistics 2010). However, as these women's experiences were highlighted in the above discussion, to create their own knowledge or learning activity in their cultural context, they do not demand huge resources. Village women can manage their informal literacy learning by themselves. They require a particular skill and knowledge at a specific time in their space to improve their everyday life. They are aware of gender disparity and/or disadvantage of being 'illiterate', yet they create their own strategies to tackle these issues.

The informal learning/literacy that the village women engage in is based on everyday life, their needs and their space, and it conflicts with what the formal adult literacy programme will offer to literacy learners. It would be best to explore how the formal adult literacy programme could be coordinated with village women's actual needs and assist to improve self-defined existing practices.

There was no evidence of a mechanism for young (formally) educated people to come back to informal learning about traditional strategies to overcome everyday issues in the Maasai community. Therefore, there needs to be an informal learning opportunity or mechanism for young (formally) educated people to gain hands-on experience in the cultural and traditional knowledges. I am not suggesting here that classic primers should be replaced by culturally relevant ones; rather, I offer ideas on how educators can integrate culturally relevant learning materials in order to relate curricula to learners' lives.

182 *Conclusion*

Especially needed as women's leaders are Maasai women and coordinators for outside organisations, because they analyse issues from both insider and outsider perspectives. This defined perspective brought about a positive impact on other women in their communities. In their women's group, an illiterate woman became a secretary or a vice-chairperson with the support of other female members. As some village women said, they needed to acquire the basic writing skills to record minutes or microfinance literacy, and they were encouraged by colleagues to work on it together. This case suggests that if there is a devoted human agent like these women's leaders in the community, it will generate a space for women who share knowledge and skills to bring about a social change in traditional communities. All of them are talented women who work towards local continuous sustainability of learning at the grassroots level.

The research also suggests that women's leaders could act as local facilitators to connect village women to the government and other external organisations. Moreover, women's leaders did not force behavioural change onto people in the community. In the case of FGM practice, some leaders shared the negative consequences of the FGM practice with local people, and tried to save girls who were forced to undergo the practice, leading to an arranged marriage, to escape the situation with their knowledge, networks and legal support. They knew the power of information and knowledge, yet did not force people to adopt new knowledge in the community.

As proposed by Campos (1997),

> it is the duty of the State to create favourable conditions for civil society. This statement starts with the excluded to organize itself into self-generating enterprises. It is only in this way that the most intractable problem of poverty can be solved without the need of direct intervention by the State. The legislation for favouring the creation of such enterprises, however, is sorely needed.
> (cited in Carmen and Sobrado 2000, p. 9)

Women's group activities though informal learning/literacy are continuous and sustainable activities for water, food and culture. Development initiatives at the village level are logical and practical. Therefore, local efforts should be supported by comprehensive national action, and external organisations should be supportive rather than distractive to village women. Basic human needs such as water and food should be made accessible by external aid. This should be connected to the nation, in the sense of giving appropriate rights around water and food, land relations. Access to and control of livelihood resources and the decision-making body ought to be considered.

Supporting Carmen (1996) and Foley and Michl's (1999) views, development practitioners should be aware that people have the autonomous capacity to construct knowledge and act upon knowledge. Transformative knowledge curriculum in "programmes" cannot be "provided" or "transmitted" by external professionals to adult learners. Individual learners ought to be treated with respect, and their organic knowledge must be encouraged and supported.

Although, through the findings of this study, it is evident that the nature of informal learning and literacy shown in women's grassroots groups is highly effective in poverty prevention, one could be concerned about the evaluation of aid organisations' assistance for local women's informal learning and literacy. As the research findings have demonstrated, the outcome of informal learning and literacy is highly measurable if the evaluation were to be undertaken via a longitudinal analysis of children's education, nutrition and health, HIV/AIDS, maternal health, reduction of FGM and early marriages and gender equality issues. How local women assist each other through self-determined learning to overcome everyday life issues can be evaluated based on the prior mentioned aspects of literacy. If other organisations or governments are intent on running effective adult literacy programmes, the following recommendations are made:

- Learners should be supported to take initiatives in their learning processes, including the production and selection of the content of learning materials, the recruitment of instructors and the schedule of literacy classes.
- External aid workers or government officers and community workers together should become part of the educational process, actively working on analysing their own community issues, how these are challenged, and how new insights result through learning by doing.
- Adult basic education should include not only alphabetical literacy, but also recognise the importance of health and nutrition, gender issues, the negative effect of girls' early marriages and FGM on schooling, and include microfinance literacies in programmes.
- A regular in-service training course or seminar should be organised for local literacy instructors so that they can build teaching and learning materials matched to learners' needs. Also the instructors can facilitate an open discussion forum about culturally sensitive issues such as FGM, women's unequal heavy work-load. In addition, the local instructors can plan a lesson on small-scale business in the curriculum to create a discussion among participants, not as an external class activity.
- The establishment of technical mentors by the government would be helpful for adult education instructors to solve classroom issues and provide needs-based appropriate learning instructions.
- Learners' informal learning based on previous knowledge and experiences should be supported, especially, the preservation of traditional Maasai ornament production and house construction.
- Cultural identity and dignity should be at the core of informal learning/ literacy and development projects, sustaining traditional solidarity and togetherness.

- Informal learning and literacy should be supported for people to become a local change agent through a space created to raise people's voice. People should be encouraged to discuss in the space in which they become creative and critical about their real life situation in order to find the solution for improving their well-being.
- Gender issues should be paid special attention to within adult education and literacy and development programmes, considering togetherness and harmony.
- Women participating in grassroots development programmes should be encouraged and supported to discuss goal settings for their future, education, small businesses and financial management opportunities.
- Gender equality education should be organised for men with local facilitators based on their context.
- There should be an educational mechanism for young educated people to come back to a village for acquisition of local knowledge, culture and tradition. Young educated people should have opportunities between both formal literacy learning and informal and traditional learning to acquire hands-on problem solving skills.
- The cooperation between government, international aid agencies and NGOs should have local facilitators who understand local communication channels to disseminate information on development issues in a local context.

Directions for future research

This research presents avenues for future scholarship on women's literacy and development. First, the research demands that we reconsider what literacy means and what literacy does from local people's perspectives. As this research has demonstrated, the concept of literacy and the process of acquiring literacy differ among individuals and region to region. This research also revealed that women's groups in Narok generated a space for village women to raise their voices on community and family issues and were effective in creating collaborative and cooperative informal learning and literacy among the members. This research has also contributed to the scholarship on the discourse of women's literacy and empowerment by examining village women's informal learning mechanisms and its impact on well-being.

While this study focused on women's views on literacy and community development, it would be useful to explore men's perspectives on informal learning, literacy, gender equality and development as it would allow for possible transformative strategies for men to embrace gender equality.

It would be beneficial for future scholarship to investigate characteristics of women's groups as informal institutions and revisit how widespread they are. Future research could explore the different women's groups and the relationship between group structures, group strategies and group sustainability. Future research could also consider the question of the relationship between the types of women's groups and their effectiveness – are some groups more effective than others? In order to answer these questions effectively it would be both interesting and challenging to continue studying some of the groups observed for this research over a more extended period of time.

Conclusion

This research supports Spivak's (1985) postcolonial feminist argument that subalterns can speak from where a space is made available. Women in this study created a space to raise their voice comfortably without changing their identity or social class. They organised small-scale projects based on their needs. In the process of conscientisation (Freire 1970), the subaltern village women became able to analyse issues and act upon solutions, they constructed and re-constructed knowledge. This research also supported Carmen's (1996) view that, within an increasingly competitive and globalised world, people use local resources, expertise and opportunities to organise the collective goals of the people. Drawing on internal motivation, small-scale development programmes such as income generation, health and education were autonomous, demonstrating an autonomous development approach (Carmen 1996). As Pradervand (1989) and Mohanty (2003) suggested, when acting in solidarity, women have power in the male dominant system. In addition to their manageable size and significant voice, through solidarity and collaboration, women acquired various literacies to improve their well-being. Beyond their weak formal status, they could use the power of the collaborative to lead a social change.

The women who participated in this research promoted cultural values in order to create a harmonious society in the village. Supporting African feminism (Tamale 2006) as well as a diversity of feminisms (Mohanty 2003), this research demonstrated that women accommodating men's self-pride attempted to build a relationship in which men and women played different roles accordingly and effectively. Moreover, women had their own resistance to gender inequality by forming groups to create a forum to bring about solutions to social issues. This grassroots women's movement was linked with feminist legal activism on FGM, land tenure and early forced marriages. Local facilitators such as female teachers were an effective bridge between the village and the nation. Also, education decisions made by the Kenyan government did not appear to correspond with the decisions made by local communities' representatives. Adult education is becoming more uniform, and it was also viewed from the perspective of global competition, attempting to produce mass-literates.

For those who are poor and excluded, "the solution is not provision, delivery of services or other forms of assistance. What is needed, instead, is an opening up of opportunities and spaces for group/organizational learning capable of pulling them out of their predicament and flourish" (Carmen and Sobrado 2000, pp. 10–11).

On the one hand, while gaining self-help skills are expected through the new adult literacy programme by the government, the learning methodology and curriculum used for the programme is still conventional, in which adults are required to learn a set of subjects of primary education that lead to a certificate. This banking concept of education, as it is called by Freire (1970), does not encourage adult learners to be critical enough of government policies, rather it leads to illiterate adults accepting government policies and keeps them in their situation. On the other hand, women in Narok made it clear that they were able, without the literacy curriculum imposed by the government, to be critical about social issues through needs-based informal learning and to become truly self-reliant.

Through a postcolonial feminist perspective, analysis was raised to a broader level of conceptualisation, one which is required to understand how socio-economic, historical and political factors interact with race, class and gender to influence the interviewed women's learning and empowerment experiences. The relationship and complexities between the effect of traditional and historical forces, together with the present socio-economic, political and environmental factors have influenced the women's learning and community development activities. Accordingly we must work towards taking into account the wider context of the women's everyday lives and voices that influence the marginalised women's experiences. Narayan and Harding (1998) encourage us to think of postcolonialism and feminism as "thinking spaces" that open up transformations in social relations and in the ways we think about them.

The researcher is not suggesting reduction of technical support or financial aid to formal education and literacy. However, this research has shown that community-based education and development strategies for poverty alleviation at the level of the micro-economy should be developed and supported by government and external donor agencies' policies. Adult education should not be governed by market theory or mass-production.

The knowledge gained from this study will contribute to develop adult education programmes that address women's everyday experiences and issues in Kenya that are understandable, accessible and culturally appropriate for women. This will help to ensure the women can access educational services and resources in a timely manner to promote self-directed learning and to improve quality of life. Interventions must involve multiple sectors to address the determinants of effective adult education in a particular socio-cultural context.

The goal of adult education should be opened up to democratic debate and create a space where local people can and are supported to conduct cooperative learning. A people-centred learning system is important for raising the level of well-being in society as a whole. The promotion of social harmony, solidarity, cooperation and mutual-support should be encouraged in both formal and informal adult education so that people's development can become continuously sustainable.

References

Allen, A. (2008). Power and the Politics of Difference: Oppression, Empowerment and Transnational Justice. *Hypatia*, 23(3), 156–172.
Alsop, R., Bertelsen, M., and Holland, J. (2006). *Empowerment in Practice from Analysis to Implementation*. Washington, DC: World Bank.
Bartlett, L. (2008). Literacy's Verb: Exploring What Literacy is and What Literacy Does. *International Journal of Educational Development*, 28(6), 737–753.
Barton, D., Hamilton, M., and Ivanic, R. (eds). (2000). *Situated Literacies: Reading and Writing in Context*. London: Routledge.
Bhabha, H.K. (1994). *The Location of Culture*. London: Routledge.
Carmen, R. (1996). *Autonomous Development: Humanizing the Landscape. An Excursion into Radical Thinking and Practice*. London: Zed Books.
Carmen, R., and Sobrado, M. (2000). *A Future for the Excluded: Job Creation and Income Generation by the Poor: Clodomir Santos de Morais and the Organization Workshop*. London: Zed Books.
Crenshaw, K. (1989). Demarginalizing the Intersection of Race and Sex: A Black Feminist Critique of Antidiscrimination Doctrine, Feminist Theory and Antiracist Politics. *University of Chicago Legal Forum*, 1989: 139–167.
Foley, D.K., and Michl, T.R. (1999). *Growth and Distribution*. Cambridge: Harvard University Press.
Freire, P. (1970). *Pedagogy of the Oppressed*. New York: Continuum.
Gandhi, L. (1998). *Postcolonial Theory: A Critical Introduction*. New York: Columbia University Press.
Government of the Republic of Kenya. (2007). *Kenya Vision 2030: A Globally Competitive and Prosperous Kenya*. Nairobi: The Government of Kenya.
Hodgson, L.D. (2001). *Once Intrepid Warriors: Gender, Ethnicity, and the Cultural Politics of Maasai Development*. Bloomington: Indiana University Press.
Kabeer, N. (1999). Resources, Agency, Achievements: Reflections on the Measurement of Women's Empowerment. *Development and Change*, 30(3), 435–464.
Kenya National Bureau of Statistics. (2010). *Economic Survey 2010*. Nairobi: The Government Printer.
Mohanty, C.T. (1984). Under Western Eyes. *Boundary 2*, 12(3), 338–358.
Mohanty, C.T. (2003). *Feminism without Borders: Decolonizing Theory, Practicing Solidarity*. Durham and London: Duke University Press.
Narayan, U., and Harding, S. (1998). Introduction. Border Crossing: Multicultural and Postcolonial Feminist Challenges to Philosophy (Part1). *Hypatia*, 13(2), 1–6.
Nyerere, J. (1968). *Freedom and Socialism. A Selection from Writings and Speeches, 1965–1967*. Dar es Salaam: Oxford University Press.
Ogunyemi, C.O. (1985). Womanism: The Dynamics of the Contemporary Black Female Novel in English. *Signs*, 11(1), 63–80.
Pradervand, P. (1989). *Listening to Africa: Developing Africa from the Grassroots*. New York: Praeger.
Said, E. (1978). *Orientalism*. London: Routledge & Kegan Paul.
Said, E. (1989). Representing the Colonized: Anthropology's Interlocutors. *Critical Inquiry*, 15(2), 205–225.
Spivak, G.C. (1985). Can the Subaltern Speak? Speculations on Widow Sacrifice. *Wedge*, 7/8(Winter/Spring), 120–130.

Spivak, G.C. (1988). Can the Subaltern Speak? In C. Nelson and L. Grossberg (eds), *Marxism and the Interpretation of Culture*, Basingstoke: Macmillan Education, pp. 271–313.
Tamale, S. (2006). African Feminism: How Should *We* Change? *Development*, 49, 38–41.
UNESCO. (2003). *Education for All: Is the World on Track?* EFA Global Monitoring Report 2002. Paris: UNESCO.
UNESCO. (2003). *Gender and Education for All: The Leap to Equality*. EFA Global Monitoring Report 2003/4. Paris: UNESCO.
Wane, N.N. (2008). Mapping the Field of Indigenous Knowledge in Anti-Colonial Discourse: A Transformative Journey in Education. *Race, Ethnicity and Education*, 11(2), 183–197.
World Bank. (2012). *World Development Report 2012: Gender Equality and Development*. Washington, DC: World Bank.
Young, I.M. (1997). Unruly Categories: A Critique of Nancy Fraser's Dual Systems Theory. *New Left Review*, 222, 147–160.
Young, R.J.C. (2001). *Postcolonialism: An Historical Introduction*. Oxford: Wiley-Blackwell.

Index

Page numbers in **bold** denote tables, those in *italics* denote figures.

Achebe, Chinua 13, 21, 60
act of knowing, development of 157
adult education 97, 102, 139, 174; certificate-oriented learning 2, 5; classes in Narok *127*; curriculum for 2, 5, 175; development of 3; directions for future research on 184–5; Freire's approach to 3, 158; goal of 186; imposed by UNESCO 39; informal learning and 26–31; and initiatives to reduce adult illiteracy 79; Kenyan policy on 79–81; Knowles's views on 143, 157; life-long learning 29; literacy programme on 81, 181; 'non literacy' aspects of 38; primary school education 2, 80; quality of 26; recommendations on 180–4
Adult Education Donor 80
adult literacy *see* adult education
African cultural practice 2, 4, 6, 34, 37, 40, 46, 58, 135, 141, 147, 161, 163, 176
African feminism 59–62, 126, 177, 185; Oyewumi's view on 61; significance of 63
African feminist scholarship 60
African identity 15
African womanhood 59
African women 58; Western feminists' views on 59
agency, concept of 44
agricultural training programmes 103, 179
alphabetical literacy programme, certificate-based 158
animal trade 120
anti-colonial movements 11

autonomous 4, 6, 31, 35, 158, 172, 173, 182, 185

being poor, concept of 128
Bhabha, Homi 11, 15, 63, 104, 170
black feminist movement 45
black people: humanity of 13; oppression of 11, 13
black women, discrimination of 45, 47, 60
British colonisation 4, 124; legacies of 10; schooling and language education 27
British East Africa Company 78
British imperialism 13

'capacitation (learning)' process 35, 104
cash economy 82, 121, 147
certificate-oriented learning 2, 5, 80
child brides 102, 176
Children's Act No. 8 of 2001 84, 86
child sponsorship programme 46, 84
Christianity 11, 58, 91, 124, 177; gender-based hierarchy of 124
Christian missionaries 13
classroom learning 157
collaborative learning 32, 101, 105, 109, 112–14, 116, 153, 158, 178
collective empowerment 43, 45–6, 48, 109–10, 127, 141–4, 162, 168, 179
colonial schooling and language education 27
coloniser–colonised power relationship 16
communication channels 141, 171, 184
community-based organisations 5, 68, 173

Index

community development 4, 29, 161; agents of change 32; impact of literacy on 7; women's capacity for 32, 112
Conrad, Joseph 13
conscientisation, idea of 35–6, 91, 145, 168, 175, 185
cooperative learning 104–5, 128, 134, 143–4, 162, 168, 186
Crenshaw, Kimberle 45–6
critical thinking, process of 36, 157, 169, 179
cultural hybridity, idea of 170
cultural identity 14, 59, 183
cultures: conservation of 123–4; of poor countries 20

Dakar Framework for Action on Education for All (2000) 1, 33
decision-making processes 1, 38, 44, 126, 144, 161, 170, 179; women's participation in 6, 10, 16
de Morais, Clodomir Santos 34, 103
development: of capacity 110; of community 1–2, 4, 6–7, 9, 18, 29, 32, 41, 47, 56–7, 67–8, 71, 79, 86, 90–3, 109, 112–15, 126, 128, 133–4, 141, 153, 161–3, 170–1, 174, 176, 184, 186; of country 3; economic 11, 81, 108, 111, 148, 156, 159; social 78–9, 93, 156; women 148–9, 152
Diallo, Nafissatou 15
division of labour 34, 104, 106
domestic violence 156, 159–60
dowry murders 58

early marriages, cultural practice of 2, 14, 83–5, 86, 94, 101–2, 135–6, 144, 147, 156, 161, 163, 171, 183
educational attainment 1, 33, 38, 135, 153, 160
Education for All (EFA) 1, 33
education system: banking concept of 157; British system of 12; 'capacitation (learning)' process 104; certificate-oriented learning 2; colonial schooling and language education 27; development programmes 12, 17; European models of 12; female education 135; formal education 31, 101, 139; Kenyan Certificate for Primary Education 5; medium of instruction 28; Ministry of Education of Kenya 2; non-formal education 27, 30; primary school education 2, 33; quality of 1, 26; traditional indigenous knowledge 12; Western-style 31
emancipation of women, key objective of 2, 10, 140
entrepreneurial literacy 34, 104
ethnography 36, 57, 63, 64, 66
exclusion, power of 110

faith-based organisations 31
family planning 83, 117
Fanon, Frantz 10–12; *Black Skin, White Masks* (1967) 11; on oppression of 11; perspectives on decolonisation 11
female education 135
female genital mutilation (FGM) 2, 46, 58, 83–5, 140, 161; affect on girls' school performance 84, 183; awareness raising programmes 84; Children's Act No. 8 of 2001 84, 86; circumcision 84; complications regarding 84; as cultural beliefs of modesty and femininity 83; cultural practices of 163; eradication of 135, 140, 145, 161; girls' decisions regarding 84; law prohibiting 84; National Plan of Action for elimination of 84; negative aspects of 135; peer-group pressure for 84; prevalence of 83
female grassroots entrepreneurs 147
female labour and productivity 31
female power, in socio-cultural areas 60
feminist research: African feminism and 59–62; data analysis 71; data collection in the field 63–71; establishing rapport 62–3; ethical considerations 72–3; ethnography-based 64; interviews 66–7; on literacy discourse 64; on Maasai women's thinking and behaviours in literacies 64; process observation 65–6; recruitment process of research participants 68–71; research participants **70**; selection of field sites and research participants 67–8; on women's everyday life 57–9
feminist scholarship 9, 42, 59–60
feminist theory, postcolonial 9–22; concept of 11; emergence of 11–18; and informal learning 172–3; knowledge construction 19; literature and discourses on 12; methodological framework of 11; objectivity of 18–21; 'womanism' perspective of 15
food security 172–7

forced marriage 83, 185
formal education in Africa 37, 101, 139; beneficiaries of 31
Freire, P. 3, 35–6, 101, 128, 142, 148, 157–9, 162, 168, 175, 179, 186

gender discrimination 47, 174
gender disparity, through an unequal workload 81, 108, 111, 124, 181
gender equality 1, 6, 33, 59, 61, 79, 144, 145, 156, 159, 180, 183–4
gender hierarchies: of Christianity 124; within the family 119
gender inequality 103–4, 111, 125, 173; in educational attainment 33; in poor countries 10; women's capacity in overcoming 152
gender reconstruction, process of 61
government and NGO officers, narratives of 152–60; about views of the future 160; activities to improve women's well-being 158–60; analysis and discussions of 156–60; John's story 156; learning activities 157–8; literacy, concept of 160–2; Moses's story 154–5; Sankale's story 153–4
government literacy centres 80, 154
Gramsci, Antonio 16
grassroots development programmes 184
grassroots organisations 41
Green Belt Movement 44, 61
Gross Domestic Product (GDP) 3
Guha, Ranajit 16

Hall, Stuart 15
health education, community-based 140
HIV-AIDS infections 94, 103; effects of 135; transmissions through sexual intercourse 104
home finances, management of 121
house construction, role of women in 98, 102, 124, 125–6, 183
household chores, in Maasai community 117–20; gender hierarchies within the family 119; household security 117; man's activities from Monday to Friday 118–20; Wangui's observation on 117; woman's activities from Monday to Friday 117–18
household security 115, 117
human development 6–7, 33–4, 38, 56, 173, 177

Human Development Index 78
hybridity, process of 15, 170

illiterate adults 2, 35, 80, 186
incidental learning 28
income generation 39, 81, 128, 136, 147, 152, 154, 185; women's capacity in 152
independency of women 44, 137, 160; economic independence 60, 144–7; feminism and 60; impact on well-being of their family 101; self-empower and 46; self-learning 102; through microfinance activity 142
Indian women, dowry related harassment of 58
informal learning 1–4, 7, 90, 112–13, 126, 128, 162, 184; and adult literacy 26–31; application of 28; competences gained in 28; definition of 27–8; effectiveness of 30, 33; elements of 32; formalisation of 30; impact on women's power and influence 4; impact on women's well-being 33–6, 173–6; interpersonal values of 30; key themes of 115–26; Maasai women's experiences in 9, 16, 26, 47; nature of 6; opportunities for 31; postcolonial feminist theory and 172–3; quality of 26; recommendations regarding 180–4; role in development of professional skills 28; as self-directed learning 28; self-empowerment via 34; significance of 32; socio-cultural perspective of 36–40; and traditional education in Africa 28, 32; women's empowerment and 40–7; women's learning in Africa 31–2
informal literacy 91, 93, 113, 133, 143, 150, 161, 162, 181
inheritance law, in Kenya 83
institutionally validated agency 148
international non-governmental organisation (INGO) 84
interpersonal relationships: between men and women 111; power balance in 111
intersectionality, idea of 45–8, 145, 152
interview 1, 57, 63, 66, 67, 98, 106, 113, 133, 134, 137, 139, 146, 157, 171, 179

job creation 35
joint liability loan 115

Kenya: Adult and Continuing Education programmes 79–81; British colonisation of 124; Department of Adult Education 79–80; historical background of 77–8; Human Development Index 78; initiatives to improve education and people's well-being 78–9; initiatives to reduce adult illiteracy 79; map of 69; Mau Mau movement 78; Ministry of Education 2, 79–80, 85; Ministry of Gender, Sports, Culture and Social Services 79–80; Ministry of Health 79, 84; social pillar of 78; Vision 2030 78–9, 180; women's development in 79–81
Kenya Adult Learners Association (KALA) 153–4, 157
Kenya Certificate of Secondary Education (KCSE) 155
Kenyan Certificate for Primary Education (KCPE) 2, 5, 80, 155
Kenyatta, Jomo 78
Kikuyu Central Association 78
knowledge: construction of 19; ownership of 61; production of 19, 101, 107, 114; sharing of 32; traditional indigenous 12; transfer of 103
Knowles, M.S. 113, 142–3, 157

leadership 61, 109, 123–4, 126, 133; patriarchal 78; women's capacity for 32
learning, critical reflection on 114
learning literacy, process of 112
legal marriage, minimum age for 82, 159
life skills, capacities of 115, 127, 157, 176
lifetime learning 27, 29
literacy 1–4, 7; balance between orality and 40; benefits for women from 39; certificate-based alphabetical literacy programme 158; in context of international development 172–3; definitions of 34, 82; entrepreneurial literacy 104; everyday literacies 35; in formal literacy programmes 34; Freire's perspective of 35–6; government officer's perspective on 160–2; for human development 38; impact on people's standard of living 161; impact on women's empowerment and agency 38–40; John's concept of 159; New Literacies see New Literacy Studies (NLS); role in one's life 34; social aspect of 103; as social skill 36; socio-cultural view of 35, 36–40; Street's concept of 36; of women 1, 39; from women's group leaders' perspective 148–50
literacy learning 36, 91, 100, 113, 133, 157, 161, 163, 173, 181, 184
literacy programmes, certificate-based 163, 175
'lived' experiences, of colonisation and postcolonial life 12

Maasai communities, in Kenya 6; Christianity, impact of 11; gender roles in 18; male-dominated 114; struggle against colonisation and social justice 11
Maasai women in Kenya 77; access to health services 83; activities from Monday to Friday 117–18; community development activities 79; educational opportunities 83; FGM and early marriages 83–5; household chores 117–20; informal learning 4, 33–6; knowledge of family planning 83; learning strategies 79; minimum age for legal marriage 82; policy of adult and continuing education of 79–81; reproductive role of 83; situation in Narok County 81–5; traditional clothes 82; well-being of 152; see also village women, narratives of
Maathai, Wangari 44, 61–2
male dominance, production and protection from 115, 120–1
marginalised social groups 41
marginalised women: knowledge construction 19; social inequality experienced by 9; status of 16
marriage, in Maasai community: arranged marriages 83; child brides 102; early marriage, practice of 102, 163; forced marriage 83; Marriage Act of 2008 83; minimum age for 82; polygamy 82
Mau Mau movement 78
'merry-go-round' system, concept of 108–9, 115, 137, 142
microcredit programmes 41–2, 142
microfinance 41, 141, 170; conducted within the women's groups 115; defined 115; for joint liability loan 115; 'merry-go-around' activity 137;

strategies of 115; village-based 112, 116; village women's method of 142
Millennium Development Goals (MDGs) 1, 33, 161
Ministry of Education of Kenya 79–80, 85; literacy programme 2
money management 41
Moyers, Bill 13
Mudimbe, V.Y. 13

Narayan, U. 20, 58, 181, 186
narrative (analysis) 1, 71, 91, 92, 93, 94, 95, 96, 97, 98, 99, 100, 105, 109, 126, 133, 134, 135, 136, 137, 138, 153, 154, 156, 173
needs-based development programmes 7
needs-based learning 105, 109, 157, 186
New Literacy Studies (NLS): concept of 36–40; Irvine's view of 37; nature of 37; postcolonial curriculum 37; programmes for women 38–40; Street's approach to 36–7
non-formal education 27–8, 79–80; benefits of 30; of schooled girls in Ghana 30
non-governmental organisation (NGO) 27, 61, 84, 110, 159
numeracy skills 5, 30, 34–6, 109, 128, 154, 176

observation (process) 18, 56, 57, 64, 65, 70, 71, 90, 102, 105, 107, 114, 115, 116, 128, 173
on-the-job training 32
oral culture societies 40
orality, significance of 143
out-of-school youth 2, 79–80
Oyewumi, Oyeronke 59, 126, 143; view on African feminism 61; womanism, concept of 60

Pan-African Green Belt Network 44
Papen, Uta 32, 34, 39
patriarchal system 31, 103, 105, 141, 143
patriarchy, notion of 4, 10–12, 16–17, 21, 44, 48, 58, 60, 85, 93, 106, 110, 114, 125, 128, 144, 147, 168, 177, 179
people-driven literacy programmes 163
polygamy, practice of 82, 152, 176
poor countries 2, 10, 20, 21, 26, 27, 33, 34, 40, 41, 64, 104, 170
postcolonial theory 19, 60; for promoting women's equality 9, 11–18, 20–1, 145, 170; poverty alleviation 41, 112, 139, 161, 186
power 2, 4, 6, 7, 9, 10, 11, 12, 13, 15, 16, 17, 20, 26, 29, 31, 32, 36, 37, 38, 41, 42, 43, 44, 47, 57, 58, 60, 61, 78, 82, 107, 109, 110, 111, 119, 123, 124, 128, 141, 143, 145, 146, 149, 151, 157, 161, 162, 169, 170, 172, 173, 176, 179, 182, 185
practical learning, importance of 157–8
Praxis, process of 103–4, 108, 111
primary school education, for adult learners 2, 5, 33, 80
problem-based learning 113–14
problem solving skills 3, 35, 127–8, 184

quality of life 2, 186

rainwater harvesting 122
recommendations, on adult literacy programmes 180–4
resource management: in conserving culture 123–4; in drought-stricken area 121; of household 106–7; male-dominated 115; in securement of water 121–3

Said, Edward 10, 13, 15, 169; *Orientalism* (1978) 12
school management, women involved in 123
self-confidence 34, 38, 43, 103, 105, 113, 161
self-development, process of 159, 162
self-directed learning 4, 26, 28, 32, 114, 186
self-empowerment 102, 145, 161; impact of literacy on 112; process of 91; via informal learning 34
self-esteem 38, 113, 145, 161
self-help group 107, 114, 136, 154
self-learning 102, 174
self-representation, notion of 20, 170
sexual differences, social negotiation of 58, 159
social and economic development, politics of 11
social exclusion 115
social identities 46, 47; politics of 11
social inequality 174; experienced by marginalised women 9; gender as determinant of social 124
social justice 11, 26, 32, 34, 36, 61, 104, 110

social protection programmes 81
social spending 41, 112
social welfare services 31
'space,' notion of 109
Spivak, Gayatri 9, 16, 63, 102, 114, 150, 169–70, 185; on power of exclusion 110; 'space,' notion of 109; strategic essentialism, idea of 19, 92
standard of living 145; impact of literacy on 161; sustainable 172
Steady, Chioma 59
story-telling 28, 32
strategic essentialism, idea of 19, 59, 92
Subaltern Studies Group 10, 16
Sustainable Development Goals (SDGs) 1, 33

teacher-centred learning 157
Thiong'o, Ngũgĩ wa 14, 21, 27, 60
Third-World Women 45, 57–8
traditional birth attendance (TBA) 94, 99, 103, 109, 135
traditional indigenous knowledge 12, 61, 103; informal education and 28
transformative knowledge 105, 182

unemployment: poverty due to 34
United Nations Educational, Scientific and Cultural Organisation (UNESCO) 80, 158; adult literacy imposed by 39; definition of informal learning 27; notion of literacy 34
United Nations Entity for Gender Equality and the Empowerment of Women (UNIFEM) 80, 84
universal primary education (UPE) 33

value of education, in women's lives 5
verbal communication 28, 104
village-based literacy 68, 112
village ethnographic communities 172
village women, narratives of: about their future 113; Agnes's story 99; analysis and discussions of 101–13; background of the research site 91–2; of conserving culture 123–4; cultural influences 93; farming and employment opportunities 113; gender disparity through an unequal workload 108; group activities 107–11; household chores 117–20; impact of group activities on well-being 111–13; knowledge production 101; on learning/literacy and well-being 113–14; learning processes as informal learning/literacy 101–5; Luisa's story 100–1; Maria's story 94–5; Mary's story 94; Nahiegu's story 97–8; Namelok's story 97; Namunyak's story 96; narratives of 92–101; Naserian's story 95–6; on practice of early marriage 102; process observation and 114–26; production and protection from male dominance 120–1; productive role of women in the village 124–6; resource management 121–3; resource management of household 106–7; Resson's story 96–7; Rhoda's story 98–9; social injustices 93; on theme of women's responsibility 110; unequal social relations 93
vocational training 80

water management 121–3
Western feminism 60; feminist movements 103; Mohanty's views on 58; political project of 57
Western missionaries 11
womanhood: African 59; idea of 45
womanism: African feminism 59–62, 111, 126; idea of 14, 57, 60; Ogunyemi's views on 60
women entrepreneurs 31–2
women in Narok 178–80
women of colour 14, 20, 45, 170
women's emancipation, in Africa 33, 39, 153; strategies for 39
women's empowerment 1, 17, 34, 126, 156, 172; collective action for 43, 109, 144; concept of 40–5; in context of development 90; definition of 42; forms of 42–3; Freire's approach to 101, 159; Friedmann's view on 40–1; gender inequality and 10; impact of literacy on 38–40; individualistic idea of 42; intersectionality of ethnicity, class, gender and poverty 45–7; Kabeer's view on 41; key objectives of 10; Maathai's view of 44; microcredit, role of 41–2; power-over 42; power-to 43; power-with 43; in relation to international development 7; self-empowerment *see* self-empowerment
women's group leaders: analysis and discussions of narratives of 139–46; gender issues 133; group activities and informal learning 139–46; impact of

group activities on well-being 146–8; involvement in women's groups 134; Joan's story 135–6; literacy, concept of 148–50; narratives of 134–9; notion of informal literacy/learning 133; opinions about women's situation 150–2; on overcoming women's inequality 150–2; postcolonial feminist perspective 134; power-to empower the women 145; Rose's story 136–7; Ruth's story 137; Sara's story 137–8; Teresa's story 138–9; views about the future 146

women's responsibility, themes of 110, 117

women's self-directed learning and literacy 26

women's voices, significance of 4, 9, 17, 30–2, 56, 61, 63, 91, 101, 143, 159, 163, 169–71, 180

women's well-being: impact of group activities on 111; impact of literacy on 33–6, 173–6; and problem solving skills 35; women's roles in improving 176–8

World Vision 46, 84–5, 135, 140, 147

Printed in the United States
By Bookmasters